Xmas 1990.

Merv

find th

Love, M.

BESIEGED

BESIEGED

A DOCTOR'S STORY OF LIFE AND DEATH IN BEIRUT

DR. CHRIS GIANNOU

KEY PORTER BOOKS

Canadian Cataloguing in Publication Data
Giannou, Chris
Besieged: A Doctor's Story of Life and Death in Beirut
Includes bibliographical references.
ISBN 1-55013-219-9

1. Giannou, Chris. 2. Shatila (Lebanon: Refugee camp). 3. Palestinian Arabs – Lebanon – Beirut. 4. Lebanon – History – 1975- . 5. Surgeons – Lebanon – Biography. 6. Surgeons – Canada – Biography. I. Title.

DS87.53.G5 1990 956.9204'4 C90-094133-2

Key Porter Books Limited
70 The Esplanade
Toronto, Ontario
M5E 1R2

Maps: William Laughton
Typesetting: MacTrix DTP

Printed and bound in Canada

90 91 92 93 94 6 5 4 3 2 1

Discontent is the first step in the progress of
a man or a nation.

— saying found in fortune cookie,
Chinese restaurant, New York City

Committed to the future —
Even if that only means "se préparer à bien mourir."

Dag Hammarskjöld

Even if Death is always there,
it is second,

Freedom always
is first

Y. *Ritsos*

Contents

A Note to the Reader

This book is a record of a particular event in contemporary history, a people's struggle to survive and overcome immense and terrible hardships. It is not an academic treatise. For the reader who wishes a more detailed and scholarly history of the Middle East, I include a selected bibliography.

I have tried to tell a human story and have simplified the politics and history without, I hope, being simplistic. I am not objective, but have tried to be fair throughout. I am not non-partisan; I was an active participant in the incidents recounted herein, as well as an observer. But my partisanship is not uncritical.

Something drew me, a Canadian surgeon, to Shatila's struggle, its pain and heroism. Something compelled me to stay with these "wretched of the earth," longer than I ever imagined. I have been through several wars in Lebanon over the last ten years, and North American acquaintances often ask me why I would choose not only to live there, but to keep going back. This book is an attempt to answer that question, for myself as much as for the reader.

In the public debate in the West since the outbreak of the *Intifadah* in December 1987, many people, regardless of their sympathies concerning the Israeli-Palestinian conflict, want to know more about the Palestinians — what life is like in a refugee camp; how refugee society is organized; what refugees think; how they live. This book is highly personal, but it is also an attempt to enter that debate and influence it to help people better understand the feelings and motivations of Palestinians and, in so doing, to advance the cause of a just and equitable peace.

I have changed certain characters and especially names where present circumstances would endanger the lives of those concerned. I have omitted certain details, for brevity, and again out of concern for the security of those involved. But I believe that these changes and omissions do not alter the essence of the story, a story of ordinary people doing extraordinary things.

Many friends were surprised that I had the patience to sit down in one place long enough to finish this work; I owe it to them. Moral support to continue with endless rewrites and recuperation came from Stuart Schaar, Nubar Hovsepian, Paula Newberg, Dr. Saundra Shepherd, Rachel Burd, and Rick Salutin. My thanks to Jackie Swartz, Leyli Shayegan, Karen Judd, Carole Saltz, Sheldon Fischer, Elisa Petrini, and Susan Schindehette, whose editorial comments and interest helped the novice writer far more than they realize. Carol Stock was instrumental in the most trying task — the first regurgitation of endless, dense, painful detail. Leila Musfy, who could not visit me in Shatila, graciously helped with the maps in Washington. To Régine Ponson, I owe a great debt: for her friendship, courage, and the use of her personal photographs and memoirs. My gratitude goes to the Blue Mountain Center (N.Y.) writers' and artists' colony, for generously allowing me to avail myself of the premises at a most critical point.

I am fortunate to have found in my editor, David Kilgour, an understanding and sympathetic person who became enthralled with the project and deftly cleaned up my mess. There are others too numerous to mention who, by showing a continuing interest in the eventual result, have proved the best of stimuli.

After considerable thought, I decided against a formal dedication for this book. The book itself, I realized, is the dedication I make to the people of Shatila and all other refugee camps and all those other self-sacrificing souls around the globe who by their example have given me much more than I can ever hope to repay.

Prologue

Shatila Refugee Camp, West Beirut,

April 3, 1987

A RESOUNDING THUD, FOLLOWED BY THE STACCATO OF small-arms fire, pierced the silence. In the hospital emergency room, we looked at each other in silent understanding – the enemy militia had once again attacked the United Nations' food trucks. And once again, we would stand by and watch the cartons and sacks of rice, sugar, oil, flour, and canned goods go up in flames. We heard shouting near the hospital and knew that the frenzy of work would allow us to forget – forget one exhausting twenty-hour day too many; forget the debilitating diet of fewer than 1,000 calories a day; forget the frustration of the seemingly endless siege.

I could hear the screams growing louder and louder as people quickly approached the hospital. The scene was all too familiar: emaciated young men in rags carrying a wounded body on a hammock stretcher strung between two poles. They burst through the door, a band of children and the curious following behind, straining to see the wounded woman. It was Somaya, lying pale on the stretcher, her long dark robes splotched red; two men cradled her young children in their arms.

I could guess what had happened. After being cloistered for months in underground bomb shelters, some families had gathered in a dangerously exposed spot near the periphery of the refugee district, eager to watch the arrival of the food convoy. The enemy militia encircling the refugee camp had opened fire. Now families and gawkers had noisily converged on the hospital, gathering in the waiting room, impeding the movements and work of the hospital staff. I gave them a long, cold stare and a few shouted orders, and the milling crowd cleared the area.

I directed the men carrying Somaya's children into the out-patient clinic. A large piece of shrapnel had decapitated one child. The other had a black and red gash in place of a right eye. There was nothing I could do for them.

I went back to the emergency room and quickly examined Somaya. The other doctors and nurses swarmed about her, cutting away her clothing, inserting intravenous lines, and withdrawing blood samples. They administered analgesics, antibiotics, and antitetanus serum. Under the dim glow of the battery-run neon lamp overhead, I saw that shrapnel had hit her in the chest and abdomen. It was a kind of injury that had become routine. X-rays were not necessary: the penetration of the shrapnel was only too obvious. Besides, we had to conserve our dwindling electrical supply.

Somaya needed an operation, and as the only surgeon in the camp, I would perform it. I ordered two units of blood. With insufficient fuel to run the electric generators, the laboratory technicians would have to cross-match the blood without electricity, using instead a system involving a fluorescent lamp powered by a car battery. Appropriate technology – Western medicine fuelled by desperate improvisation.

Somaya had been a neighbour. With her three children, she lived on the second floor of the house just beside the hospital pharmacy. Her husband had disappeared in the 1982 Massacre of the Sabra and Shatila refugee camps in Beirut. Over the previous eighteen months, her pallid, toothless face and those of her three young children had become a familiar sight in the narrow alleyways around the hospital.

"Dr. Giannou, Dr. Giannou, where are my children?" Somaya babbled. I tried to calm her, told her not to talk, it was bad for her, but she went on. "We were standing by the house of Abu Kamal, watching the trucks arrive. The children were crying from hunger. Then there was a flash, and the ground heaved up. Where are my children, my children?"

I walked the ten steps from the emergency room to the out-patient clinic of our cramped makeshift hospital, where a nurse was wiping the blood from the two tiny disfigured corpses. How could I tell Somaya that two of her children were dead? How could I bury yet another two bodies? Shatila had been under siege for so long; there had been so many bodies, so much blood. And so many tears that we could not yet allow ourselves to shed.

A scrub nurse announced that everything was ready, and two hospital workers-cum-orderlies carried Somaya down to the underground operating theatre. Once again, we would perform an operation without electricity, one fluorescent lamp functioning on a car battery and a series of flashlights and camping lanterns providing the only lighting. Yet again, I would have to do what surgeons avoid doing – operating on a friend. Somaya lay naked and limp on the operating table. I went to work on the belly that had given birth to the now lifeless bodies in the room upstairs.

Shatila had been under siege for 131 days – the latest, most murderous and devastating of a series of battles. The War of the Camps, as it was called, pitted the inhabitants of Palestinian refugee camps in Beirut against the Lebanese Shi'ite Amal militia and their Syrian backers. The militiamen thought that they could overrun the squalid refugee district, control it and its independent-minded population *manu militari*. First they tried to bomb the inhabitants into submission. Then they attempted to starve them by destroying the desperately needed provisions carried by UN trucks. But this was Shatila! The Palestinian refugees had withstood the infamous Massacre of Sabra and Shatila in the summer of 1982, and for the last two years, since 1985, they had withstood the possibility of yet more. Shatila: symbol of resistance in the face of oppression, massacre, poverty, siege, and yet more massacre.

It is impossible to understand Shatila and its symbolic significance without understanding at least some of the dizzying political complexities of life in the Middle East. Shatila is but one of many Palestinian refugee districts scattered around several countries in the area. During the first Arab-Israeli war between 1947 and 1949, after the creation of the state of Israel and its rejection by the Arab nations, about 900,000 Palestinians fled their homes, some to avoid the armed conflict, others forced out militarily or by fear after a number of well-publicized massacres carried out by extremist right-wing Jewish underground groups. UN Resolution 181 of 1947 partitioned British Mandate Palestine into the Jewish state of Israel, an Arab Palestinian state, and the international zone of Jerusalem. Due in large part to a tacit agreement between the Israeli leadership and the King of Jordan, the Palestinian state never saw the light of day. In spite of yearly United Nations' resolutions calling for their repatriation or compensation, 900,000 refugees remained scattered, homeless and stateless (unlike any other contemporary refugees).

In 1949, the world community created the United Nations Relief and Works Agency (UNRWA) to deal with these refugees. There were more than 100,000 Palestinians in Lebanon (equivalent to ten percent of that country's population at the time, and by 1982, some 250,000 were registered with UNRWA), as well as hundreds of thousands of others in Syria, Jordan, the West Bank, and the Gaza Strip. UNRWA set up a series of refugee districts in these areas, signing ninety-nine-year land leases with the Arab governments' approval. Originally the districts consisted of tent encampments – thus the name "camps." UNRWA established fifteen such refugee camps in Lebanon. One of them was Shatila, named after the wealthy Lebanese man who donated a plot of land out of a sense of solidarity with the destitute refugees.

The tents eventually gave way to shacks of wooden panelling and zinc sheeting, followed in turn by one-storey, flat-roofed cinderblock buildings without indoor plumbing, running water, or electricity. At first, large tracts of empty land separated the urban area of Beirut from the refugee districts of Shatila and the nearby camps of Sabra and Burj el-Barajneh. Over four decades, due to uncontrolled urbanization, a rural exodus of poor villagers flooded Beirut and swamped the small, isolated refugee camps in a sprawling suburban slum. Slum merged with refugee district: both had the same drab concrete buildings, same hodgepodge of paved and unpaved roads and alleys, same labourers and shopkeepers, same alienation and poverty. Poverty does not recognize arbitrary borders, and the outlines of the original refugee districts had long since been forgotten. With time, the region around Shatila housed a raucous mix: Palestinian refugees; poor Lebanese; and migrant Egyptian, Syrian, and Kurdish manual labourers. The poor had come to live with the poor. They created a sorry slum belt around Beirut and provided a plentiful source of cheap labour for the needs of the sophisticated and luxurious inner city. Interspersed amidst the raw cement and mortar exteriors of the shanty-town hovels were solidly built, eight-storey middle-class apartment blocks with smoothly finished façades. A struggling sub-middle class tried to "cross the street" into the better apartment houses.

For some twenty years, the Palestinians remained the wards of the UN and the Arab state system. UNRWA provided and oversaw basic services in the refugee districts – education, health clinics, water purification, sewage and rubbish disposal. At first, the overwhelming majority of Lebanese received the refugees with an outpouring of sympathy. But as the years passed, and the refugees, unable to return to their homes, became a permanent feature of the Lebanese social landscape, sentiments changed. Some Lebanese profited from this source of cheap labour; others feared that the entrenchment of a largely Muslim population would tip the scales of Lebanon's political system. Christian Armenian refugees, who fled to Lebanon after the genocide in Turkey, never provoked such alarm. On the contrary, although as numerically strong as the Palestinian refugees, *they* were accorded full Lebanese citizenship.

Except in Jordan and the West Bank, where they hold Jordanian passports, Palestinian refugees have no citizenship. They carry a travel document, *laissez-passer*, given out by their host government. In Lebanon, the government also controlled the kinds of employment open to the refugees, usually limiting them to the most menial labour. To maintain the Palestinians' status as "non-permanents" – refugees who would theoretically eventually leave the country – the government prohibited them from building concrete roofs to cover their cinderblock houses, the theory being that you could not build a second storey if your roof was made of zinc sheeting. Resentment of such treatment increased over the years, just as it did among disenfranchised and poor Lebanese. Intermarriage between Palestinians and Lebanese helped the process of integration, but was largely a phenomenon of the poorer classes.

However, the Palestinian refugee population, in Lebanon as elsewhere, never became an underclass. Through education and entrepreneurial flair, they became upwardly mobile, and openly chafed at their status as wards of Arab states. Over the years, through locally formed Popular Committees, they had already begun helping administer camp services that had once been the sole province of UNRWA. But by far the most momentous step in the development of Palestinian nationalism came in 1968, when the refugees took control of a small, politically insignificant body called the Palestine Liberation Organization.* In an era of world-wide decolonization, Palestinian nationalism was irrepressible. The Palestinians' hunger for national identity and self-determination would never be the same.

This hunger had been fed by a sense of intense frustration at seeing many countries in Africa and Asia achieve independence while the

*Although the PLO was founded in 1964 by the League of Arab States, Palestinian political factions assumed control of it only in 1968, subsequent to the Arab defeat in the 1967 Six-Day War.

very existence of a Palestine people was denied. The frustration was coupled with a sense of euphoria created by the wave of anticolonial guerrilla wars of the 1960s and 1970s – Algeria, Vietnam, the Portuguese colonies of Africa, Zimbabwe, Namibia, South Africa. The times added Palestine to the list and prompted some Palestinian factions to engage in headline-capturing, sensationalist exploits – airplane hijacking, hostage taking, bloody suicide commando attacks, blind violence. The press lapped up the stories of terrorism, reinforced the prejudices and stereotypes, and the Palestinians gained publicity of incalculable value. This publicity also bestowed on them a reputation for violence which they have not lived down to this day.

By 1975, the refugee camps in Lebanon had become largely autonomous, relying on UNRWA and the Lebanese state only for public utilities. The PLO and its various factions had established a presence in all camps, including Shatila. Through institutions like the Popular Committees, the Palestine Red Crescent Society (PRCS), and General Unions, it provided everything from kindergartens for preschoolers, and vocational training for teen-agers, to disability payments for wounded guerrilla fighters and pensions for retirees. The seed of an economic base was planted in public-sector textile factories that gave jobs to widows and orphans. Revolutionary Courts tried thieves and traitors; ideologues taught political science; military veterans trained young fighters. A people without a state had become adept at improvising the socio-economic structures necessary for its survival. The once fledgling PLO emerged as a kind of state-in-exile, and in the midst of Lebanon's civil disintegration, it became a state within a state.

The collapse of Lebanese state institutions during the civil war that began in 1975 brought an end to all the restrictive laws pertaining to working Palestinians, and further growth in the PLO's power opened new avenues of employment and development. The restrictions returned after 1982, but by then an entire generation had grown up without them, and whatever the distinctive accent of their parents, the younger generation of Palestinians melted into the mosaic of Lebanese regional accents. Were it not for the political rhetoric, pro- and anti-Palestinian, the Palestinians in Lebanon would have become much like the Lebanese Armenians – a distinct society within Lebanon's ethnic and sectarian pluralism but participating fully in its social, economic, and political life. As it happened, the Palestinians did participate, but there was no consensus as to what form their participation should take; commerce was acceptable (business is business, after all), but not integration or citizenship, or political power – the Lebanese could not even agree how to parcel out power among themselves.

Until the 1970s, the traditional cliché had it that Lebanon was the Switzerland of the Middle East, and Beirut the new Paris. The free-wheeling, open, and tolerant atmosphere attracted politically persecuted writers, publishers, and painters from throughout the Middle East. Beirut was a capital of artistic, intellectual, and political exiles, as well as bankers, merchants, and businessmen. A special tacit code designated every café with the political leanings of its clientele. Pan-Arabists, Communists, monarchists – a gentleman's agreement of tolerance gave everyone and every tendency ample living space.

But underneath the tranquil surface lay a plethora of problems. Deeply entrenched religious, social, economic, and political divisions mark Lebanon's social fabric, the sequelae of colonialism, decolonization, and the secular ideologies that swept the Middle East in the 1950s and 1960s. The differences are not simply Christian versus Muslim. Tensions exist between rich and poor, right and left, sectarian and secular, rural and urban; political traditions of the feudal clan compete with modernizing democratic aspirations, creating a generational gap between an elderly traditional political caste and a group of young militia leaders. "The Events," as the civil war is called in Lebanon, broke out in 1975 and generally polarized the country between two contending camps: a right-wing, mostly Maronite Christian grouping of militias and political parties (Phalangists), and a left-wing coalition of Lebanese secular parties and militias (socialists, Communists, and pan-Arab nationalists), mostly but not entirely Muslim, called the Lebanese National Movement (LNM). The Palestinian refugee community (about a tenth of the population) and its political representation, the various factions of the PLO, entered the fray on the side of the LNM.

The right-wing Maronites, traditionally the advantaged group politically, socially, and economically, feared both the results of demographic changes that had made Muslims the majority community in Lebanon and the increasingly active political role of the PLO and its secular, left-wing Lebanese allies. The latter wanted a more democratic form of government, not one based on religious affiliation.

Civil war ravaged the country, with contending militias and troops perpetrating massacres and counter-massacres. A whole society became a string of contending militias; every interest group armed its followers or hired mercenaries, and the combatants often fell far short of their leaders' heroic rhetoric.

War carved up the city of Beirut, indeed the whole of Lebanon, into different fiefdoms. An ever-shifting series of alliances among warlords, revolutionaries, traffickers, businessmen, politicians, and militia leaders created, at times, an apparently intractable confusion. Each major coalition controlled some part of the country. The president of the republic held no real power, his sovereignty extending, literally, only as far as the ornate wrought-iron gate of the Presidential Palace.

Lebanon's particularity was its position as crossroads, transit and meeting point between the European West and the Arab Middle East; it was a vibrant society open to many cultural and political influences, a resonance box upon which the swirl of regional events drummed out conflicting rhythms. As a result, local factors were only one element in the many that created the divisiveness of the Lebanese scene. Not content with all the local contradictions of a fractious and fractured society, various groups invited foreign involvement, for ideological or financial reasons, and regional conflicts soon complicated a difficult enough situation, at times overshadowing local problems.

In early June 1976, the right-wing Phalangist militia faced imminent military defeat when Syrian troops entered Lebanon, at the invitation of the Lebanese Maronite president, to help put an end to the civil strife. They attacked the PLO-LNM coalition. Two years later, Israel launched a limited invasion, siding with the Phalangists for its own reasons, one of which was to destroy the growing power of Palestinian groups. Outraged, Syria switched allegiances to the PLO-LNM.

By 1980, violence had degenerated into killing, looting, and extortion for base motives – territorial supremacy, criminal greed, grudges, and revenge – under a veneer of political justification. Many combatants could no longer articulate what they were fighting for, beyond shop-worn slogans or narrow community interests. Lebanon had become a post-apocalyptic society where the only law and order came, literally, out of the barrel of a gun and, sometimes, from the memories and social reflexes of a distant past. Beirut had fallen into a bizarre, finely tuned, complex form of near-total anarchy.

In June 1982, Israel invaded Lebanon to destroy the military, political, and socio-economic infrastructure of the PLO and put into power an acquiescent Lebanese government. The strategic goal of the invasion, an attempt to suppress the raucous Palestinian population of the occupied territories of the West Bank and the Gaza Strip, who had been demonstrating and throwing rocks for months, proved a total failure, as future events would show.

The Israeli army overran southern Lebanon, and after the evacuation of Palestinian troops and cadres in late August, Ariel Sharon, Israeli defence minister and mastermind of the invasion, imposed his candidate in the presidential election, providing Lebanese civil strife with a breath of fresh air.

The new president was a Phalangist, but no one wins for long in Lebanon. In the crucible of Lebanese politics, the bickering factions could conceivably elect only a compromise candidate, and a Phalangist president constituted anything but a compromise.

Following the assassination of this Phalangist president-elect by a Lebanese political foe, Israeli troops occupied West Beirut – now emptied of Palestinian fighters – took military control of the area and allowed the right-wing Christian Phalange militia to enter the undefended refugee districts. Despite U.S. guarantees and assurances for the physical security of the civilian population, massacres at Sabra and Shatila took place. Resistance was impossible; the Phalangist militiamen indiscriminately slaughtered the inhabitants. More than 3,000 Palestinian and Lebanese residents of the area died or disappeared, carried away to unknown destinations in the backs of Phalangist trucks. A world-wide public outcry, including protests in Israel, followed what Palestinians and the entire Middle East came to call "the Massacre." Israeli soldiers evacuated West Beirut, but handed over power to the Lebanese army controlled by the Phalangist government, a party to the civil war and the traditional enemy of many people in West Beirut.

This army spent most of 1983 tracking down and imprisoning many Palestinian and Lebanese activists. The Phalangist government's repression proved so extreme that West Beirut finally erupted in the uprising of February 6, 1984. Militiamen dug up their arms caches and went into the streets, the army dividing along sectarian lines. Between them, militiamen and nationalist soldiers expelled the Phalangist government-controlled troops from West Beirut.

In southern Lebanon, the Israeli army met with an ever-increasing popular guerrilla resistance to its occupation and finally withdrew in stages (1983-85) from most of the territory conquered in the 1982 war. The general situation in the country resembled that which had existed before the Israeli invasion, but with one notable exception. The PLO had represented the main political and military force in West Beirut and the south; now its leadership and many of its cadres had evacuated the city and the south. The Palestinians found themselves in a position of extreme weakness. But the ordinary people now had an active and ongoing tradition of resisting those forces whom they regarded as their enemies.

In Phalangist-free West Beirut in 1984, everyone was busy reorganizing: para-military militias flourished again, as did various left-wing Lebanese secular parties, the sectarian Muslim Shi'ite Amal Movement, the fundamentalist pro-Iranian Hizbollah, Palestinian groups within and outside the PLO, and numerous semi-feudal war-lords, local political chieftains and "community leaders," gangsters and street gangs with or without an ideology. Reorganizing meant recruiting – militiamen, party members, administrative personnel, thugs – rearming, opening offices and bureaux, re-establishing social services, and controlling "turf."

The strongest of the different Palestinian groups within the PLO was (and still is) Yassir Arafat's Fatah (reverse acronym for Palestine National Liberation Movement, and also a word meaning "the opening onto a new future"). Financially powerful, through contributions from oil-rich Arab states and judicious investment of funds, it enjoyed the most popular support. But since 1983, Arafat and the Syrian government had been at loggerheads. The Syrians disagreed violently with Arafat's leadership, considering him too moderate, and with the PLO weakened by its departure from Beirut and dispersal throughout the Arab world, Syria seized the moment in 1983 to attempt to impose its tutelage on the Palestinian leadership. Its goal was to control, politically and militarily, the PLO. The Syrians helped foment and then supported a dissident movement within Fatah and ultimately within the PLO itself. Although all Palestinians recognized the legitimacy and symbolic value of the PLO in terms of Palestinian national identity, some groups withdrew their recognition of the legitimacy of Arafat's leadership.

The Palestine National Salvation Front (PNSF), gathering the more radical and pro-Syrian factions, was the ultimate outcome. They criticized, with some reason, the corruption and nepotism of the PLO state-in-exile and disagreed with any political moderation that might entail the cessation of the "armed struggle," a negotiated settlement of the Arab-Israeli conflict, and recognition of Israel. Although they did not agree entirely with each other, and each faction had its own conflicting strategic goals the groups composing the PNSF found it expedient to join with Syria in opposing Arafat's leadership. (Syrian *realpolitik* had more to do with timing, regional power politics, and Syria's role and position, than with ideology.)

The ever-more fragmented Palestinian scene included yet other groups: the Democratic Front for the Liberation of Palestine (DFLP) and the Palestine Communist Party held an intermediate position between the pro-Syrian PNSF and the Arafat loyalists. Although also critical of organizational lapses, these orthodox Marxist groups had a more pragmatic and realistic political platform than the PNSF.

The majority of ordinary Palestinians, however, jealous of their relative political independence within the PLO, resented the Syrian intrusion. The trusteeship of Arab regimes did not interest Palestinians. During the period 1949-67, Arab states had controlled the West Bank and Gaza and had not allowed the Palestinians to organize as an independent political entity with freedom of action; as a result, the organizing they did was clandestine. The Arab state system considered the Palestinian cause the Arab cause, and Palestinians its wards; in fact, all too often the Palestinians in any given Arab country were no better than hostages in the hands of cynical and despotic regimes who thought little about using them as pawns in various inter-Arab rivalries, and especially in political conflicts with the Palestinian leadership. Almost twenty years later, the Palestinians felt that they had sacrificed too much and paid far too high a price to return to the political conflicts of any Arab state again.

The Palestinian refugee camps of Lebanon constituted the weak pressure point in this struggle for influence, and Syria had its local proxies lean heavily on them. In December 1983, their actions culminated in the battle of the camps in Tripoli, Lebanon's second city, between Arafat loyalists and Syrian-supported dissidents. The Syrian army participated in shelling the refugee districts and the city. With its formation, the PNSF became the semi-official representative of the camps in northern and eastern Lebanon, where Syrian control was preponderant.

The Syrians had no desire to allow the Palestinians and their political rival, Arafat, to re-establish a political base in West Beirut after the uprising in February 1984 that expelled the Phalangist-controlled army. But, for reasons of political propriety, Syria could not intervene directly in the city, and instead called upon its local ally, the sectarian Shi'ite militia, Amal. Supported by the Lebanese Army Sixth Brigade, Amal militiamen were the most powerful military force in West Beirut. It was their task to control the Palestinians and their left-wing Lebanese secular allies. Easier said than done. Lebanese socialists and nationalists continued to occupy large areas of West Beirut. Entrenched inside their refugee camps, the various Palestinian groups increased in strength, escaping more and more from any external authority. In light of this, control of the Palestinians meant control of the refugee camps themselves, militarily if necessary.

And so, in May 1985, Syria gave the green light to begin what became known as the War of the Camps. It started as a street skirmish – not an unusual event in Lebanon, where a traffic accident can and often does degenerate into a full-scale battle with heavy machine guns and rocket-propelled grenades – and turned into a surprise massive assault against the refugee districts of Sabra, Shatila, and Burj el-Barajneh.

During this assault, the second massacre at Sabra took place. Amal militiamen overran the Sabra refugee camp on May 31, 1985, and took prisoner 700 young Palestinian men, who simply disappeared. There has been no news of them to this day.

By October 1985, war had clearly redrawn the boundaries of the Shatila refugee camp – all 200 yards by 200 yards of it – that a shared poverty had previously erased. Those who had survived the infamous Massacre of Sabra and Shatila confronted the prospect of an even more horrendous massacre, but they vowed to fight and resist. This time, they would not go to the slaughter without a struggle; anyone who wanted to conquer Shatila would have to go in over the dead bodies of its inhabitants.

By the time I arrived in Shatila in 1985 to set up a Palestine Red Crescent Society (PRCS) hospital, I knew the Middle East well: I was a five-year veteran of war surgery and a seventeen-year veteran of what might best be described as a Third World odyssey.

My road to Shatila had been a long and tortuous one. In 1968, at the age of nineteen, I had arrived in Mali, West Africa, to teach English and mathematics. Like many other North American students of the time – idealistic, appalled by racism, assassinations, and political horrors at home and by the war in far-off Vietnam, caught up with the plight and promise of a newly reawakened Third World – I was drawn to the struggle for political and social justice. The maelstrom of student protests, the upheavals of Québec's *Révolution tranquille*, the headiness of civil rights marches in the American deep South, the Prague spring, and African decolonization monopolized my attention. I felt the immediacy of incidents thousands of miles away as my mind tuned in the world, the global village. Nothing seemed extraneous.

But I also had another, more personal cause: in early adolescence in Toronto, I had made the decision to go into medicine. My heroes and role models were deeply committed doctors – Albert Schweitzer, Norman Bethune (the Canadian who served with the International Brigades in Republican Spain and then with Mao Zedong's Eighth Army Corps, eventually dying of septicaemia contracted while operating on the wounded in the mountains of China), and Ernesto Che Guevara, whose political activities make many people forget that he was a doctor. Their selfless dedication coincided with my own yearnings – a passion and philosophy that endless discussions at home had cultivated. Adolescent fantasies? Romantic dreams? Whatever they were, they shaped the man to be. In Mali there were no romantic fantasies. I saw with my own eyes what those doctors had had to deal with – poverty, malnutrition, ignorance, inadequate medical care, oppression – and I knew that this was where I had to be.

There was something else too. The son of Greek-Macedonian immigrants to Canada, I had always felt like an outsider growing up in the WASP Toronto of the 1950s and 1960s; complacent, staid "Toronto-the-good," quiet, clean, and "white"; a village of a million people who prided themselves on their tolerance and open-mindedness, their civilized way of life and lack of racism. Hypocrisy ruled that world, of course. There were simply not yet enough people of colour for Toronto's true colours to show. Acutely aware of being the child of immigrants who spoke broken, heavily accented English, I attended an élite and prestigious school for boys, where the few "ethnics" – Jews, a Pakistani, and myself – found ourselves outnumbered by the WASPs; we felt surrounded by the establishment. We had to do better than the WASPs and speak English better than they. The more I saw and learned, the more disillusioned and embittered I became with Canadian society and North American values and perceptions.

In Mali, though the details of daily social life were different, the spirit of the place made me feel right at home. The Malians I met were desperately poor and immensely proud. Grinding poverty, death, political and social crises ravaged the country, yet I found the resilience, optimism, intellectual honesty, and generosity of the people overwhelming. My friends engaged in impassioned philosophical and political discussions, much as my father and maternal grandfather had, their voices often rising with emotion. Anything worth talking about, they talked about with passion. They extended their hospitality without question, welcoming me as if I were a cousin from another village, taking me into their homes, feeding me, including me in family celebrations and feast days. In Mali, I found the camaraderie that I had longed for growing up in Canada. I also found the justification of the values that my family had given me: a sense of justice and compassion, an ethos of principles that mandated personal responsibility towards society. Humanity, not dollars or prestige or class, counted.

That year in Mali, after a coup d'état overthrew the radical nationalist government, one of my students died during an epidemic of cerebro-spinal meningitis, and I myself fell ill with malaria and then hepatitis. I felt the vortex of events swirl about me. Even the pathology that racked my body seemed strangely congruent with outside events. The young Malian doctors who treated me, newly graduated from modern French state-of-the-art hospitals, complained bitterly. They had trained in facilities where they lacked nothing and now faced the constant struggle to adapt, innovate, make do with what little they had. They hoped that, somehow, they would be able to overcome the maddening frustrations of practising medicine in circumstances for which they had not been prepared. Because of what I learned from them, I decided to study medicine in Algiers, where conditions and equipment would be more like what I would have to work with if I stayed in the Third World.

In Algeria, newly independent after a long and brutal anticolonial war, I learned more than medicine. Always a political animal, I immersed myself in the rich debates of a country just emerging from French rule. The totality of the revolutionary experience forced my Algerian friends to question every shibboleth in politics, literature, cinema, and the social sciences. The country seethed with massive cultural, social, and political contradictions and I found myself in the midst of one.

I fell in love with an Algerian woman, and my relationship with her overshadowed all else. We had a Romeo-and-Juliet romance, overwhelmingly passionate against inordinate odds and opposition. Saida and I wanted to marry, but in nationalistic Algeria marriage to a non-Muslim foreigner was taboo. In the face of threats, emotional blackmail, and finally expulsion, we fled Algeria, married, and moved to Cairo to pursue our studies.

Cairo was a revelation, a teeming cosmopolitan metropolis, capital of a 7,000-year-old society – from pyramids to Abd el-Nasser's High Dam. Only a year had passed since the death of Nasser, and Cairo was a centre of pan-Arabism, imbued with a sense of Egypt's manifest destiny as a leader of the Third World. When we arrived in 1971, we saw Soviet military and economic advisors everywhere. When we left in 1980, American and Israeli tourists and businessmen had taken their place. We lived through and observed the historical transformation that occurred in Egyptian society, from Nasser to Sadat. In the meantime, we learned Arabic and completed our studies, Saida in linguistics at the American University and I in surgery at the National Cancer Institute.

The University Hospital clinics were like a pathology museum, from tuberculosis and leprosy, to malnutrition and morbid obesity. Peasant women arrived for examinations and held in their cupped hands huge breasts of rotting malignant flesh, the putrid odour overwhelming even some of the more experienced clinicians. I felt a sense of helplessness as I observed the mass of misery, and with it, rage. I knew all about this, in theory. Now I faced it in practice.

And practise was what I sought to do next. By 1980, both Saida and I had completed our masters' degrees. My Cairo medical education had been perfect training for me, involving as it did constant improvisation and adaptation to fit whatever conditions I might find. But where to go?

For various reasons, Lebanon and the Palestinian refugees there attracted us. It was nearby, and we had a few friends there. I had met quite a few Palestinians and Lebanese during my years in Algeria and Egypt, and fellow classmates, both in Algiers and in Cairo, had become our best friends. More than that, the Palestinian cause drew me: a people dispossessed and vilified as terrorists both in Israel and throughout the Western world – "victims of the victims," in the words of Professor Edward Said.

My views on the Israeli-Palestinian question represented to me a convergence of my ideas and emotions about contemporary political events. The Holocaust had been a unique event in human history, in more ways than one. The Nazis had massacred millions of Jews, while the soon-to-be victors, the Allies, looked on. Great Britain, Canada, the United States watched and allowed only pitiful refugee quotas of several thousands of Jews per year (in Canada, under the slogan "None is too many"), while hundreds of thousands clamoured for entry. Then, partly to expiate their sense of guilt, partly for crass imperial interests, these same Allied victors, supporting the former victims, victimized another people, the Palestinians. By the 1970s, the self-justification of the injustice was all too apparent in the new anti-Arab, anti-Palestinian racism that depicted the victims only as "oil-sheikhs" or "terrorists."

Besides, the view of the Middle East from Africa seemed more congruent with UN documents I had read as a student than with the views of the North American media. As early as 1965, I had been introduced to the Palestinian question when I participated in a high-school model United Nations General Assembly, where we studied UN documents and engaged in debates. Western media had defined problems in the Middle East in terms of Israel and Egypt, or Israel and the Arabs. At the mock assembly, I studied UN resolutions from the 1940s and 1950s that dealt with the rights of Palestinians. Palestinians? I realized that an entire people had disappeared from public discourse. Western public opinion had forgotten that the Palestinians existed.

I had seen Lebanon once before, for several weeks in the summer of 1973. At first view, the cosmopolitanism and sophistication, the bookstores and cultural activity, the intellectual and political ferment, the tourism and *joie de vivre* gave the country a marvellous allure. But a basic contradiction of poverty and political disenfranchisement for the majority of the Lebanese people whose labour created the conditions for the life-style of the minority lurked beneath the tolerance, erudition, and sophistication.

After years of civil war, revolutionary hopes of wiping clear the veneer of sophisticated, cultured tolerance, based on privilege, gave way to primitive bestial intolerance. This was the Lebanon that I met, the result of so many betrayed hopes and dreams, when I returned to work there in 1980 as a surgeon with the PRCS.

I worked at the Gaza Hospital in Beirut, the main surgical hospital of the PRCS and informally the Ministry of Health of the sizable semi-state apparatus that the PLO had become. The hospital bordered the Sabra refugee camp, just to the north of the general slum area that was known as Shatila, taking its name from the refugee camp that formed its heart and core.

I often walked through the maze of alleyways of the refugee camps and surrounding areas that first year, visiting patients and friends, or simply going from the Gaza Hospital to the PRCS administrative offices at Akka Hospital a mile away. Walking along the main road, Sabra-Shatila Street, between the two hospitals, friends told me: this is Sabra, this Shatila, the other side of the street is not part of the camp. It all looked the same, one continuous swath of ramshackle shanty town and humanity.

In 1981, Saida left for London to pursue a Ph.D., and I went to southern Lebanon. Several years later we divorced, and there was no one to tie me to any place other than where I was – Lebanon.

We worked hard in the PRCS hospitals where I was posted, honing our skills in field hospitals under combat and siege. Depending on which war it was, I remember dashing across the Lebanese countryside in an ambulance dodging Israeli, Phalangist, or Syrian bombs. During the Israeli invasion of Lebanon in 1982, the Israeli army took me prisoner, an experience I will never forget – only the intervention of the Canadian government secured my release. In 1983, in Tripoli, northern Lebanon, under siege at the hands of anti-Arafat Palestinian dissidents and the Syrian army, I was charged with the medical care of six Israeli prisoners of war in the custody of the PLO, dodging Syrian bombs this time in order to reach my patients. Such are the ironies of war.

After a year and a half in PRCS hospitals in Cairo and Sanaa, North Yemen, after hearing of the slaughter in Shatila that summer, in October 1985 I asked to be posted there.

LEBANON

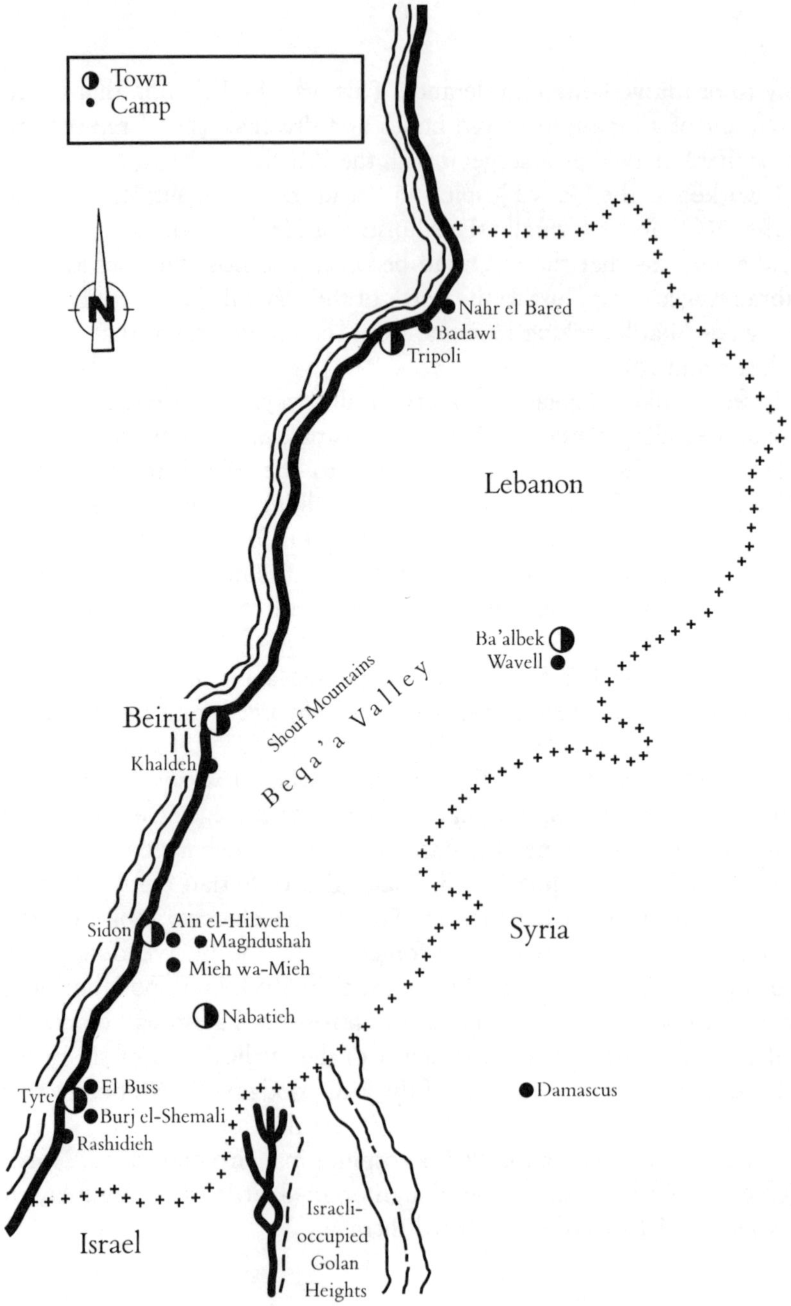
Town
Camp
N
Nahr el Bared
Badawi
Tripoli
Lebanon
Ba'albek
Wavell
Shouf Mountains
Beqa'a Valley
Beirut
Khaldeh
Sidon
Ain el-Hilweh
Maghdushah
Mieh wa-Mieh
Syria
Nabatieh
Tyre
El Buss
Burj el-Shemali
Rashidieh
Damascus
Israel
Israeli-
occupied
Golan
Heights

BEIRUT

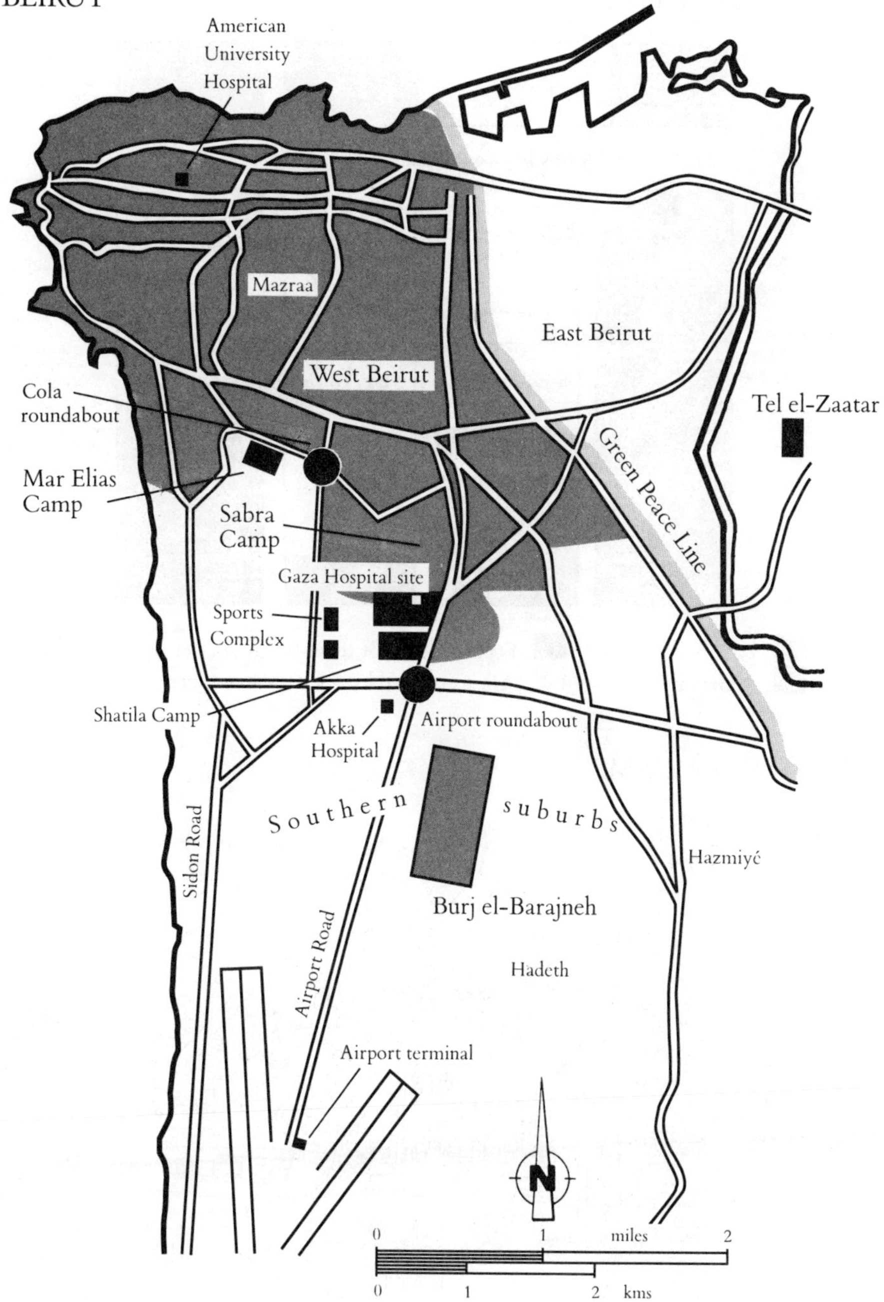

American University Hospital
Mazraa
East Beirut
West Beirut
Cola roundabout
Tel el-Zaatar
Green Peace Line
Mar Elias Camp
Sabra Camp
Gaza Hospital site
Sports Complex
Shatila Camp
Akka Hospital
Airport roundabout
Southern suburbs
Sidon Road
Hazmiyé
Burj el-Barajneh
Airport Road
Hadeth
Airport terminal
N
0
1
miles
2
0
1
2
kms

THE HOSPITAL

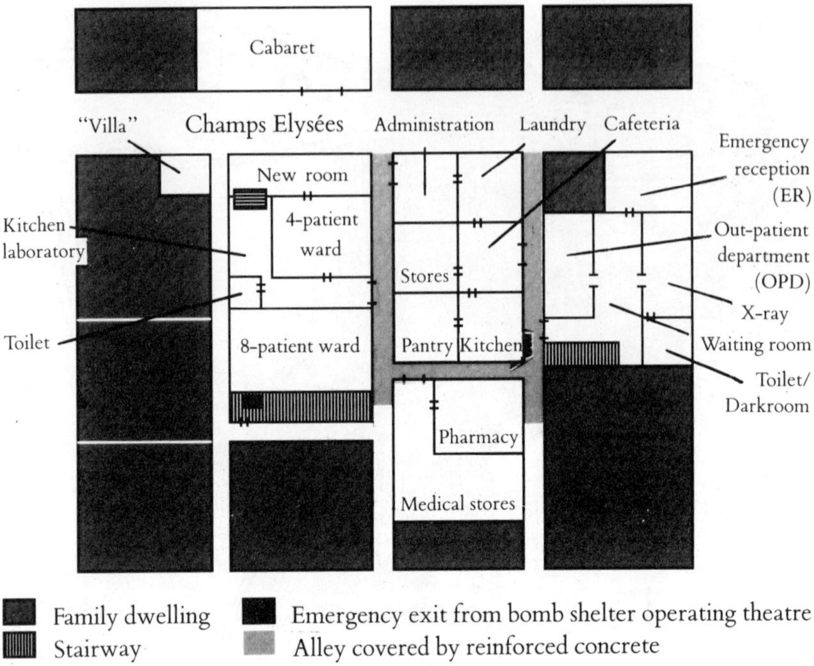

SHATILA CAMP

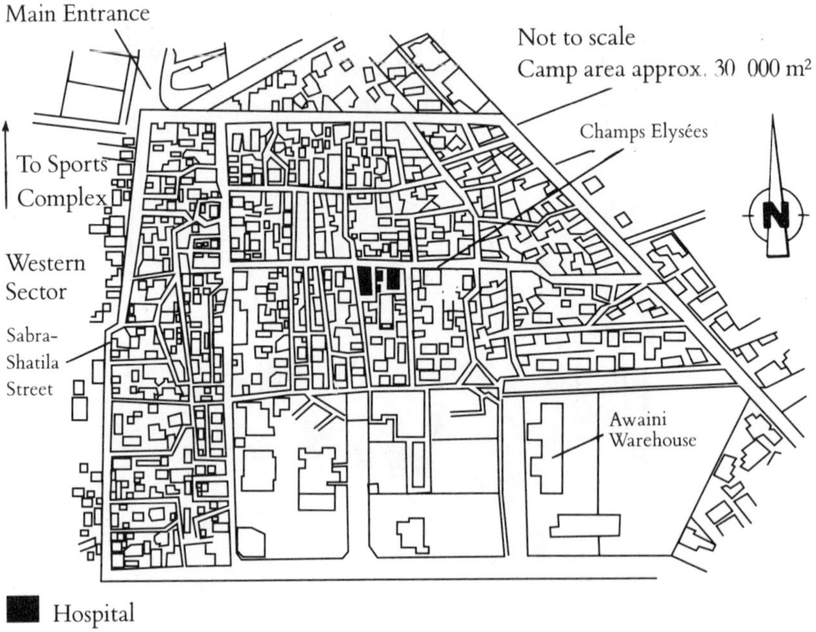

1

"After All, This Is Shatila"

October 27, 1985

I FELT ANXIETY MINGLED WITH NOSTALGIA AS THE airplane swooped low over the sea into Beirut International Airport. The plane trip from Sanaa, North Yemen, to Beirut via Cyprus took only four hours but covered centuries in changing social realities. Snow already capped the peaks of the majestic mountains beyond the city. I looked down on the familiar sights of Beirut, scenes of some of my most cherished and most bitter memories: of good friends and good times, tainted like everything else in Lebanon by memories of war and suffering. My emotions swung back and forth, mirroring, I thought to myself, my comings and goings to and from Lebanon. I had not seen West Beirut since the Israeli invasion of 1982, since before the Sabra and Shatila Massacre.

Two Lebanese friends met me at the airport. Nothing new here: the usual contingent of bandoleered militiamen and soldiers, heavily armed yet lackadaisical about security, and the usual good-natured but nervous jostling of travellers. Customs agents pretended to carry out their duties in a country where everything imaginable was available cheaply through smuggling. The routine only served to enrich the agents by means of the traditional baksheesh. Some things in Lebanon had remained the same.

My friends accompanied me into town. They had been members of the Communist Party, but now belonged to the pro-Iranian Shi'ite fundamentalist party, Hizbollah. I didn't ask too many questions about their change of allegiance. Nonetheless, only Hizbollahi could guarantee my safe passage through the Shi'ite southern suburbs of Beirut and through the checkpoints of Amal, the mainstream Muslim Shi'ite militia. My companions explained, not without a little dark humour, that if the militiamen at a checkpoint asked too many questions, they would simply reply that I was their "Western hostage." There had not been any "Western hostages" the last time I was in West Beirut, when the Palestinians and their leftist Lebanese allies held sway. Decidedly, if some things in Lebanon had remained the same, others had changed.

I was dropped off at an innocuous little hotel in the city. For security reasons, no one knew the date and time of my arrival. I contacted a "safe" person in the PRCS administration; within an hour a clerk and a chauffeur, whom I knew from 1980 at the Gaza Hospital, picked me up at the hotel. Their Mercedes bumped along the rutted road on the way to Shatila. Bearded Amal militiamen and Lebanese army soldiers, nonchalantly carrying their weapons, sat at sidewalk café tables or ambled about the surrounding alleys. We passed the towering hulk of the gutted Gaza Hospital and the Sabra refugee camp, surrounded by the middle-class eight-storey apartment buildings and two-storey slum dwellings of the "Lebanese" Sabra. I stared in disbelief at the remains. Bullet-riddled blocks of tenement buildings and the Sabra market, flush with food stalls and wooden carts piled high with fruit and vegetables, bordered a swath of crushed concrete slabs and twisted iron bars that spread out like a large parking lot. The militiamen and soldiers had flattened the flimsy ramshackle refugee camp buildings with bulldozers. In fact, it *was* a parking lot; a large grey-green tank was stationed right in the centre of what once had been a refugee sanctuary. The tank's turret pointed towards Shatila, some 400 yards off.

We drove past the last Amal checkpoint without any trouble – the militiamen knew my friend the clerk and could expect special favours when they brought their families for treatment at one of the PRCS clinics – and parked on Sabra-Shatila Street, the major thoroughfare that bounds the western edge of Shatila. A long, relatively straight road, in contrast to the tortuous alleyways that emptied into it every few yards, S-S Street led from the Gaza to the Akka Hospital about a mile away. One- and two-storey flat-roofed cinderblock houses lined both sides, unfinished exteriors displaying their skeletons of bricks and cement mortar, wooden window frames interspersed with rolled-up aluminum door shutters opening onto tiny grocer shops, sandwich counters, barber and hair-styling salons, car mechanics' workshops. Here and there, like an oddity, was a three-storey solid building with a smooth-finished façade, tell-tale remnant of a more prosperous family, a more prosperous time. All constructions, however, wore the pitted acne-like markings of bullet holes.

The street surface had once been paved. Now, every rainfall turned the dust of its ruts, pot-holes, and bomb craters into a quagmire. An attempt had also once been made to add a sidewalk on each side, about a yard in width – a futile and vain project. What remained of the pedestrian sidewalk became porches for the tiny dwellings; the mass of bustling pedestrians invaded the street, vying for passage with the stream of cars and pick-up trucks that clogged the six-yard-wide roadway, large enough for two-way traffic. In spite of the squalor and in contrast to the spectrum of dull greys, grey-browns, and mud-browns of the slum-scape, the people were dressed neatly and cleanly, most in modern Western clothing; blue jeans were the favourite among men, but natty pleated trousers and the latest fashionable loose-fitting shirts were also conspicuous; bright reds, greens, and yellows marked the skirts and dresses of the women, also modern but with hemlines modestly below the knees, for the most part; a few people, usually the more elderly, male and female, preferred the traditional flowing dark robes, the head covered either by a scarf or the ubiquitous plain white or checkered black and white or red and white Arab *keffieh*, the head-dress popularized by Palestinian *fidayeen* ("self-sacrificing" guerrilla fighters).

Carrying my one suitcase, I followed my companions into a labyrinth of alleyways, turned a sharp corner, and found myself in a narrow street clogged with a boisterous crowd stretching some fifty yards between two-storey cinderblock houses riddled with bullet holes. A din of children's voices, clanking metal, and welders' torches greeted us. The atmosphere immediately became claustrophobic; the two-storey dwellings seemed to tower over the minute alleys. Apart from the modern Western-style dress and traditional garb, the fashion parade here in the depths of the refugee district now included military grey-green camouflage. Passing Shatila's only mosque we turned left and about thirty paces on arrived at a nondescript, two-storey, pock-marked building that had been set up as a clinic. Having delivered me, the clerk and chauffeur left. I would not retrace my steps to West Beirut and the airport, or even leave the physical boundaries of Shatila, for twenty-seven months.

In the alleyway outside the clinic a throng of some thirty people surrounded me. I hugged and kissed each of them on both cheeks, as is the custom. I knew many of the staff, had worked with them at the Gaza Hospital, in southern Lebanon, or Tripoli. It was good to meet these old friends again after all that they and I had gone through over the last few years. I was pleasantly surprised to see so many of them – they had survived, were still alive! – here in Shatila. I would not be alone. We hugged, joked, slapped backs, and reminisced. Many had survived the Sabra and Shatila Massacre of September 1982. They had been working at the time in either the Gaza or the Akka hospitals and owed their lives to the intervention of medical volunteers from Europe and America. Other friends had not been so fortunate. One of the two doctors slain that September had served under me as an intern during my residency at the National Cancer Institute in Cairo; two ambulance drivers, also martyrs of the Massacre, had been part of my staff in Nabatieh, in southern Lebanon in 1981-82; still others had been imprisoned during the Israeli invasion of 1982. But the experiences I'd shared with these friends had bonded me to them. We were all back together again in Shatila, and it felt like a family reunion.

During the first round of the War of the Camps, in May 1985, no medical facilities whatsoever had existed in Shatila. After the ceasefire, personnel from the Palestine Red Crescent Society had entered the camp and set up a clinic. The staff knew that I had come as the new hospital director and that I had a good deal of experience in setting up a field hospital; quite a number of them had previously established similar facilities with me. They were also happy and relieved that a surgeon had finally arrived. It seemed that no other surgeon had been willing to come to Shatila.

One of the few people I didn't know personally was Dr. Mohammed Khatib, the acting director of the clinic. A general practitioner, and one of the two doctors stuck in Shatila during the horrendous first round of fighting the previous summer, he was an eccentric, overweight, jovial fellow about my age, with bad teeth, and an even worse chain-smoker than I. The inhabitants of Shatila recognized him as their poet laureate and chess champion, but all of this I found out later. I didn't want to waste time on the niceties now, so we plunged right in. Dr. Khatib and I stood aside and had the first of many long discussions well into the night, discussions about politics, war and health, love, medicine, and poetry. He described to me what he had attempted in organizing the new hospital and some of the problems he had faced. I found him unassuming and unpretentious. He could easily and understandably have felt some jealousy at my taking over as hospital director. But in fact, relief shone in his face. He knew that I had more medical and administrative experience than he and was eager to learn and co-operate.

Dr. Khatib was still suffering from nightmares about some of the wounded who had literally died in his arms because he was unable to help them. He had no surgical experience and few medical supplies at his disposal during that first battle. He had vowed then that he would never find himself in such a situation again, and now he particularly wanted me to teach him some simple but potentially life-saving surgical procedures. I called up the words of the Dean of the Algiers Faculty of Medicine when he answered a question that some students had raised about the relevancy of a course on new developments in neurochemistry. "What usc is such knowlege, given the state of our technological development and the needs of our people?" the students had asked. "We are underdeveloped," began the young dean shyly and with a boyish grin, "but we do not have to teach and practise underdeveloped medicine. You will learn the new as well as the old; your genius will be to determine when and where to use each." I repeated his words to Dr. Khatib. "We do not have to practise underdeveloped medicine, even in the simple surroundings of Shatila."

Dr. Khatib and I became close friends over the next twenty-seven months, and his co-operation proved instrumental not only in helping to set up the hospital, but also in dealing with the camp's inhabitants and different political leaders. He lived in Shatila and the people all respected him. The long list of Shatila's martyrs would eventually include the names of his two children.

The PRCS had rented two houses for the clinic and future hospital; they were separated by a third uninhabited one, its roof blown away. Dr. Khatib showed me around. Externally, nothing distinguished these buildings from the others in Shatila. The first house was two storeys high, flat roof, the only large window on the ground floor covered over by a pile of sandbags that reached nearly to the second storey. There were four rooms on the ground floor. We entered through a short corridor that contained a toilet and small niche under the staircase that served as kitchen. The corridor gave onto a central waiting room with wooden benches and doors to the other three rooms. Workers had recently whitewashed and then repainted in hospital green the walls of all the rooms. A few posters from the

World Health Organization (WHO) and UNICEF dealing with breast-feeding, the treatment of infantile diarrhea, and vaccinations hung on the walls.

The emergency reception, about four and a half by four yards, contained two cots for receiving patients; a series of wooden shelves filled with one-litre plastic sacks of intravenous fluids; a metal cupboard for phials and ampoules of emergency drugs; and a table along one wall with dry-heat sterilizer, small autoclave, and paraphernalia for dressing changes. The second room, about the same size, served as the pharmacy and also as a place for unoccupied staff to sit and drink tea or coffee and chew the fat. Shelves containing different medications covered three walls, and a small window, used to dispense prescriptions to patients, looked out onto the entrance corridor.

The third room, furnished with an examining couch, simple wooden table, and two chairs, functioned as the out-patient clinic. The furnishings and decor of the entire place, like the people, were frugal and simple.

Leaving this building, we followed a narrow alleyway, walked around the uninhabited house, and came upon a large three-storey building. Men on the roof were constructing a fourth storey. This structure, located at almost the exact geographical centre of Shatila, appeared to be one of the most solidly built in the camp. The PRCS had rented the ground floor from a member of the Executive Committee of the General Union of Palestinian Workers, Abu Mohammed Faramawi (in keeping with tradition, he was called Abu Mohammed – the father of Mohammed, his first-born son), whose family now lived in the storey above. The third storey was empty and unfinished, raw concrete and plaster, with laundry lines strung from empty window- and door-frames. Faramawi had had the prescience to accept an offer made by the PLO in 1975 to construct underground bomb shelters in the refugee camps of Lebanon. He later explained over coffee that he and his family were the only ones in Shatila who had agreed to leave the camp for a year, while the PLO demolished his home, dug a basement bomb shelter, and then rebuilt the dwelling in a very solid fashion. Since then, people in Shatila had often used this bomb shelter to seek safety from shelling. The shelter measured eight yards long by three and a half wide. A wall extended over just half the width, more or less dividing it into two rooms. My colleagues had planned to use the space as an X-ray department.

The ground floor of the building comprised two rooms, a kitchen and a small bathroom. Dr. Khatib and other staff had thought to use the larger of the two rooms as an operating theatre and the smaller, which could hold up to four hospital beds, as an in-patient ward; the kitchen was to be the nursing station. Whitewash and hospital green met the eye here as well. Various pieces of equipment, surgical instruments, aluminum drums, and sterilization boxes filled the two rooms to overflowing. The prospective operating theatre contained an air conditioner, placed in what had formerly been the living-room window. It was the only air-conditioned space in all Shatila. Meagre as it all was, dispersed between the two buildings, this already constituted, along with a reasonable supply of medicines and dressings, far more than what had been available the summer before.

After our visit to the clinic and hospital-to-be facilities, Abu Mohammed Faramawi invited Dr. Khatib and me upstairs for the traditional welcoming coffee. Large calloused hands vigorously shook mine. Faramawi had been a house painter and then dabbled in construction work, including the fourth storey-in-progress of his building. Of medium height and build, dark and moustached, he was in his early fifties. An autodidact, Faramawi had a long history, as he began to recount it, of political activism. He had risen to prominence in the Workers Union but, before that, he had been responsible for administrating the medical services of the Popular Front for the Liberation of Palestine (PFLP) in Lebanon. Now he listened intently while I described my plans for the future field hospital. He and his wife took great pride in living in Shatila, their home for thirty-odd years, and were adamant, like Dr. Khatib, in remaining there with their seven children. They wore the identity of Shatila like a badge of honour: its squalor, its suffering, its Massacre, its resistance and determination to overcome all and build a better, more just life. His wife, Oum

Mohammed ("the mother of Mohammed"), had worked in the PRCS as chief housekeeper of the obstetric and gynaecology department of Gaza Hospital when it was still functioning. She would soon assume similar functions in Shatila. Somewhat corpulent, a vivacious and conscientious woman, Oum Mohammed quickly adopted me. She often rummaged through my affairs on the sly, searching for dirty laundry to wash, to save me the time and effort, or put aside a plate of food when I was kept late and missed meals.

We talked about The Situation – our situation in Shatila. In order to function in Shatila, I had to understand all the factions, military and otherwise, represented in its population. The strongest of the different Palestinian groups was Yassir Arafat's mainstream Fatah, the central component of the PLO, funded by Saudi Arabia, Kuwait, other oil-rich Gulf states, and their relatively wealthy and not inconsiderable Palestinian immigrant populations. The Palestine National Salvation Front (PNSF), the "opposition," was composed of six smaller, more radical factions, funded by Syria and Libya. Between the Arafat loyalists and the PNSF lay the orthodox Marxist Democratic Front and Communist Party. Faramawi and Dr. Khatib both had close connections to the Popular Front for the Liberation of Palestine – Marxist, pro-Syrian and part of the PNSF, but defiantly Palestinian nationalist. As Faramawi put it, "We recognize our Arab political background, but Arab regimes have too often betrayed us, exploited our refugee situation for their own political agendas."

The current War of the Camps involved the Palestinian inhabitants of the refugee camps and the Lebanese Shi'ite militia, Amal. They had formerly been allies, and, ironically, various Palestinian guerrilla groups had trained many of the Amal cadres before 1982. The political upheaval in Lebanon after the Israeli invasion undid old alliances and created new ones that reflected the new balance of power. The Shi'ite community had assumed a new importance, and its sectarian Amal Movement had since become Syria's preferred ally and proxy militia in Lebanon, doing its political bidding. The Palestinians felt the desertion of Amal to the Syrian side as yet another of the many betrayals that they had faced at the hands of their Arab brethren.

I asked what had happened in Shatila that last summer, and Faramawi related how only 120 young men had defended the camp against an onslaught of thousands of well-armed militiamen backed by the tanks of the Lebanese Army Sixth Brigade. "Some days, our young boys had only ten bullets per man. Fifty-two of the 120 died."

The two general practitioners in the camp at the time had no surgical experience, no hospital, and no medical supplies. Dr. Khatib described how they had gone searching the houses, gathering a few capsules of Ampicillin here, some tablets of aspirin there. He had horror stories to tell of that first battle. All too often, he had few or no supplies to alleviate the suffering of the wounded as they awaited death in the oppressive summer heat.

"What did you do?" I asked.

"I gathered the wounded in the mosque. I spoke to them gently and fanned them while they died."

Shatila somehow staved off the disaster that had befallen Sabra, not 400 yards away, in that first battle and siege of thirty days. Much of that time, the TWA airplane hijacking at Beirut airport and the death of an American navy diver monopolized media coverage. The War of the Camps disappeared from the international news wires. Cynics (including Faramawi and Dr. Khatib) believed that elements close to Amal had staged the hijacking, precisely in order to bury under a cloak of media silence the screams of the besieged in Shatila and Burj el-Barajneh.

After a Syrian-brokered cease-fire between Amal and the pro-Syrian factions in the PNSF, numerous pronouncements and communiqués repeated that the belligerents would not renew the War of the Camps, that Amal and the PNSF were allies against Arafat's "deviationist line." Amal had not attained the goal, however, of controlling the Palestinians and the Arafatists.

The refugee districts of Shatila and Burj el-Barajneh remained stubbornly defiant of external control. Soldiers and militiamen encircled Shatila and the much larger Burj el-Barajneh. They held a tight noose around the camps, controlling and regulating the entry and exit of goods and people. But, unable to enter the defended camps, they could not control what happened inside them. Thus Shatila stood there, in defiance of the stranglehold around it, like a fish bone stuck in the throat – and the Amal leaders and their Syrian backers wanted badly to swallow that bone. Further rounds of skirmishes, battles, and sieges of the refugee camps were in the offing. Faramawi and Dr. Khatib believed that Syria and Amal, under the guise of fighting Arafat's Fatah, had targeted all Palestinians. Amal militiamen had seized unarmed Palestinian civilians in West Beirut, holding them hostage. Their fate – beatings, rape, torture, and often death. Everyone expected more.

I understood that, during hostilities, Shatila's inhabitants would not have access to the Gaza and Akka hospitals of the PRCS. Their distance from Shatila, though tantalizingly close (less than half a mile away), made them of little use. Fighting would block off the roads and render evacuation of the wounded impossible, as had been the case with Dr. Khatib's patients in the mosque. With the prospect of future battles and sieges looming before us, we had to render Shatila as self-sufficient as possible, including an autonomous medical unit, if we were going to resist. And that resistance would determine our very survival.

I remembered walking through the alleyways of the region, visiting friends, colleagues, and patients, when I was chief resident at Gaza Hospital in 1980. The general area the people then called Shatila included the camp itself plus the surrounding slum areas, all told, about a mile square. Now I asked, why so much emphasis on Shatila? What made Shatila so important? "Geographically," said Faramawi, "Shatila controls a vital juncture between West Beirut, the political capital, and the huge southern suburban slums, stronghold of the Lebanese Shi'ite community. Three rival groups, each with its militia, compete for the allegiance of the Shi'ites – the sectarian pro-Syrian Amal Movement, the fundamentalist pro-Iranian Hizbollah ('Party of God'), and the secular pro-Syrian *and* pro-Palestinian Communist Party. Hizbollah refuses to fight us as a matter of principle. So do the Communists. Amal knows that the War of the Camps is unpopular even with many Shi'ites. There is much friction between them and the other groups. They want to control the others, just as they want to control us, at the behest of their Syrian mentors. And they want to get it over with as quickly as possible."

Faramawi took another sip of coffee. "Amal sees us as a threat to this vital juncture; during fighting, our snipers can easily block the roads, cutting off West Beirut from the suburbs. Also, Shatila is the smallest and poorest of all the refugee districts in Lebanon. Topographically, it is located in a depression, surrounded by a series of small hills. The sports stadium complex on the western ridge of hills overlooks the entire region. It bristles with heavy weapons looking down on us. For all these reasons, the Amal leaders believe that Shatila is the easiest camp to overrun and the most difficult to defend." He hesitated, then continued, his voice rising, "And after all, this is Shatila! We're a symbol of persecution and resistance to persecution. If Amal and the Syrians can destroy the symbol of steadfastness and resistance, then other Palestinians, they hope, will lose faith and confidence. And it will be that much easier to control them." His voice lowered, he spoke slowly, pausing after each word. "But ... we ... refuse ... to ... surrender! We'll always refuse to surrender, to submit to someone else's yoke! We have no country. My children, like over half Shatila's inhabitants, have never seen Palestine. We are refugees. But Palestine exists in our hearts and minds. We are poor. They belittle, malign, and despise us, call us terrorists. But we, too, are human beings. We, too, have our human dignity and our pride. We, too, have our dreams."

We finished our coffee, and Dr. Khatib and Faramawi took me on a tour of the camp. Crowds thronged the web of alleyways, some only a yard and a half wide and made even more tangled over the years as families enlarged their homes, adding a few precious inches to their dwellings, eating away at the already narrow alleys. We passed under "bridges," extra rooms built over alleyways between buildings; the soggy unpaved passages underneath never saw the sun. I winced at the humidity and the sickly-sweet fermenting scent of the open sewers.

Middle-aged, heavy-set women balanced overloaded shopping bags on their heads, carefully but nonchalantly skirting the open sewers, pot-holes, and bomb craters. Swarthy muscular men in blue jeans or military camouflage trousers carried lumber, iron bars, sacks of cement, pushed wheelbarrowfuls of gravel and sand, breaking and further twisting the amazing cobweb of above-ground water pipes. This was the feverish activity of rebuilding, for the nth time, the battered squalor of Shatila, heavily damaged by tank and artillery fire in the summer's fighting. And, as usual in the Third World, there was the ever-present swarm of children. Children underfoot everywhere: running, shouting, throwing stones at each other, squabbling, falling over one another and rolling in the dust, carrying groceries, playing at war – seemingly general raucous anarchy. Apart from local variations, the scene could have been Bamako, Algiers, or Cairo.

Originally peasants in Palestine, most of the camp's inhabitants had become labourers – painters, carpenters, electricians, plumbers, and masons. Abu Mohammed Faramawi was typical. A few had commercial interests that they had established in the urban areas of Beirut. Over the years, many had left to find work in the oil-rich countries of the Gulf, sending back monthly cheques that supplemented the incomes of the families in Shatila. The younger generation had greater opportunities for education. In fact, education constituted their major focus of attention; for many it was the only means of escape from the tedium and poverty of refugee life. In one of the ironies of contemporary history, Palestinians boast a higher percentage of university graduates than any other people in the Middle East. Denied most other kinds of employment by the Lebanese government, the generations born in Shatila graduated as engineers, doctors, and teachers and found jobs in Lebanon or the Gulf. And as their socio-economic status improved, they themselves moved out of the camp to establish residence in Beirut. By 1985, only a few professionals like Dr. Khatib chose to live in Shatila.

We passed by the two UNRWA schools, one primary, the other secondary. They had been badly damaged during the first round of fighting, but reconstruction was underway. In the meantime, Faramawi's children, along with all the rest, left the camp every day to attend UNRWA schools set up in West Beirut. The unstable security situation interrupted classes frequently, and students could have a continuous education only if their families moved out of Shatila and settled in the city. Many of the high school students, however, participated in the defence of the camp. As a consequence, they were torn between leaving Shatila to further their education and remaining within the confines of the camp to help defend their homes and families. Many did not face this dilemma simply because they did not have enough money to resettle in expensive West Beirut. Homes in the refugee district allocated to families by UNRWA were at least rent-free.

Several people had opened vegetable and fruit stands and even a grocery store inside a transformed house – all four by three yards of it. One carpenter had set up shop and a few enterprising individuals had established welders' workshops. But the vast majority of the population left the camp to find gainful employment in the city. Limited means and limited space severely restricted economic activity within Shatila itself, and for most goods and services the camp depended on the outside world.

Each spot we visited – the mosque, the schools, the carpenter's shop, the water reservoir – had a story to tell, etched in pain, stained in blood. My two new friends were survivors of battles, shellings, the Massacre, the siege. They knew all the stories and anecdotes of death, horror, and heroism.

We walked along the camp's periphery, clambering over the rubble – broken slabs of concrete spilled onto former alleyways and streets; broken homes collapsed onto themselves; two-storey buildings telescoped like accordions into a mass barely six feet high. We looked at a group of Amal militiamen opposite, seated around a makeshift table just beyond the corridor of devastation and debris, not twenty yards away, lazily drinking their afternoon tea. We eyed each other warily, with obvious hostility, before we moved on. The stretches of destruction, flattened buildings, and debris-strewn streets constituted the military fronts bordering three sides of the camp. Beyond, I could see constructions similar to those in Shatila, then taller, better-built buildings – apartment houses and administrative offices. We had quickly covered the camp's geography. It really was only 200 yards by 200 yards (the equivalent of four small city blocks or four North American football fields, less than an acre). The pressures generated by the natural population increased over the last three decades and improving incomes had caused many to move out of the refugee camp into the surrounding slum areas and even into residential districts of Beirut. The Palestinian population in the area, Dr. Khatib told me, had reached more than 8,000 people before the summer of 1985. We would now have to deal with and provide medical services for about 3,500 people. The others had fled, during and after the first battle, to other refugee districts in the north or south of the country if they had relatives there, or to squatter buildings and basement shelters in areas of West Beirut controlled by the Socialist Party, where they were uncomfortable but safe.

We reached the fourth side of the camp, to the west, bordered by Sabra-Shatila Street, where my drivers had parked the car. I knew this street well. The widest street in the neighbourhood, it ran from the ten storeys of reinforced concrete of Gaza Hospital to the north, with its spacious underground operating theatres and bomb shelter, squeezed among seven- and eight-storey apartment buildings at the periphery of the Sabra camp, past the tall gracious minaret of the Sabra mosque, past Shatila, and on towards the mass grave of the victims of the 1982 Massacre and the Akka Hospital at the airport roundabout. I had walked this street often, going from Gaza to the PRCS administrative offices at the Akka Hospital complex. But, in my time, there had been no mass grave, and the Sabra camp had been a bustling hive of activity, just like Shatila, only larger and better built. I remembered the narrow meandering streets and alleys winding downhill from the built-up areas of West Beirut. During the heavy winter rains, the natural depression around Sabra and Shatila was often flooded. Three feet of water regularly submerged the stretch of S-S Street that traversed the gully. I waded across it many times to get to Gaza Hospital. People often transformed fruit vendors' carts into rafts to float across.

Faramawi explained, as we crossed the now dry street, that the camp's combatants controlled the immediate area between Sabra-Shatila

Street and the sports stadium perched on the hill – "the western sector," a distance of 400 yards. A mixed population had inhabited this region. It included poor Lebanese – mostly Shi'ite villagers – Palestinian refugees, and migrant manual labourers of several nationalities. I had often driven on the highway now hidden from view on the opposite side of the hills, past that stadium complex. The highway was one of the major routes connecting West Beirut to the southern suburbs, and beyond to southern Lebanon; it was the route that the camp's snipers could cut off, if necessary. My last view of Beirut in the summer of 1982, as I sped by in an ambulance, scrambling to return to my hospital in the deep south, was of Israeli supersonic aircraft bombing the Palestinian and nationalist Lebanese military installations buried within the depths of the stadium's massive concrete structures.

I studied closely the silhouette of the sports complex atop the ridge of hills, dominating the entire region with its soaring parapets and the solid immensity of the bowl-shaped stadium. The Amal militia and supporting units of the Lebanese army now manned the fortified positions within its hulking mass, armed with artillery, multiple rocket launchers, and tanks. The militiamen and soldiers had previously aimed the guns' barrels at East Beirut, "the enemy," not two miles away as the crow flies. Now the barrels pointed ominously at Shatila in the gully below.

I mused on the irony of the fate of this sports stadium, the modern inheritor of the ancient tradition of gladiators and the circus: the Beirut sporting complex had truly reverted to the gladiators.

This "western sector," with its mixed Lebanese-Palestinian population and one- and two-storey cinderblock shanty-town dwellings, was not unlike Shatila itself except that the houses were slightly more spacious and many had a small garden; the sector was now empty, except for combatants hidden silently in alleys and houses. The buildings showed the traces of war – bullet pock marks and shell holes – but the damage was less severe than in Shatila. The first battle of the War of the Camps the previous summer had depopulated it. Families had fled the area and dared not return. The western sector now constituted a major battlefield between the contending forces. The most advanced lines of the camp's defenders were within ten yards of the sports stadium's ramparts. The opposing fighters, Palestinians and Lebanese, often called out to each other by name, for many had been neighbours and friends in the not-too-distant past. The horrifying, bloody reality of civil strife now pitted them against each other, at calling distance from one another.

But the Shi'ites of Amal were not simply blind proxies of the Syrians. By the 1970s, the Shi'ites constituted the largest and poorest community in the Lebanese fabric, living mostly in rural areas of the south and Beqa'a Valley, and in the sprawling slums around the Beirut refugee camps. The community had suffered tremendously since the late 1960s, when they received Palestinian guerrilla fighters with open arms. Shi'ite villages in southern Lebanon bore the brunt of Israeli reprisals for Palestinian guerrilla attacks. Israeli policy was simple: deny the guerrillas popular support by exacting a very heavy price for it from the civilian population.

Politically, large sectors of the poor Shi'ite community had been members of the Communist or revolutionary pan-Arab parties and ideologically supported the Palestinians. Socially, they lived together with them in the slums of Beirut and intermarried. Many even became members of Palestinian factions, but the political power of the PLO reflected itself most on the Sunni Muslim urban dwellers of Beirut, Tripoli, and Sidon, the traditional mercantile class and second community, after the Maronites, in Lebanese politics.

Pushed by poverty, and following a millennial Phoenician tradition, many Shi'ites had emigrated to Africa and Latin America to pursue commercial activities. They made fortunes and returned to Lebanon, where they did not have political power commensurate with their demographic strength and new wealth. Resentment with this continuation of political disenfranchisement among the Shi'ites grew, fuelled by the well-known corruption and high style of living of certain Palestinian political élites before the 1982 evacuation of Beirut. It was an easy matter for the new ambitious Shi'ite bourgeoisie and the Syrians to turn many of the alienated poor against their immediate slum neighbours – the Palestinians of Sabra, Shatila and Burj el-Barajneh.

Faramawi, Dr. Khatib, and I slowly walked back to the tumult of Shatila from the eerie silence and emptiness of the scarred western sector. It had been a long day. We walked without speaking. They had already said enough. We knew that our predicament was grave. Completely surrounded, outgunned, topographically dominated, aware of the frailty of the infrastructure, crushed by the stories of mutilation and death, certain of more battles and sieges, I wondered if I really understood what I had gotten myself into. But, after all, this was Shatila! I would make their predicament, that of Abu Mohammed Faramawi and Dr. Khatib and their families and friends, mine.

2

The Four-Day Battle

EVERYONE IN SHATILA UNDERSTOOD THE SIEGE SITUAtion and the danger it posed. Everyone listened intently to the repeated speeches and communiqués of the Amal and pro-Syrian Palestinian leaders. Everyone wanted to believe the announcements proclaiming the end of hostilities between the refugee camps and the neighbouring Shi'ite slums, the end of the War of the Camps. Everyone hoped against hope that the announcements were true. No one was convinced that they were.

As part of the official policy of reconciliation after the first cease-fire, Amal, which controlled the roads, had granted the camp's inhabitants permission to rebuild. They carried in cement, bricks, sand, and gravel, and intense and hectic activity clogged the narrow alleyways as men transported all manner of construction materials, rebuilding entire sectors of the refugee district.

The men of the camp, many of them skilled workers, carried out the reconstruction themselves. This provided work for them as well as new shelter for their families and indicated the sense of self-sufficiency that Shatila was developing. Everyone had one thing in mind, one purpose – to prepare better services and better means to resist in the inevitable upcoming battle. In addition to repairing homes, the two schools, the mosque, and the hospital, they constructed two underground bomb shelters and then erected four-storey buildings above them. Taller than most other buildings, they afforded greater protection from any future bombing or shelling; a number of buildings now reached four and five storeys, especially in the centre of the camp around the hospital complex. Directly across the street from Faramawi's building, the owners, like him, were constructing a new fourth storey, which cast its shadow onto the hospital.

The construction workers had learned well the lessons of Lebanon's civil war. They built strategically located walls and roofs of reinforced concrete, with iron rods forming a scaffold-grid. Faramawi and others explained to me that the important factor was not the actual diameter of the iron rods used, but rather the density of the grid. The men wove the rods into a lace-like network of close, tight spaces before pouring the cement. Iron bars of only a quarter inch in diameter can stop a mortar shell or rocket-propelled grenade if interwoven tightly enough.

The UNRWA bureaucracy distributed money for reconstruction based on a census of family members and an estimate of the extent of damage to homes. The pro-Arafat PLO set up a committee of its cadres and independents – engineers, masons, respected community members – to supervise purchases from a special PLO reconstruction fund and the distribution of building materials. The other factions were invited to participate, but only the relatively neutral and non-extremist Democratic Front (DFLP) and Communist Party did. The PNSF coalition refused any co-operation with the Arafat "deviationists."

Nonetheless, the committee considered it everyone's right to receive the necessary bricks, mortar, cement, iron bars, and so forth necessary to reconstruct damaged or destroyed homes, regardless of political affiliation. Committee engineers determined the quantities of materials to be distributed to each family. Many thought that the quantities decided upon did not meet their due; there was constant squabbling over cement and iron. This added another topic of conversation, complaints, and arguments to the lengthy nightly home discussion sessions that formed the favourite social pastime among families.

While reconstruction proceeded in the camp, I occupied myself with organizing medical services. I thought the original set-up of the hospital totally useless. I could just imagine the difficulties inherent in transporting the wounded from the emergency room along the alley, down the stairs to the shelter for X-rays, and then back up the stairway to the operating room. Also, the layout of the proposed operating theatre did not allow for the sterilization or stocking of surgical instruments, and four beds were far too few to have in the hospital's main building.

I explained to Dr. Khatib my plan of action. I described to him some of the conditions we had dealt with in south and north Lebanon in previous years. We had to take into consideration the type of weapons that might be used against the camp, in order to assure the safety of the hospital. We were not a "M.A.S.H." unit far from the battlefield with helicopters delivering the patients. On the contrary, we were right in the middle of a battle zone and could expect direct bombardment of the hospital should hostilities break out. We would have to reinforce the hospital buildings through various means and spent the next several weeks doing so.

One of the things I had learned on several battlefields was to secure the operating theatre, preferably underground. The only place available was in Faramawi's building. We transformed the basement shelter from proposed X-ray department into operating theatre. Next, we had to set up miniature versions of different services. "To organize the placement and distribution of the different hospital departments," I explained to Dr. Khatib, "walk through the buildings as though you were a wounded patient. Follow the different steps involved in managing the patient:

first, the emergency room; then, X-rays and lab work; next, the operating theatre; and finally, post-op recovery and ward."

We would have to make do with the small and cramped emergency reception; no larger room was available. The old out-patient department next door to the ER became the X-ray service. In its five and a half by three yards, we managed to place a table for patients to lie on, a portable X-ray machine that would meet most of our needs, and a large aluminum box equipped with heaters and a fan to dry our films. The adjoining small toilet served as darkroom; three receptacles for fixer, developer, and rinse water to treat the X-ray films replaced the sink. The PRCS bought our portable X-ray machine, a real delight, in West Beirut and brought it into Shatila in the back of a pick-up truck. It was an excruciating, back-breaking task to unload and wheel it through the narrow alleyway.

The ground floor of the first building now comprised the emergency reception (ER), X-ray department, out-patient clinic in the original pharmacy, and waiting room. Thus, we organized an integrated emergency reception area. The ER had two examination couches, the out-patient clinic another two and an obstetric table, and the central waiting room place for three more couches. These provided the necessary space for receiving up to eight wounded at one time during a battle and room for consultations and dressing changes in peace time. The X-ray facilities immediately off the central waiting room meant a minimum of movement for any wounded patients. The laboratory we put elsewhere, since it did not, unlike the X-ray service, have to be in close proximity to the ER; the patient does not go to the lab, only a phial of blood. All the necessary resuscitation and prep work could now be done more efficiently in one place. Also, I had learned from experience that not all the wounded needed operative intervention in the theatre. Our integrated reception area allowed for minor surgical procedures without disturbing the rest of the hospital. Economy of space became an overriding principle.

This left the pharmacy to replace. Cramped as the camp was, the only solution to this game of musical chairs was to rent a third building between the first two and off to the side to provide for the pharmacy and medical stores. Dr. Khatib and I joked about the size of the hospital and the refugee district – the Shatila sardine tin.

With the operating theatre in the shelter, the large room on the ground floor of Faramawi's building became a new ward, accommodating an additional eight beds, half of which were hospital beds and the other half ordinary cots. We now had a total of twelve beds in our two-ward hospital, one room for men and another for women patients. We transformed the former kitchen into our laboratory – all four by three and a half yards of it. But at least it contained a sink, water piping, and ceramic counter top to wash slides, test tubes, and other equipment.

The head of the PRCS construction crew, another fellow whom I knew from my days at the Gaza Hospital, came regularly to Shatila. He was my contact with the central administration of PRCS located at Akka Hospital and understood me very well. My nervous, nail-biting hyperactivity suited him and, within a month of hard work, his construction workers had prepared the bomb shelter/operating theatre. They plastered over and painted in standard hospital blue-green the raw, bare concrete walls and ceiling; ceramic tiles covered the floor, and electrical wiring and fixtures were installed.

Plumbing hadn't existed in the original basement, so we laid pipes and set up a sink where we could scrub up and wash the surgical instruments. The workmen tediously excavated a hole in the floor of reinforced concrete, breaking up the cement and cutting the three-quarter-inch iron bars by hand with a hacksaw. This served as a sewer for the water from the sink, as well as that used to mop the floor after operations. A sump pump evacuated the dirty water through another set of pipes, back up the stairway to be drained to the outside. We sank an aluminum box into this excavated hole to function as a receptacle for the dirty water and to prevent the blood and waste from seeping into the cement. The box, with sealed cover, reached one inch above the level of the floor, and a slot was cut out of one of the protruding sides to receive the effluent from mopping up.

The half wall dividing the shelter into two rooms, each four by three and a half yards, assisted in its functional organization. We set up the first room with metal shelves along the two side walls to accommodate boxes of surgical instruments, gowns and towelling, and other supplies; the sink and sewage receptacle in one corner; and a small table upon which rested our sterilization equipment – dry-heat oven and small autoclave (a sterilizer operating on the same principle as a pressure cooker). A patient trolley on wheels completed the furnishings. On the other side of the half wall, at the far end of the shelter, we created the operating theatre itself. This included an operating table, a side lamp, an anaesthesia apparatus, a suction machine, and a diathermy (an apparatus that coagulates blood in small vessels using an electric current). We almost broke our backs again lugging the operating table down the narrow, twisting staircase. A niche in the far corner, with ladder and emergency escape hatch (bomb shelters always have a second exit should shelling block the principal one), contained cylinders of oxygen and anaesthesia gas. Every available bit of wall space held metal shelves for suture material, drugs and medications for the anaesthetist, and intravenous fluids. Within a week of completion of the construction crew's work, the operating theatre staff had set up, organized, and furnished the theatre. Six Palestinian nurses, four of them newly graduated from the PRCS nursing school, worked under the guidance of Régine to set up the operating theatre.

I had first met Régine Ponson during the Tripoli fighting in 1983. An experienced French scrub nurse, she had come with the numerous European medical volunteers who had arrived to supplement the local PRCS staff in northern Lebanon. At first, she knew nothing about Lebanon or the Palestinians. Having worked previously on the French Caribbean islands of Martinique and Guadeloupe, and fleeing the dreariness of routine in France, Régine had joined a volunteer medical group to do humanitarian work and ended up in the midst of a vicious and morally bankrupt war. She stayed on in the refugee camps of Tripoli after our evacuation and enjoyed the hectic life of setting up a new hospital. Like many European volunteers, she especially enjoyed the universal hospitality with which she was met by the poor but generous people of the camps.

Régine's politicization had developed rapidly, as is nearly always the case with European volunteers who over the years have worked and lived among the refugee population. There is a certain genius at work in the unfailing fortitude, the conviviality, the *joie de vivre* of a community that has lost so much, a community that lives in such instability, yet has retained its dignity, in spite of or perhaps because of everything, that makes it all the more touching and endearing. I wasn't surprised to find Régine again in Shatila. Having once worked in a Palestinian refugee camp, she had been bitten by the "bug" and had returned for more of the same.

She was an attractive, large-boned woman in her late thirties, with a happy but quiet disposition. Extremely hard-working, conscientious, and well-organized, she revelled in setting up the operating theatre from A to Z and teaching the Palestinian staff the basics of sterilization techniques, folding and wrapping surgical gowns and towels, and all the nitty-gritty of keeping the theatre spotless and clean, in spite of the fact that there was no door to close off the operating area from the stairway leading down to the shelter. It was largely her perseverance and discipline, which she instilled in her colleagues, that kept the theatre and equipment up to the necessary level of cleanliness, if not total sterility. Later, we performed major operations in war trauma cases, which are contaminated and dirty wounds – the bullet entering the flesh carries with it fragments of clothing and sucks in dust – yet had an infection rate of less than five percent. This compared well with a normal standard of three to five percent in major, well-equipped Western hospitals dealing with elective surgery.

Régine made friends quickly with a number of families, widows, and militants of the General Union of Women. She was immensely popular and spent her evenings on an endless round of meals, coffee, and sweets, visiting one house after another. She complained to me later about having put on too much weight in Shatila. We became, in time and through many trials and tribulations, close confidants, knowing that in each other we could find a receptive and sympathetic ear when the situation got difficult or complicated.

Looking at our new, shining operating theatre, three problems confronted us. First, the ceiling of the shelter was only six and a half feet high. With the side lamp placed in position over the operating table, I could not stand straight while operating and had to work hunched over. This would have a telling effect on my back after innumerable hours spent in the theatre, but there was no solution apart from the massages of the hospital's physiotherapist.

Second, the entrance to the stairway leading down to the shelter gave directly onto the street. This would expose patients and staff to shelling and sniper fire while going from emergency room to operating theatre. We had to make a passage leading from the interior of the hospital to the shelter stairway. Directly under the projecting second-floor balcony, the construction crew closed off a part of the street with walls of reinforced concrete. This created a new room that enclosed the stairway entrance. They then knocked a hole in the original wall of the building, opening a new doorway and passage from the four-bed ward to this new room. A reinforcement of the balcony completed the protection of the new route – from emergency room to hospital, through new room to stairway and down to the shelter. We used the newly constructed room for undressing and changing into surgical green, and the theatre staff now had a sitting room in which to drink coffee and pass away the time, or sleep.

The last problem involved the stairway itself. Like all entrances to underground bomb shelters, an abrupt double turn skewed the stairway, preventing shrapnel from travelling directly downstairs to injure people hiding inside if a shell landed at the doorway. We had to carry our patients down to the operating theatre on a hammock stretcher hung between two wooden poles, gingerly manoeuvring the tight corners. To facilitate passage, we knocked out chunks of the wall to accommodate the poles. Chipping away at the walls of reinforced concrete was also a tedious task, but we finally lopped off the necessary pieces at the turns to allow stretchers to pass with a minimum of discomfort and trauma to patients and stretcher bearers alike.

The first round of fighting had destroyed the homes of Dr. Khatib and many cleaning women, nurses, and technicians, who now had to live either in the hospital or outside the camp. The owners of the rooms on the second storey above the emergency reception area had left. We rented these rooms as living quarters for Régine, Dr. Khatib, and the nursing and cleaning staff who lived in the hospital. If sleeping quarters for the staff and myself were still a problem, so was space for all the support services necessary in a hospital. We stuck the kitchen into one cranny, the laundry into another.

The destruction of the Sabra camp and many of the houses in Shatila had forced many families to take up residence in West Beirut, squatting in public buildings or unfinished construction. Some had found refuge in large underground bomb shelters in parts of the city controlled by the Progressive Socialist Party (PSP) of Walid Joumblat. They lived there in horrendous, overcrowded conditions, but they were safe. These squatters included many of the PRCS personnel now working in the hospital, as well as others with social or political responsibilities in the camp, who had to commute daily to Shatila.

Life for these people was precarious. They went about their affairs not knowing when Amal militiamen would subject them to further repression or exactions. The non-resident hospital staff often complained of the dangers involved in simply walking along the 400 yards of street past the Gaza Hospital to reach Shatila. They all had stories to tell of how, while skirmishes raged around Shatila, Amal militiamen picked up people on the street or entered Palestinian homes in West Beirut, looting, raping, and taking hostages.

Rabiha, like Dr. Khatib, had lost her home. She too lived in the hospital. Her eyes squinted badly from an uncorrected childhood defect, so that when she looked at you, it seemed as though she was staring in the opposite direction. In her mid-thirties, this forlorn but sturdy woman held the post of chief housekeeper of the hospital. Oum Mohammed Faramawi soon joined her in sharing these duties. Rabiha's situation symbolized that of the majority of Shatila's inhabitants. Divorced years previously, she had eked out a meagre existence with her fifteen-year-old child. The first battle had cost her not only the hovel she lived in, but also her son. He was among the 700 missing from Sabra, where he had been visiting a friend when the fighting began. Rabiha continued her duties in Shatila, believing it her utmost duty to remain there, steadfast. She lived on the hope that her son was still somehow alive somewhere – in prison, perhaps, in West Beirut or Damascus.

Rabiha exuded a mixture of sadness, a sense of loss, and the will to survive, to overcome and to hope, if only for her son's life. Like Abu and Oum Mohammed Faramawi, and so many others, she wore the identity of Shatila like a badge of honour. Untiring in walking back and forth between the camp and the market-place, she organized a cohort of young cleaning women to daily run the gauntlet of the main street to fetch food and supplies for the hospital. Rabiha knew the Amal militiamen well, many by name, since they had been frequent patients at the Gaza Hospital where she had worked when it was functioning. She told me of several staff members who had fallen victim to the political gangsterism, as she called it, of the militiamen on the main street. Which explained why, once having finished their work for the day, many of the staff preferred not to leave Shatila after dusk for security reasons and therefore remained and slept in the hospital.

I had to take all this into consideration. I was responsible, as hospital director, for the security of my staff, and for cajoling and convincing them to continue working in Shatila, and I was responsible for providing them with the necessary minimum of physical comfort while they served there. I pored for hours over work schedules, which became one of my most important administrative tasks, trying to arrange timetables that would pose the least security risk to the hospital workers commuting daily. I had to make allowances for where people lived, for pregnant staff, and for those with young children and still maintain sufficient personnel on hand within the camp to cover the needs of the hospital. A skirmish could break out at any time of day or night, and often did, rendering it impossible for anyone to enter the camp and leaving us to make do with whatever personnel were present. I put far more people on afternoon or night shifts than was necessary, simply to make certain of their presence in Shatila.

In addition to myself, our roster included at different times two assistant surgeons and from four to ten general practitioners. We counted between twenty and twenty-five nurses, a third of whom were male, and always present were at least one X-ray and two laboratory technicians, as well as a couple of pharmacists. We always had a small army of workers and cleaning women, many of whose homes had been destroyed and who preferred to sleep and live in the hospital residence rather than stay with their families in squatters' quarters in the city. We never lacked for staff, but having all these people on the hospital premises meant I had to deal with providing sleeping quarters, food, and laundry and toilet facilities for them. Every and any place was deemed suitable for sleeping quarters – the X-ray room, ER, outpatient department, laboratory, pharmacy, as well as the formal residence on the floor above the ER. The logistics at times seemed surreal.

I myself first slept in the four-bed ward, then in the eight-bed ward; when these became functional, I moved over to the pharmacy. In a couple of months, we rented the uninhabited building, the one without the roof, located in the centre between the three others containing emergency reception, pharmacy, and wards. Workmen had since rebuilt the roof, and we used the building for the hospital kitchen, laundry, cafeteria, food store-room, and administration. I now slept in the pantry among the sacks of potatoes and rice and piles of onions.

This situation did not last too long, and in early 1986, just over two months after I arrived in Shatila, I finally moved into a three-yard by three-yard, one-room, second-floor apartment with adjoining toilet and shower, located in a building just next to Faramawi's. Furnished with a reed mat, two mattresses on the floor, and a plastic-covered clothes rack, the place enabled me to get away from the confines of the hospital and obtain as much privacy as possible under the circumstances. When I named it "the villa," the joke going the rounds of the hospital staff about the limited geography of Shatila now put it that we had a "villa inside the sardine tin."

The four separate buildings were welded into a single unit by a system of wrought-iron tube scaffolding that covered the three hospital alleyways. The scaffolding supported metal sheets and a double layer of sand bags. The essential miniaturized services were all in place by the end of 1985, and although the four buildings may not have physically resembled a hospital, the complex functioned as one. With time, we made small improvements here and there, brought in new equipment, and learned lessons under fire in a series of minor skirmishes and battles that helped us improve services even further. It was not a sprawling modern complex like the American University Hospital, nor even the old ten-storey, 150-bed Gaza Hospital; but from ER to OR; food stores to laundry; staff residence to one-room administration with three desks for the secretary, accountant, and myself; everything was there – even if one had to walk along the hospital alleyways in knee-high rubber boots because of rain flood waters or backed-up sewers.

It was Ali Abu Toq's men who had constructed the protective scaffolding and painted the hospital. Ali, the pro-Arafat Fatah and PLO leader of Shatila, was one of the first people outside the hospital staff to greet me. I had known him since 1981, when he had been responsible for building the fortifications of the Beaufort Castle in the area of Nabatieh in southern Lebanon. The towering parapets of this Crusader castle perched on the summit of a stupendous precipice overlooking the Litani River effectively controlled any movement on the unfolding plain below. Ali and his men spent weeks and months pouring cement. That summer, Israeli airplanes spent hours bombing the handful of men within the fortified structures, but to no avail: there were almost never any casualties.

During 1981 and 1982, I met repeatedly with Ali and his fellow battalion officers. The Fatah "Jermouk Battalion" had an excellent reputation known throughout Lebanon. It differed radically from the majority of Palestinian troops, recruiting mainly among Palestinian and Lebanese students at the American University; the officers were all university graduates and many worked on masters' or doctorate degrees, so it acquired the nickname of the "Students' Battalion." The battalion imposed a strict discipline on its troops, and its relationship with the civilian Lebanese population was superb. Lebanese Shi'ite farmers came to Ali and his fellow officers to solve disputes over sheep, chickens, or rent. The battalion motto read: "A revolution without a sense of morality is but theft and hypocrisy." When Israeli troops stormed the Beaufort Castle in the 1982 invasion, they engaged in one of their most difficult battles ever. The next day, Israeli radio commended the fallen Palestinian defenders, praising their tenacity and courage. It was one of the few occasions I have heard Israeli radio speak about Palestinian fighters without referring to them as terrorists.

I had worked with Ali again in Tripoli and we had become close friends. Thickly bearded, short, supple, and built like an athlete, he radiated confidence. His eyes gleamed with a pragmatic optimism, his voice was quiet and compassionate, but he could be iron-hard and ruthless when faced with insubordination among his men, or disrespect among them for the civilian population. The Fatah men in Shatila were not used to Draconian discipline, and Ali's prison cells were never empty. The epitome of the committed professional revolutionary, he selflessly sacrificed himself and his own and his family's comforts for the cause of his people. Groups of camp dwellers, delegations of women or elderly men – the notables – met regularly with him, asking for financial aid or intervention in some squabble. Widows and orphans made the daily pilgrimage to his offices for assistance. He charmed them all. Little children ran after him in the alleyways just to say hello or touch his hand.

Ali was a military, political, social, and administrative genius, a leader of men and women who commanded their love and respect. Smuggled into Shatila several months after the first battle to take command, he was the head of the Arafat Fatah faction and the PLO not only for the camp but for all Beirut, in spite of his physical isolation in encircled Shatila, and was well-known for supporting political positions contrary to those of his leadership. His independence and nonconformity knew no bounds. He was one of a group of fellow officers who had undergone their military training in the Soviet Union, but he had also been to the People's Republic of China and was very fond of organizing voluntary work days. A platoon of his men, ordinary Shatila inhabitants, regularly cleaned the streets or emptied the rubbish dump, constructed houses or bomb shelters. Following Ali's example, self-sufficiency became the leitmotif of all activity in Shatila.

In January 1986, just over two months after my arrival, we all reaffirmed that conviction. Throughout the fall and winter, a series of night skirmishes had occurred between the encircling Lebanese Shi'ite militiamen and the Palestinian defenders of the camp. Usually these lasted only several hours: someone threw a hand grenade, or shot the occasional rocket-propelled grenade (RPG) and a stream of small arms fire ensued. A joint Lebanese-Palestinian security committee spent hours trying to end such incidents, re-establish a cease-fire, and run down the culprits responsible for the outbreak of shooting. In early January 1986, yet another skirmish occurred, but no cease-fire. The Amal militia shut off the road leading into the camp. No one could enter or exit. The siege was on.

The small arms and automatic rifle fire into the camp hit the upper storeys of the buildings, making a distinctive sharp "crac." Families took refuge in the ground floors of houses. Young men rushed from their homes, dressed in a hodgepodge of camouflage uniforms, civilian clothes, or even pyjamas, bandoleers of cartridges and belts of ammunition magazines and grenades slung across their chests. Most carried AK-47 (Kalashnikov) Soviet assault rifles, although some had U.S.-made M-16s or RPG launchers. Everyone stored their weapons at home; in Lebanon, no respectable home would be without a rifle or two, or several grenades. Almost every man in the camp had his own revolver. The men scurried about, sometimes passing through the hospital alleyways, en route to their posts. The battle fronts were along the perimeter of the camp, where I had strolled with Abu Mohammed Faramawi and Dr. Khatib that first day.

Each political faction had an allotted area of the battle-front periphery as its military responsibility. Normally, only a few fighters on guard duty manned the fronts. Now, everyone scrambled to his respective position as each faction, pro- or anti-Arafat or neutral, posted a platoon or two of men at every critical point. Although only 120 men had defended Shatila during the thirty-day siege of the previous summer, the camp now bristled with more than 1,000 armed combatants. Some had been present the previous summer but had been unarmed, others had arrived after the cease-fire. They often joked about the overcrowding at the fronts in the tiny area of Shatila. "Would you kindly move over so I can fire a shot?"

Amal snipers rendered movement around the camp hazardous. Within hours of the onset of hostilities, representatives of the political factions, Popular Committee, and Union of Women came together and formed special teams to deal with the logistical problems. One team went about marking alleyways exposed to sniper fire. They made special passages through adjacent houses, knocking door-sized holes in interior walls to allow movement from one area to another under cover. A team of women and men in the bakery prepared bread in an open hearth oven, sliding the loaves of pita bread in and out with long wooden paddles, while others delivered food to the fronts. Another group, along with the hospital workers, took care of starting up the camp's electric generators. The Amal militiamen had cut the municipal electricity supply as well as the access road.

The hospital became a centre of frantic activity. The seventy-five staff members present gathered in the emergency room or in the wards. Those who had been at their homes or visiting friends in the camp quickly rushed back, dodging snipers' bullets. Nurses pushed aside tables and chairs and wheeled into place extra examination couches, transforming all three rooms of the clinic – ER, out-patient department, waiting room – into one large emergency reception area. I posted the doctors and nurses among the eight available couches, waiting for the wounded to arrive. Dr. Khatib sat in a corner, calmly smoking away, surrounded by a small group excitedly recounting where they had been, how they had reached the hospital, how many times they had stumbled over the ever-present network of above-ground water pipes, how many bullets had struck the walls directly over their heads. The doctors, nurses, cleaning women, technicians, workers kept up the droning nervous chatter, everyone finding reassurance and a sense of security in sheer numbers.

And so we faced our first major battle. I had profited from the previous minor skirmishes that occurred throughout the fall months. Now I gathered the general practitioners and ER nursing staff to repeat once again the routine we had developed. At the Gaza Hospital in 1980-81 and in Tripoli in 1983, we had received massive casualties in very short periods; more than 100 wounded might arrive at the hospital within half an hour. One of the most difficult problems, I learned, was the naturally felt reflex of convergence. All the medical personnel automatically rushed to deal with the first wounded patient that arrived. Then, when the second and third patients made their appearance, the mass of doctors and nurses broke up and scattered pell-mell among the wounded. By the time the hospital received the last of the wounded, the staff had forgotten and neglected the very first. Only organized self-discipline could ensure that doctors and nurses would stick to their assigned couches and not rush to meet the patients. They had to learn to wait for the wounded to come to their stations, thus preventing the chaos that resulted from too many doctors and nurses falling over each other.

I guessed that Shatila and its population were too small to suffer mass casualties in a short period, but even three or four wounded at one time would create havoc in our cramped quarters. I had established a protocol and training programme, and a number of the nursing staff who had battle experience helped to train the less experienced doctors. I assigned one nurse to test for sensitivity to, and then administer, penicillin to all the wounded; another did the same for the antitetanus serum; a third injected the analgesics. Each of the main couches for receiving patients had a team of one doctor and two nurses. They would strip the patient, set up the intravenous lines, and draw blood samples, which a nurse collected and then delivered to the laboratory technician. The staff learned to overcome their convergence reaction. If only one patient arrived, then only one team worked. The others waited patiently at a distance so as not to interfere.

As the sole surgeon, I would move about the patients, making quick examinations and diagnoses, give advice, and supervise any surgical work that the GPs performed. All the while, I would mentally perform a triage of the patients to decide who most urgently needed surgical care in the operating theatre, who was less seriously injured and therefore could wait or be operated on by the GPs, and who was so severely hurt that not much could be done.

This is standard procedure in any mass-casualty situation. Surgeons face some of the most difficult dilemmas in medicine when deciding which patients to operate on first and which must simply be left to die. One applies the classical rules of trauma surgery to make what may seem to be a moral judgement, or at least, a judgement with moral consequences. Of course, in a large modern hospital, with many operating theatres and scores of staff, one doesn't usually confront such a situation. But, in an earthquake or war, a delicate balance can exist between available surgical facilities and the number of wounded. In Shatila, we had two scrub teams, one surgeon, and one theatre. The balance could be very delicate.

The protocol and training served us well. Over the four days of the battle, we received eighteen wounded, six at one time on the final day. Young men weighed down doubly with ammunition belts, rifles, and stretchers carried their wounded comrades into the reception area. Chaos erupted as relatives, friends, and onlookers streamed into the hospital – also experiencing the natural human reaction of convergence. The hospital workers tried to remove the crowd from the waiting area and entrance while the nurses and doctors manoeuvred around the milling gawkers. I finally confronted the crowd. With screams and shouts, insults and cold stares, I got their attention. "Doctors, leave all the wounded to die! Don't treat anyone until everybody gets out!" Silence. I stood my ground. The people thought I was bluffing. I continued to simply stand there; none of the other personnel moved. The wounded men's comrades finally forced the crowd to leave, begging them to let the hospital staff get on with their work. Eventually, we trained even the camp inhabitants so that my silent presence standing before them, arms crossed, was enough to make them withdraw.

The staff, freed from the encumbrance of the curious, quickly set to work on the six wounded men. Clothing cut from the bodies lay strewn in blood puddles on the floor. Bullet cartridges rolled on the concrete. One of the workers gathered up clothing, ammunition, and weapons and piled them in a corner. Intravenous infusions went up; blood samples passed by, hotly clutched in expectant hands. I moved from patient to patient – only one serious case. But what a case: a half-dozen high-velocity bullets had slammed into his two thighs, which had swollen to huge proportions; his pulse and blood pressure were barely measurable. I examined him quickly; head, chest, and abdomen clear. "Massive bleeding. Probably hit the blood vessels along with the fractures. No time for X-rays. He'll be dead, exsanguinated, before the films are developed." I barked out my findings, half to myself and half to my colleagues who were busily pumping fluids into him.

To the operating theatre quickly. The hospital workers carried his stretcher around the alleyway, through the hospital ward, down the staircase, onto the trolley. Onto the operating table. Cardiac arrest. Pump him full of plasma, fluids, blood; heart massage. A beat returned. No time to scrub, surgical gloves. Open up both thighs; clamp one artery, one vein. Pack fractured bones and minced muscle with large sterile sponges. Stabilized. More blood.

Several hours later, exhausted, we relaxed in the ward. He was alive. "I thought we had almost lost him there, for a moment."

Dr. Khatib smiled. "Six months ago I did lose people like him. Two months ago we would have lost him. Now, things have changed."

Meanwhile, feverish diplomatic activity among the various Lebanese, Palestinian, and Syrian political leaders led to a cease-fire. Sabra-Shatila Street reopened and people once again passed in and out of the camp. We busily set to work to correct the gaps in our preparations. The Four-Day Battle had shown up weak points. And, despite declarations to the contrary, everyone in Shatila knew that they could expect further fighting. After a relative calm of several weeks, the skirmishes recommenced, culminating in a major battle in April 1986. Once again, but this time for twenty days, the militiamen totally blocked off the encircled camp.

3

Preparation: Rivalry and Co-operation

AMINA HURRIED INTO THE HOSPITAL EARLY ONE morning to see me. In her mid-thirties, wide-eyed and ebullient, constantly active, she headed the General Union of Palestinian Women for Shatila and all of Lebanon. She sat at my little table in the kitchen and shared my breakfast; between mouthfuls of white cheese and olives, she quickly explained why she had come. She wanted me to visit a patient at home, even though I normally did not make house calls in the tiny confines of the camp. Only a special situation would warrant it. Yasmine, the nineteen-year-old daughter of Oum Shakour, had been outside Shatila at the Sabra market-place when the Four-Day

Battle erupted. Amal militiamen had picked her up on the street near the Gaza Hospital.

After intense political negotiations had established a cease-fire, Amal had reopened the road leading to Shatila and released prisoners taken from among the civilian population in West Beirut. Not everyone had been as lucky as Yasmine. Seventeen Palestinians, including an entire family of six, had died, slaughtered by Amal militiamen who had stormed their homes. The mutilated bodies turned up in rubbish dumps, vacant lots, and ditches.

Yasmine's luck was tainted, nonetheless. Her swarthy features and accent gave her away as Palestinian even before the militiamen looked at her papers. The militiamen had beaten, tortured, and raped her. Released by her tormentors, she had returned to Shatila at dawn. Amina wanted me to speak with Yasmine in the privacy of her home before examining her and performing any analyses at the hospital.

I followed Amina through the narrow alleyways and entered a one-storey, two-room dwelling – home to seven people, and typical of the refugee district. Portraits of dead family members, martyrs, lined the walls; reed mats covered the concrete floor, a few pieces of threadbare furniture were stuck in corners. The family, like several I had met in Shatila, had originally lived in the Tel el-Zaatar refugee camp in the suburbs of East Beirut. They were the survivors – women and children – of the siege and massacre that had taken place in that camp between June and August 1976, when right-wing Maronite Christian militias had besieged it for fifty-four days. When the camp finally surrendered, the International Red Cross organized the evacuation of the inhabitants. The right-wing militias did not respect the Red Cross auspices and massacred the entire adult male population of about 2,500 on the road during the evacuation. Their widows had by now grown into middle age, and their children had entered adulthood. The story was well known in Lebanon, and I had heard it and met other survivors, as well as one of the Red Cross delegates involved, years previously. Oum Shakour's family were among the survivors.

Many of Shatila's inhabitants had relatives living in other refugee districts of Lebanon, and many of them moved from one camp to another. This form of internal population migration followed familial ties and economic developments, as well as the changing military and security situation in different areas of the country. The painful memories of that migration lived on in people like Oum Shakour and Yasmine and were a constant reminder of the threat now facing Shatila under siege.

Yasmine appeared delicate and frail, a large ugly blue-black swath surrounding her barely open left eye. Once my welcoming demitasse of coffee had arrived, I asked everyone except Amina to leave the room. At first, Yasmine had been withdrawn; now in the presence of only Amina and myself, she opened up and described her ordeal. "There were five of them. All bearded. The same age as my brothers. They pulled me into an alleyway. Hit me. Then pushed me into a car." A constant nervous stream of talk poured forth, at times a near-hysterical incoherent babble, then silence, followed by a cool clinical description in detail, as though Yasmine had detached herself from her body and looked on from without. "After the third man had finished, he pulled up his pants, sat down beside me, lit two cigarettes, and offered me one." The entire recital broken periodically by uncontrollable sobs and tears. Amina and I listened, not interrupting, but hugging her and stroking her hair back from time to time. While recounting her tale, she lifted her skirt and removed her blouse to show us the traces of cigarette burns and various bruises. When she had finished, I asked a few questions and performed a perfunctory examination to make certain nothing was broken and that she was in no danger, telling her that I would see her the next day at the hospital. I explained what I wanted to do and why, and what laboratory analyses would be necessary. Amina would accompany her. I wrote out a prescription for a mild sedative. She needed sleep, rest, and reassurance more than anything.

While listening to Yasmine's horrific story, I remembered vividly what I had always thought when confronted by a new patient. "What if this person were my father, or mother, or sister? How would I want another doctor, a colleague, to deal with them?" Listening to Yasmine, and thinking of my own sister, troubled me profoundly. Could I become too close, too involved, too attached? Could I, in trying to be too compassionate, get lost in my passion? Become inefficient as a doctor and worthless to my patients? Not perform enough examinations and analyses because they might be too intrusive? I pondered. A rape was a case in point. There had to be a golden mean between paralysing compassion and cold, detached, clinical efficiency. "*Pan metron ariston,*" as my father would have put it in classical Greek. "Nothing in excess. Moderation in all things. The Golden Mean." I had always managed, so far, to achieve successfully what I perceived as that Golden Mean in my dealings with my patients. Within two years, and countless Yasmines later, I would be far less sure of myself.

I later spent many a long evening over thick Turkish coffee at Oum Shakour's house, listening to the horror stories of the Battle of Tel el-Zaatar and the hardships suffered there, always keeping an inquisitive ear open to any details that might help us in our defences and organization of life in Shatila. We were all determined that Shatila would not succumb to the fate of Tel el-Zaatar or repeat the experience of Sabra and Shatila in 1982.

Yasmine's two teen-aged brothers belonged to rival Palestinian groups. The young boys argued at length, and vehemently, the policies of their respective factions. Both were students and, as members of political factions, fighters who took up arms every time the camp was under attack. Both received a monthly salary. This has become the basis of the social, economic, and political organization of Palestinian refugee camp society in exile. Each faction has a militia of part-time fighters and full-time professional *fidayeen* who undergo classical military training – topography, tactics, logistics, artillery, communications, air defence. Add to these men myriad administrative cadres, journalists, cineastes, diplomats, political theorists, health workers, engineers, teachers, public relations experts, etc., and one soon has a substantial bureaucracy.

The civil strife and war in Lebanon over the last twenty years has been the equivalent of a continual series of earthquakes, requiring "catastrophe assistance"; some families have lost their homes four or five times. The PLO and some Lebanese political groups have established an entire network of social services and aid to help reconstruct, heal, and provide livelihoods after the various military forces – Lebanese militias, PLO, Israel, Syria – have destroyed, maimed, wreaked havoc, and caused socio-economic upheaval.

The social services institutions, military and administrative cadres, have amplified the PLO-state bureaucracy. This "state" functions and governs: it has institutions; makes policy; takes social, economic, and political decisions; and is responsible, in practice, for a large number of diaspora Palestinians, especially in Lebanon, and therefore pays health insurance, old age and disability pensions, widows' stipends, and scholarships, as well as salaries and "catastrophe assistance." This assumption of responsibility to provide for one's people is the responsibility of power, and the power to provide is based on money.

Money has poured into war-torn Lebanon, and continues to do so, from various countries, each financing some faction or other to act as its proxy in the regional conflicts that are played out on Lebanese turf. Each faction pays salaries to its militiamen and cadres. At times, they are no more than bribes, but in general, the salaries are salaries, providing the sole source of income for many people. Above all, salaries mean allegiance.

In Lebanon, belonging to a faction and receiving a monthly salary was (and still is) much more of a political statement than belonging to a political party in a Western parliamentary democracy. The allegiance could cost you your life. Every family in Shatila, as in all the other refugee districts in Lebanon, included at least one member directly or indirectly affiliated with one of the political groups, and many families, like Oum Shakour's, included several people, each of whom was on payroll with different factions.

In a united PLO, factional differences could be resolved through dialogue. A divided PLO, with the legitimacy of leaders put into question, was a totally different affair. Political divisions within Palestinian ranks extended into individual families. At the same time, familial pressures and ties often tempered the divisive effects. I had encountered, over the years, many others like Oum Shakour's sons. It was this kind of sibling political rivalry that had turned the 1983 internecine

Palestinian fighting in Tripoli, between Arafat loyalists and dissidents, into a nightmare. Like stories of the American, Spanish, or Greek civil wars, brother had fought brother, and father had fought son.

Amina, Oum Shakour's confidante and Yasmine's mentor, not only presided over the General Union of Palestinian Women in Lebanon, but also was a member of the Palestine National Council (PNC) – the PLO's parliament-in-exile. As such, this remarkable strong-willed but soft-spoken woman was virtually the highest level PLO officer in Shatila, rivalling in position Ali Abu Toq, the Fatah and PLO leader for Beirut. She also presided over the arguments of Yasmine's brothers. One belonged to Fatah, Amina's faction, and listened to her obediently. The other was a dissident, and held a half-concealed contempt for her, for Arafat, and for their presumed traitorous moderation and "deviationism," tempered only by his mother's remonstrances and his obliging confession of respect for Amina's kindness towards his sister.

Amina personified Palestinian civil society. Refugee society in the diaspora, out of national self-awareness, organized itself around a number of mass, popular groupings with administrative and financial ties to the PLO. These groupings included general unions of, among others, women, workers, students, doctors and health personnel, writers and journalists, all of which provided social and educational services. The General Union of Palestinian Women was the most active in Shatila, due largely to Amina's indefatigable activity. She visited families, distributing food and powdered milk to the needy; cajoling, calming victims of rape like Yasmine; listening to complaints; and helping arrange marriages – serving as the modern militant equivalent of the traditional matchmaker. She operated a workshop, teaching the women trades such as knitting, sewing, and typing to help supplement their families' incomes. The women sold the goods they produced to Lebanese merchants to sell on the open market. Her kindergarten received the children of the women enrolled in workshop training. These services created an atmosphere of social normalcy in the camp and encouraged people to remain there. Similar Women's Union kindergartens and workshops functioned throughout the Palestinian districts of Lebanon. The Workers' and Students' unions organized services as well, training electricians, plumbers, and mechanics and obtaining scholarships for university studies.

I noticed that the contending factional leaders in Shatila, including Amina, had established a *modus vivendi* among themselves. As a rule, PNSF leaders did not meet with Fatah Arafat top leaders, but second-echelon officers, often childhood classmates and friends, did. Some served as intermediaries between the factions, as during the Four-Day Battle, to set up the work teams and co-ordinate the many services – water, electricity, distribution of building materials, or food, building of fortifications – necessary to organize life in the camp and resistance to Amal. As director of the hospital, I invoked a policy that put the PRCS above the factional rivalry. The hospital was the property of all, and everyone had equal access to it. I knew, from years of experience in other refugee districts, the kind of frictions and problems that could arise if people perceived the hospital as being too closely allied with any one group. The president of the PRCS is, after all, Dr. Fathi Arafat, the younger brother of the beloved and despised Yassir. Notwithstanding my longstanding and new friendships with many leaders of rival factions, and my own political views, my obligations went out to the people, their cause and Shatila. I had criticisms to make of everyone and every faction and did so quite freely. It was my way of being a true friend and demonstrating my solidarity.

I held an extraordinary position; since I was the sole surgeon in Shatila, every faction needed my services. In addition, I gained people's respect by demanding strict discipline among the hospital staff and the patients, the latter often unruly fighters – arrogant bravado-spouting adolescents. Non-compliance with visiting hours, smoking in the wards, disrespect towards the female nursing staff, abuse of analgesics, sedatives, and amphetamines – pain-killers, "downers," and "uppers" – are all part of the trial of practising medicine in Lebanon. (Stories abound in the country of doctors who have examined patients and even performed surgery with a gun barrel stuck between their ribs. I have been in similar circumstances.) This situation was compounded in Shatila where young people strained against the stifling geographic limits on their freedom. No one could argue with my iron discipline, since the obvious result was a better functioning hospital whose main purpose, after all, was to save the lives of anyone who might be wounded in defending the camp. From my days in Nabatieh and Tripoli, I had often faced grieving combatants intent on blind violence to soothe their pain, and I had gained a reputation for being able to stand up to any angry gun-toting young fighter and soon have him sobbing contritely in my arms.

The political leaders agreed with my tactics and discipline. The pressures of confinement, living within such a small area under siege, took their toll, presenting them with problems of drunkenness, drug abuse, and unruliness. I knew all the factional leaders and had done everything I could to gain their respect and trust. They knew that they could rely on me to play the role of go-between, effecting the liaison between different rival groups, all of whom accepted me and my mediation. This was easy enough to accomplish, since my administrative duties included arranging medical treatment for special cases in the private hospitals of West Beirut or even abroad. Every day saw a stream of political officers coming to the hospital, requesting various documents and medical reports, and my making the rounds of different factions' offices to arrange various logistical details.

All the groups, according to the size of their membership and the extent of their popular support, had a series of separate offices set up in rented houses, much the same as the hospital. Some offices performed purely administrative work, dealing with paperwork such as payrolls and aid to poor families and arrangements for the purchase of supplies in West Beirut. Others became workshops for repair and maintenance of equipment, machines, and weapons or storehouses for food and supplies. This left even less space for the already cramped living quarters in the refugee district.

The size of the groups ranged from the 1,000 members of the pro-Arafat Fatah, 900 of whom were residents of Shatila, to the half-dozen followers of Saiqa, the Palestinian branch of the ruling Ba'ath Party in Syria, whose few members were administrative or political staff, mostly non-residents of Shatila, and all of them non-fighters. The

1,000 Fatah included 600 young male fighters; the rest were administrative staff, repairmen, political cadres, and clandestine members (mostly women) who were responsible for smuggling in funds and secret political messages. Most groups had between 90 and 120 members each in Shatila, and according to their social activities and popularity, they were either predominantly Shatila residents, as was the case with the Popular Front (PFLP), or from other camps in Lebanon or even Syria, as was the case with Saiqa, the Fatah dissidents and PFLP–General Command. The dissident groups had to bring in sufficient fighters to participate actively in the defence of Shatila, the only way to maintain their political legitimacy and credibility.

Each large faction had a wireless communications centre – a converted house, or often just a single room with table, chair, CB radio transmitter to maintain contact with their political leadership in the Mar Elias camp, and car batteries to use when the electricity was cut – and a system of walkie-talkies to contact their fighters at the fronts along the perimeter of the camp. Each also had a prison – a couple of rooms in a house and another loss of living space – and a security apparatus – a group of officer-policemen and clandestine agents – whether for use in disciplining their own members, spying on other groups or on the Amal militia, or countering espionage directed at themselves by all of the above, the Syrians, and the Israelis. For many of the young men and women in Shatila, especially Fatah members, life was semi-clandestine, and the discovery that their names existed on a payroll could subject them to repression and a Syrian prison should they ever venture outside the confines of the camp and into West Beirut.

In spite of fierce political rivalry, responsible and broad-minded leaders, Ali Abu Toq and some of the PNSF officers overlooked the entry of food, supplies, and even smuggled weapons and ammunition into the camp by other rival factions. They knew that in time of war, with Shatila under total blockade, everything within the camp would be considered common property and distributed among all. Pragmatic co-operation, and even co-ordination, in times of need tempered the antagonistic public pronouncements and insults traded among groups.

That all the groups – the Palestine National Salvation Front, the DFLP, both orthodox and non-orthodox Communist parties, the Abu Nidal Revolutionary Council, and the PLO alliance of Arafat supporters – could live within 200 yards square and not destroy themselves and the camp was an accomplishment in itself. To get them actually to co-operate was a testament to people's maturity and ability to transcend divisions in order to attain a common goal – self-defence. Although all this may seem confusing to the outsider, it is actually commonplace in the Middle East. Lebanese parties and militias easily outnumber Palestinian ones. In Israel there are more than twenty political parties. Whatever their political differences, in a time of national emergency, such as war, all parties close ranks against the outside enemy.

Our lifeline to the outside world was the Mar Elias camp, two miles from Shatila, headquarters of the leadership of the various Palestinian groups in West Beirut and the political and administrative contact point for the factions and institutions in the besieged camps of Shatila and Burj el-Barajneh. UNRWA had set up offices in Mar Elias to co-ordinate its work, and the PRCS, with a total staff of 1,000 in Beirut, also established a small clinic and administrative offices there to more adequately serve the needs of the hospitals in Shatila and Burj el-Barajneh. The Lebanese Socialist Party controlled the region of Mar Elias, a small, predominantly Christian refugee district (about twenty-five percent of Palestinians are Christians) located closer to the city core. The Socialists were nominal allies of Amal in their conflict with the right-wing Phalangists of East Beirut, but also rivalled Amal for political and military influence in nationalist West Beirut. Closely allied to the Palestinians, the Socialist Party provided protection and a safe haven for them in West Beirut, so the Palestinian political leadership in Mar Elias had the freedom of movement and communication necessary to function. (The only exception was the Arafat wing of Fatah. Its rivalry with the Syrians and their allies in Lebanon meant that Fatah members had to work clandestinely in West Beirut. The Fatah leadership established their head offices in the Ain el-Hilweh camp in southern Lebanon, an area free of Syrian control.)

At the hospital, our work of preparation continued. Even in the best of times, the electrical power supply in Lebanon was an erratic affair. Numerous regular planned power stoppages occurred, as well as irregular and unplanned ones. Shatila's precarious infrastructure rendered the refugee district particularly susceptible to them. Electric generators were, and still are, standard equipment in all hospitals and other essential buildings in Lebanon. Many families bought small generators to cover the needs of their households, and there was a flourishing market for them. The smaller ones, up to 5 kilo-volt amperes (supplying about 3,500 watts of electricity), run on ordinary gasoline; the larger ones (up to 120 kva or more) operate on diesel fuel.

When I arrived, the hospital had a 15-kva muffled generator, set on wheels to make it mobile. After the Four-Day Battle, we bought a 50-kva model, also muffled. The muffling of the motor lessened the nuisance of the noise to the camp's inhabitants and prevented the Amal militiamen from pin-pointing its exact location – it would make a prime target for shelling. We placed the two generators by the mosque about thirty yards from the hospital in the uninhabited skeleton of a two-storey building. I gathered a team of four hospital workers to reinforce the surrounding walls and first-storey floor with sandbags to provide extra protection. PRCS rented the building next door as a warehouse for food, surgical supplies, and diesel fuel. Another session of digging and excavating followed, to sink the metal fuel containers into the floor, creating underground reservoirs. We fitted a hand pump to withdraw the diesel fuel as needed.

My experience had taught me that, in a war situation, one must always think in terms of alternatives. Therefore, I had the men lay two systems of electrical cables leading from each of the generators to the hospital. They buried all of the cables underground or snaked them through different dwellings en route to the hospital as an added measure of protection from mortar shells. Also, we stored an extra coil of cable for each generator in the warehouse – just in case. With the help of an electrical engineer, we devised a series of switches so that we could change easily from the public electrical supply to one generator or another, according to need. Although the engineer helped to create this special switchboard, the hospital workers and I had to learn the basics of operating it and the generators, since he would not be present in the camp in a siege. For me, Shatila became a vocational training centre. I tested my memory of high school and pre-med physics and learned about electricity, mechanics, and plumbing. I had to if I wanted to be able to provide everything necessary to function as a surgeon.

We redid the electrical wiring throughout the four hospital buildings; we would redo the wiring again and again, always learning from our mistakes. Finally, we set up a system of fuses and switches that provided two parallel networks. One functioned when the normal public electrical supply was available and we could turn on all lamps and equipment simultaneously without worrying about how much electricity we consumed. We devised the other network to function when our generator was operating, so that we could route the electric current to only those hospital areas or pieces of equipment that absolutely had to be functioning, in effect rationing our electric current and therefore fuel.

Preparation and planning involved the people as well as the equipment. Training for the hospital personnel included not only the protocol of diagnosis and resuscitation of the wounded in mass-casualty reception, but also simple life-saving procedures. Dr. Khatib relished this. The doctors practised endotracheal intubation (passing a tube into the windpipe to aid breathing) on cadavers. They assisted me, and then I them in cutting down on a vein (exposing a peripheral vein in the arm or leg to set up a secure line for intravenous fluids), a very important procedure when dealing with patients in shock from massive haemorrhage.

I also taught my colleagues how to place a thoracic drain under local anaesthesia. Many war-wounded receive shrapnel or a bullet to the chest, and it is a simple but life-saving procedure to place a tube between the patient's ribs into the chest cavity to evacuate blood and air, thus re-expanding the lung and stopping any further haemorrhage. Dr. Khatib showed special eagerness to learn this procedure, since he probably could have saved three lives in the first battle had he known how to perform it then.

I bought several standard medical and surgical reference texts for the hospital "library," and the doctors spent long hours consulting them whenever we had a difficult or unusual case. The GPs were hungry for knowledge and eager to perfect their skills. I tried to help them as much as possible, but numerous topics of internal medicine were beyond my expertise, and I myself often had to consult our dozen-odd texts.

Scheduling difficulties for the staff and security-related transportation problems prompted me to rely on the camp's permanent population as much as possible. I learned this lesson from Dr. Khatib's experiences in the first round of fighting, when no hospital existed. He and I gave a series of lectures on first aid to some young women of the camp, as well as to groups of fighters. The theoretical lectures alone were insufficient, and the women came to the hospital to learn practical tasks in the emergency room and in-patient ward. After several months, a few of them were working better than many of our regular nursing staff. They had the motivation and discipline to excel. One of them, who had lost three brothers in various wars, went on to learn the basic techniques of radiology and became the equal of our X-ray technician. These volunteers became an integral and essential part of the hospital staff. Self-sufficiency remained our priority.

We employed another group of volunteers from the General Union of Women in our primary health care programme. Amina knew a number of young women with high school education who wanted something more demanding than the trades workshop. After an intensive course at the hospital, they went about the camp, visiting mothers and housewives, many of whom were friends, relatives, and peers, teaching the basics of personal and family hygiene and assisting in vaccination campaigns. They were the Shatila version of "barefoot doctors."

The attempt to instil an understanding of basic first aid among groups of fighters had a very practical purpose. I had witnessed, far too often over too many years, the dangerous transportation of the wounded. In the heat and confusion of battle, young men would carry an injured comrade at break-neck speed on a stretcher, a fractured limb dangling over the edge. The original trauma might not have severed blood vessels and nerves, but this thoughtless and careless transport often did. I tried to explain the importance of immobilizing a fractured arm or leg and carrying the patient with all due care. Shatila was so small that transport time to the hospital was always short, and rushing was not necessary. I taught the combatants other basic techniques, such as how to stop haemorrhage with simple hand or finger pressure, and how to protect a patient in a coma or with a fractured spine. Some of the young men had enough presence of mind, self-control, and discipline to take the necessary precautions, but all too often, the very human urge to get a wounded friend to the hospital as rapidly as possible overcame them.

Impossible to tell, but our young patient of the Four-Day Battle, who had suffered the bilateral femur fracture and severed femoral artery and vein, and had gone into cardiac arrest, could well have been a victim of his comrades' haste compounding the work of the bullets.

4

Lessons in Electricity and Plumbing

SEVERAL WEEKS OF RELATIVE CALM FOLLOWED THE FOUR-Day Battle; then the nightly skirmishes recommenced, culminating in major hostilities in April 1986. Once again, but this time for twenty days, the Amal militiamen encircling the camp totally blocked us off. The camp's inhabitants went on red alert. Heavily armed men criss-crossed the camp's alleyways on their way to the fronts. Work teams organized to solve logistical problems. The bakery turned out bread; teams prepared food and delivered it to the fighters at the fronts; crews repaired the water pipes; squads of young men and women put warning signs on alleyways susceptible to sniper fire; yet others hung blankets between buildings to cut off the view of snipers, opened passages between houses by knocking doorways in walls, built sandbag fortifications. The sound of heavy automatic weapons fire and grenades resonated day and night. Families stayed indoors on the ground floors of houses, abandoning second-storey apartments because of the danger of ricocheting bullets. They passed the time listening to the news bulletins on the radio concerning the fighting and the political manoeuvring, playing cards or chess, cooking, eating, sleeping, loving – there is nothing like the possibility of violent death to bring forth the romantic impulse. Twelve died and another thirty-five were wounded in Shatila in those twenty days.

The hospital itself contained only twelve beds – sufficient for our routine, daily work – but now, as in subsequent battles, the number of wounded quickly surpassed the number of beds available. We took over part of a two-storey building, previously a co-operative store run by the PFLP and now partially deserted as it awaited the implementation of a grandiose plan to construct a new bomb shelter, co-operative, and residence. It had the advantage of being located just across the street from Faramawi's building, and its ten by twenty-five yards accommodated forty beds – camping cots for the most part, and a few surgical hospital beds. Patients with more severe injuries, such as head, chest, or abdominal wounds, remained in the hospital; when they recovered sufficiently, I transferred them to the forty-bed annex (which came to be known affectionately as "Cabaret Giannou"), where they lay alongside patients with non-life-threatening wounds. These less serious cases included fractures of major bones in traction, major soft-tissue injuries, and patients under simple observation. Patients with minor wounds, requiring little nursing care, along with those needing further recuperation from major wounds, went to offices or homes for a few days of rest and simple medication before returning to their duties.

We distributed the staff among the hospital, "cabaret," and homes, depending on the number of patients. Dr. Khatib, Mahmoud, the chief nurse, and Rabiha and Oum Mohammed Faramawi took charge of the doctors, nurses, cleaning women, and workers. Many of the doctors had no previous surgical experience, nor had they worked in the midst of a war. They learned how to dress a wound and perform minor surgery while bombs landed overhead. Kristen trained some of our Palestinian doctors in basic anaesthesia techniques.

Two Norwegian nurses in their late twenties, Venke, an ER nurse and Kristen, an anaesthetist, had joined Régine and me in Shatila in March 1986, just in time for the Twenty-Day Battle in April. I could now concentrate on my surgery, and not first have to anaesthetize the patients myself. Kristen had the calm, patient temperament of the experienced anaesthetist that was so necessary when dealing with some of the horrendous cases of war trauma with massive haemorrhage that we faced. We successfully resuscitated more than one cardiac arrest, like the fighter wounded in the Four-Day Battle, pumping fluids and blood into the patient's circulation, all the while performing artificial respiration and cardiac massage. Having recovered a heartbeat, Kristen would continue with her resuscitation and anaesthesia, while I intervened to attempt to stem the haemorrhage.

After intense contacts and discussions, Lebanese political parties, Amal, the Syrians, and the pro-Syrian PNSF negotiated a cease-fire; a buffer force drawn from various Lebanese parties together with Syrian observers took position around the periphery of the camp. During the lull following this battle, the movement of people and goods in and out of Shatila faced even greater restrictions.

We felt the noose of the siege tightening about us. During the Twenty-Day Battle, construction came to a halt. After the cease-fire, Amal withdrew permission to bring building materials into Shatila. No more large-scale building or reconstruction, no more beehive of activity, men pushing wheelbarrows, mixing cement, beating with hammers. This weighed heavily on the camp's inhabitants. Shatila's people had stocked some building materials and continued to smuggle in others. The construction of Faramawi's fourth storey and that of the building directly across from the hospital continued, as did that of Ali Abu Toq's new bomb shelter. But things were not the same.

Reconstruction symbolized normalcy, a return to peace between Shatila and the neighbouring Shi'ite slums. New buildings created military obstacles, offered protection, encouraged the inhabitants to remain and refugee squatters to return to newly rebuilt homes. Amal and the Syrians understood this. The permission to reconstruct could only signify a turning away from hostile intentions. Commerce, money, work portended peace. A ban on reconstruction foretold more war and destruction. Everyone knew it.

The lulls between rounds of fighting were consumed by preparations during the day for a possible new blockade of the camp, guard duty for the men at night, and endless visits and political discussions both day and night. Normal daily life disappeared, to be replaced by a mixture of socializing, planning, and readiness.

Early morning. The camp was just beginning to stir. I washed, made myself a coffee, and went downstairs to pace the alley in front of the hospital, slowly sipping my drink. The brisk morning air felt good, refreshing. My neighbours, the brothers Nabil and Mahmoud, both in their mid-twenties, greeted me as they passed on their way to work. I knew them well. They often invited Régine or me for a coffee or dinner. Nabil, an electrician, belonged to the pro-Arafat Fatah and was working on a house inside the camp. He feared leaving the security of Shatila. His brother Mahmoud, a mason, owed allegiance to the pro-Syrian PFLP–General Command and left Shatila every morning to work on a construction site in West Beirut. Although both were married with children, they continued to live all together in the same house; the Shatila sardine tin lacked space.

In turn, one of their wives, Nawal or Merfat, took care of the young children of both families, while the other went out to the Sabra market or West Beirut to shop and run errands. They bought goods every day – fresh vegetables and fruit for immediate consumption, dried goods, preserves for stocking. They stocked everything: rice, sugar, beans, lentils, flour, jams, corned beef, sardines, candles, radio batteries, yarn, blankets, canned beer. Nabil liked to drink.

The women spent the rest of the day doing the laundry, preparing food for the children and the evening meal for the men, exchanging gossip – who, among the camp's inhabitants, had been arrested "out" in West Beirut, what had happened on the road that day, what insults the militiamen had shouted out to the passing women. It was like running a gauntlet. Nawal also spent three afternoons a week at the Women's Union vocational centre, learning to use a knitting machine. She hoped to earn a little extra money making wool sweaters.

The men returned home before dusk; Mahmoud didn't want to risk the road at night, even with his political credentials. Before and after dinner, other friends and relatives passed by. One evening as I was passing by on my way to the "villa," I heard loud shouts coming through the window of their ground-floor dwelling. I stopped, knocked, let myself in, took off my shoes, and offered a general greeting, "*Salaam aleikoum.*" The shouting stopped while people returned my salutation. A strange embarrassed silence fell over the crowd. The room overflowed with at least twelve people in an area no more than four by four yards, sitting on mats, mattresses, and pillows scattered over the floor, with a large brass tray carrying the remains of a serving of coffee in the centre, and a television set blaring loudly in the corner.

A romantic Egyptian melodrama, always a favourite, was playing. I recognized the actors. Nabil and Mahmoud, pro- and anti-Arafat, rarely discussed politics between themselves: a tacit agreement. But the visitors didn't have the same agreement. Apparently, some incident in the film had provoked a comment by someone, and someone else had replied, provoking another comment. Soon, everyone was shouting, either crying out who was the real "traitor" or trying to get everyone else to stop shouting and arguing. "Those who want everybody to stop shouting win," I proclaimed in the uneasy silence.

"Have a coffee, Dr. Giannou," offered Mahmoud. People pushed aside to make room for me to sit down.

"Nawal, make a new pot, will you?" asked Nabil. "In any case, you'll have to excuse me, Doctor," he continued. "I have guard duty tonight." He rose, picked up his rifle and ammunition belt, and left.

I asked the others what the original incident in the film was about, and then, in a strong Egyptian accent and slang – the burlesque of the Arab world – told one of my Egyptian hospital stories. The tension eased and the group was soon laughing while I talked on. When I looked at my watch, it was close to midnight. I had to leave for a meeting with the Popular Committee.

The degree of movement in and out of Shatila was indicative of the political and military tensions between the refugee district and the surrounding militiamen. We invented all sorts of gimmicks, procedures, ruses, and work schedules to keep a constant flow of people coming and going. Normalcy, movement, commerce: all worked to our advantage. Patients coming to the hospital from West Beirut helped serve this purpose. Amal militiamen, Lebanese soldiers, and Syrian observers had great difficulty in refusing entry to Lebanese and Palestinian civilians ostensibly seeking the free medical services of the hospital.

The various political factions and the civilian population used periods of calm and the movement of people to transport into the camp great quantities of sundry and necessary items. Building materials were prohibited, but food, household goods, clothing, electrical supplies, aluminum water reservoirs, and spare parts were not. Shatila was becoming one large store-room. Ali Abu Toq's secret female Fatah members, Abu Moujahed's Popular Committee, Basel's security people, Abu Imad's cohorts, Rabiha, Oum Mohammed Faramawi, and the hospital cleaning women's "battalion" purchased all types of supplies in West Beirut – food stuffs, materials for repair work, radio batteries, flashlight bulbs, spare parts, coffee, cigarettes.

Every mother and every family in Shatila thought in terms of military logistics. During each battle and accompanying total blockade on Shatila, we had to make do with what we had, since it was impossible to move anything in or out of the camp. Every household stocked several large sacks of rice, sugar, flour, dried beans and lentils, cooking oil, canned goods, soap, matches, candles, radio batteries, and anything else imaginable. The hospital did the same – and more. Like the rest of the camp's inhabitants – and the hospital resembled a large household – we also had to provide for food, soap, brooms, mops, and other cleaning items. And since we in the hospital had to remain active – even and especially in war conditions – this meant providing for spare parts, light bulbs, extra rolls of electrical wiring, tools for repair and maintenance work, as well as sufficient fuel and air and oil filters, to keep the hospital's electric generator operating.

Foreseeing, buying, and transporting to the hospital the materials, medicines, supplies, and food we might need under all possible circumstances constituted my primary administrative concern. The PRCS central pharmacy bought us a regular three-month supply from West Beirut pharmaceutical firms. I obtained extra funds from the political factions and sent our pharmacists to buy even more goods. Also, various charitable organizations donated medical supplies and powdered milk or infant formula. We stocked thousands of litres of intravenous fluids, urine bags and antibiotic capsules, hundreds of ampoules of injectable antibiotics, and other essential emergency and anaesthesia medications. In addition, we stored large quantities of surgical tubing and drains, suture material, bandages, gauze rolls, adhesive plaster, and other items for the laboratory and X-ray department.

Knowing that the besieged camp would have to confront yet another battle, any occasion and any bundle of vegetables or other supplies was used for smuggling weapons and ammunition into Shatila. Over the quiet months of 1986, the political factions obtained millions of rounds of bullets, hundreds of hand grenades and RPGs (rocket-propelled grenades), dozens of mortar shells, and thousands of empty burlap sacks for sandbagging. Before 1982, the PLO received weapons directly from abroad, but that was no longer possible in Beirut. Still, the Palestinian factions really only needed money for their purchases. The whole of Lebanon had become a black market where arms merchants often sold to all parties and sides. All one needed to know was a name and address and the appropriate bank account number. Shatila's dwellers considered weapons and munitions just as essential as food, fuel, and medicines.

They employed great ingenuity to spirit in the military supplies. After middle age, traditional sedentary housewives in the Middle East tend to be overweight and wear bulky flowing robes. Hidden under these formless, loose-fitting garments, many a round of Kalashnikov bullets and hand grenades entered Shatila plastered under a heavy bosom or strapped to a flabby thigh. Women took to wearing old-fashioned corsets and girdles, the better to carry securely, close to their bodies, the priceless weapons of death and survival. Dozens of women plied the road to and from Shatila daily, braving insults and hair-raising incidents on the way. They took advantage of the traditional modesty of the bearded Shi'ite militiamen, knowing full well that the young men would not dare bodysearch them in public, in front of the Syrian observers. To do such a thing is considered taboo in socially and sexually repressed Middle Eastern societies. The women made repeated trips back and forth, their hands filled with grocery bags, and sacks of rice or mountains of vegetables balanced on their heads. The more people commuting, the better; the more movement, the less chance of searches and discovery. Huge bundles of spinach or other greens concealed a core of 60-mm mortar shells or RPGs that the women got from political contacts in West Beirut. A butane gas cylinder with a false bottom contained gelignite explosive. The women built up the camp's munition, as well as food, stores.

In Lebanese politics and elsewhere, as I have mentioned, money means power; payrolls, social assistance, and benefits are powerful instruments in factional politics. Political groups smuggled funds into Shatila in a fashion similar to munitions, to pay salaries and cover administrative functions. Fatah had the largest payroll and budget, but their members' presence in West Beirut was clandestine. The Amal militia and the Syrians always tried to intercept the couriers transporting the funds. The pro-Arafat Fatah formed the heart and soul of Shatila, as with other refugee districts, and money was its lifeline. Large numbers of Palestinians and Lebanese came to Shatila from West Beirut, as well as from other parts of Lebanon, to ask for assistance and social welfare benefits at the Fatah offices. Ali Abu Toq received them all personally, listening patiently to convoluted stories of grief, injury, death, abandonment, and destruction. As Lebanon slipped farther into economic crisis during 1986 due to the vertiginous drop in the value of the currency, Fatah funds stabilized the income of many families. Some complained that this was simply Palestinian "charity" replacing the foreign and international charity of UNRWA, or political bribery on the part of Arafat; others said that it was a right, a symbol of a state that did not yet exist, but for which everyone yearned. Whatever the opinion, few ever refused the funds. Shatila, the prime source for the distribution of such aid and assistance, increased the reputation and importance of the refugee district among the population not only of Shatila, but also of West Beirut and Lebanon as a whole.

Apart from smuggling, the other method of procuring weapons and strategic goods was to bribe Amal militiamen or Lebanese Sixth Brigade soldiers surrounding the camp. Members of various factions made discreet contacts in West Beirut and paid the price, and, in the middle of the night, a group of men would sneak through the militia lines at a predetermined point where they would not be challenged. The men thus entering the camp added to the number of fighters present and brought with them tens of thousands of rounds of ammunition. Or they paid off the militiamen and Syrian observers on duty at the entry checkpoint to Shatila – a decade of war and near-anarchy had created a parallel economy, more powerful and pervasive than the official one – to overlook the passage of munitions hidden amidst food supplies. Bribery was not always necessary; some militiamen and soldiers were sympathetic to the Palestinians and opposed the War of the Camps as a matter of principle. Shatila obtained their aid and abetment without any compensation, a few even acting as intermediaries between the camp and the arms merchants. After all, this was Lebanon!

Furthermore, many Lebanese members of Palestinian factions participated in the defence of Shatila. Not a few of them paid with their lives for their convictions and principles. Dr. Khatib told me how, during the first battle in 1985, one Lebanese Shi'ite soldier manning a tank in the sports stadium overshot the camp, and then deserted his position and entered Shatila to fight alongside the Palestinian defenders. He died from a sniper's bullet to the head.

Monsour was one of these pro-Palestinian Lebanese and his brother one of the main military officers of Fatah in Shatila. He had been one of the last patients on whom I operated in Tripoli in 1983, wounded by a bullet to his pelvis, fracturing his hip joint and severing the femoral artery. I was surprised to see him again in Shatila, healthy and walking about so well. One day, during the Twenty-Day Battle, I was operating in the theatre when Dr. Khatib rushed down the stairway breathless. Trying to control himself, he spoke quietly and slowly. "Monsour has been injured. I put in a chest tube, but he's bleeding badly. His condition is critical." I overcame a strong urge to rush upstairs to see what I could do for this gentle soul. I finished operating an hour later and ran upstairs, but they had already removed his body, wrapped in its death shroud.

Surgery is the epitome of curative medicine. A patient may enter the operating theatre on the verge of death and come out alive, if not whole. No alternative to the knife exists for a strangulated hernia or bullet wound to the abdomen. I have always appreciated the wonder of surgery. But although a surgeon myself, I have seen too much poverty-induced pathology – an epidemic of meningitis in Mali, rampant cancer of the bladder in Egyptian peasants due to schistosomiasis – to underestimate the value of primary health care and preventive medicine. Most of the pathology that one sees in the Third World is infectious in origin. Shatila and West Beirut were no exception. Living in insalubrious surroundings with open sewers, overcrowded housing, and unclean water supplies invited disease. Most of the 150-200 patients coming daily to our out-patient clinic complained of various contagious diseases: gastroenteritis, dysenteries, respiratory infections, tonsillitis, skin parasites and fungi. We saw many cases of rheumatic heart disease as a result of tonsillitis and "strep throat." However, in the Middle East in general, and in Lebanon in particular, the people eat relatively well, with a mixed diet containing a great deal of fresh fruit and vegetables and dairy products. We did not have to face the dire poverty and accompanying malnutrition that one sees in much of Africa, Asia, and parts of Latin America.

I did not limit PRCS health services in Shatila to the hospital and out-patient clinic. With the help of a Belgian couple specializing in primary health care, we set up a maternal and child health care centre. When they finished in Shatila, Dirk and Lieve went off to Burj el-Barajneh to do the same there. They had only just graduated from medical school, and their social activism and political opinions had quickly led them to take up primary health care and preventive medicine, first among Third World immigrant workers in Belgium, and then in the Palestinian refugee camps. They were enthusiastic, vivacious, curious, hard-working, and naïve: they reminded me of myself a few years earlier. They pummelled me with questions about Middle Eastern and intra-Palestinian politics, about the health implications of various social, economic, and security conditions. They considered me a good source – I spoke the language, looked Middle Eastern, had been around a long time, held a position of responsibility, and yet could also speak to them as a Westerner.

My advice to them, briefly, was: Observe, listen, ask discreet questions, talk about yourselves and Belgium, accept certain social practices until the people know and trust you; stay away from direct involvement in the politics of the camps. With all my experience in the region, I was only just beginning to understand certain attitudes and events. And there were all too many incidents that I thought I understood, only to receive a very rude awakening later.

Preventive medicine campaigns were extremely difficult to organize in the conditions that prevailed in Lebanon, especially in the refugee camps. The changing security situation created a highly unstable population, as people moved back and forth across the countryside, fleeing areas of armed conflict. Patients disappeared for months on end, making follow-up of pregnant or lactating women almost impossible.

UNRWA assumed prime responsibility for the vaccination of children, combining its immunization programme with its schools, keeping track of the children and making certain that at least the Palestinian child population of Lebanon was fully and duly vaccinated. These services were not available to the Lebanese, whose Ministry of Health had just about ceased to function because of the civil strife since 1975. We attempted to supplement UNRWA activities in this field and provided vaccinations for Lebanese who brought their children to the Shatila hospital during lulls between the rounds of fighting.

However, UNRWA's activities did not solve the problem of the immunization status of any given patient, even among Palestinians;

one could never be sure that an adult had received the necessary booster shots. This was especially critical when dealing with war trauma. Medicine considers war injuries contaminated. All patients with contaminated and dirty wounds, whether civilian or military in origin, anywhere in the world, should receive extra protection against the danger of one of the most deadly related diseases: tetanus. We had to bring in the necessary supplies of vaccine and serum, and we conducted campaigns, with the active participation of the factions in the camp, to administer booster tetanus shots to all the fighters – those at greatest risk. The administration of these shots also gave us the opportunity to determine everyone's blood group.

War tended to override all other considerations in Lebanon. Many people whose war injuries involved bones, tendons, and nerves suffered disabling sequelae. These handicapped abounded in Shatila – young people with near-paralysed arms or legs, deformed hands, wounds oozing from chronic osteomyelitis (intractable bone infections not responding to standard antibiotic and surgical therapy). Many young men dared not leave the boundaries of the camp to seek specialized care in more sophisticated hospitals in West Beirut. Some needed only intensive physiotherapy, and we set up such services in our simple field hospital. Others required corrective operations that we attempted to perform by bringing orthopaedic surgeons and neurosurgeons on contract with PRCS into Shatila on as regular a basis as possible. Still others who required specialized procedures – microsurgery, for instance – had to be spirited out of the camp at night, threading their way through the Amal lines, and out of Beirut to other areas of Lebanon from where they could leave for further care abroad. Funding was never a problem, since all of the camp's inhabitants were involved in some way or other with one of the political groups. The different political factions, along with PRCS, covered all costs incurred, especially for war-related injuries. The PRCS and the PLO had a comprehensive medical insurance programme.

Western health professionals, like Lieve and Dirk, had worked with the PRCS in Lebanon and elsewhere for a number of years. Different solidarity groups sent volunteers who usually came for a three- to six-month stint. The Scandinavians were the most active. In 1985-86, their group, Norwegian Refugee Aid (NORVAK), had several medical teams working in refugee areas in northern and southern Lebanon, as well as in the Beirut camps. A British group, Medical Aid for Palestine, also organized health personnel to help out in the camps. In late 1985 and 1986, two extraordinary people co-ordinated these different volunteers and helped them with the inevitable problems of adapting to a new and different society and culture.

Sol-Britt, originally a nurse and now NORVAK co-ordinator, visited me every week or so in Shatila. She fitted the physical stereotype of a Swedish woman – tall, lithe, blonde, and blue-eyed. Sol-Britt was only twenty-two years old, but she had a winning smile, a calm disposition, a stuttering knowledge of Arabic, and great loads of patience. She needed them all in her daily travelling throughout Lebanon, passing through the armed checkpoints of all the militia groups, and she often showed tremendous courage driving through war zones. Her ambulance, target of more than one bullet, proved of the utmost importance for transporting medical and surgical supplies to us in Shatila, as well as to other camps and Shi'ite villages in South Lebanon. On her weekly visits, Sol-Britt came to me for advice and information about the developing political and security situation. She had to deal with administrative problems with the PRCS in Beirut and in the South; cultural shock among some of the volunteers who had difficulty in adapting to Middle Eastern society; and planning to be done to meet the health needs of the camps' population during the coming difficult time.

Oervind, in his mid-thirties, Sol-Britt's Norwegian counterpart, eventually replaced her. "Really! These Scandinavians!" I thought, when I first met him. "Another tall, physically fit, blue-eyed, blond-haired Nordic." He was gentle, mild spoken, but intensely committed; as a man, travelling about the country was even more dangerous for Oervind than for Sol-Britt, especially once the hostage-taking started in earnest. But he never shirked from what he considered to be his duty and both Sol-Britt and he gave me great help and support in my sedentary existence in Shatila.

Sol-Britt and Oervind regularly gathered together the foreign volunteers from the North and South and brought them into Shatila for discussions and consultations. This was quite an adventure for many of them to whom the mere name "Shatila" conjured up images of squalor, massacre, siege, and death. Sol-Britt told me that some of her colleagues who thought nothing of braving the anarchic conditions of West Beirut were appalled at the idea of coming to Shatila. I asked her to tell them that Shatila was one of the safest places for a Westerner to be in Lebanon. But both Sol-Britt and I knew that the problem was not the 200 yards square of Shatila; it was the road through the Amal militiamen to get there. Régine, Lieve, and Dirk enjoyed the volunteers' company and went with them when they left, using the occasion to go out on the town, as much as that was possible (and it still was) in the craziness of West Beirut. How ironic and paradoxical: for Régine, West Beirut was dangerous; for the others, Shatila fitted that description. Of course, they were all right.

Like a magnet, Shatila drew foreign and international non-governmental organizations (NGOs) that wished to help the besieged camp's population. Delegates from OXFAM, Save the Children, the Middle East Council of Churches, and other groups active in Lebanon all came during the intervals between the repeated rounds of fighting and siege, offering medical supplies and other help. The International Committee of the Red Cross (ICRC) was especially active in bringing us aid and keeping a tally on our activities. I had co-operated with ICRC delegates over the years and we had developed a good working relationship; with some, I became fast friends. They were quite impressed with our little field hospital and the degree to which we maximized our medical services in such cramped quarters, and they brought every new delegate to Lebanon to visit the hospital of Shatila.

UNRWA and UNICEF aided Shatila's Popular Committee, as well as the hospital and preventive medicine programme and like the International Red Cross, many UN personnel took delight in bringing their colleagues to see the hospital. We held numerous meetings throughout 1986 with various UN technical experts to discuss arrangements for problems such as water supply, sewage, and electricity.

RÉGINE PONSON

Shatila mosque, its balcony refurbished, after the brief period of reconstruction in the fall of 1985.

BISAN PRES AND PUBLICATION INSTITUTE LTD., CYPRESS

An alley in Shatila. Note aboveground water pipes.

RÉGINE PONSON

View of three hospital buildings and the Champs Elysées during the Six-Month Battle. Faramawi's balcony is in the foreground.

The newly-constructed antechamber under Faramawi's balcony. Note the sandbags, stretcher poles and mattresses piled on the stairwell entrance to the operating theatre.

RÉGINE PONSON

NASR ABU KHAROUB

Amal position (circled) overlooking the devastated periphery of Shatila. Tunnels from the camp reached the base of this building.

RÉGINE PONSON

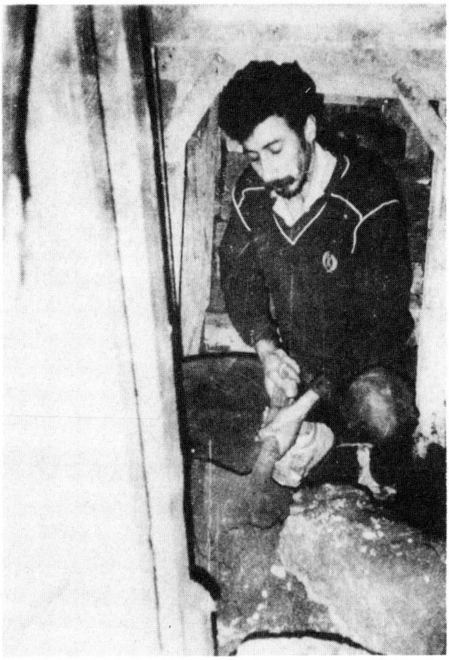

Digging a tunnel with a sawed-off shovel.

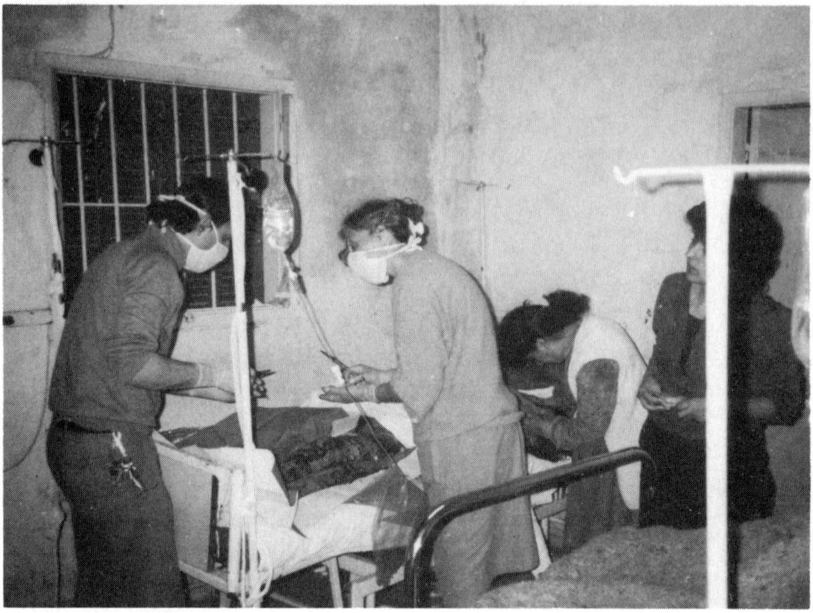

RÉGINE PONSON

Régine assists me in changing the dressings of a burn victim in the ward.

Operating-theatre backache: stooping under the overhead lamp during an operation.

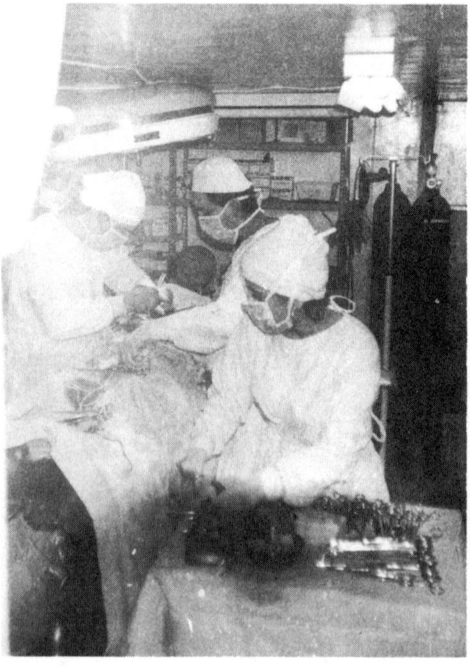

RÉGINE PONSON

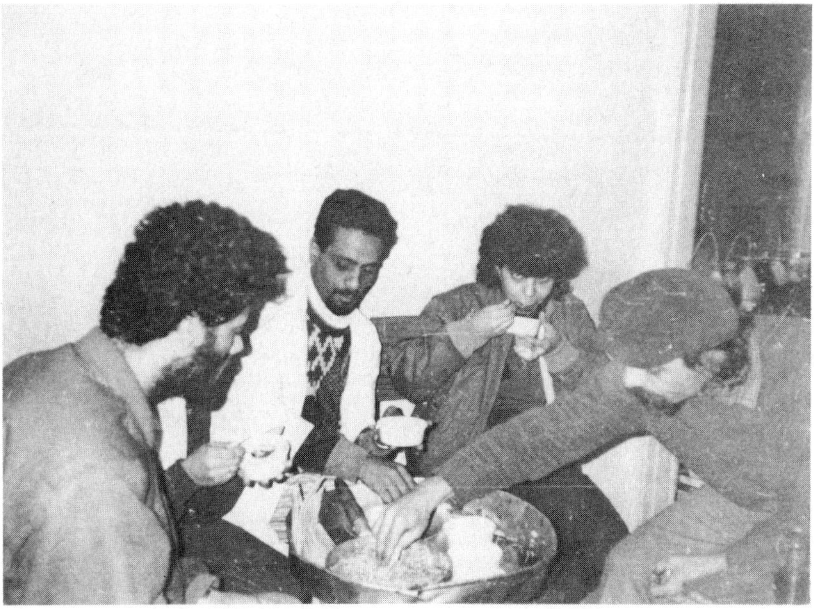

RÉGINE PONSON

Sharing a midnight meal with the night-shift nursing staff.

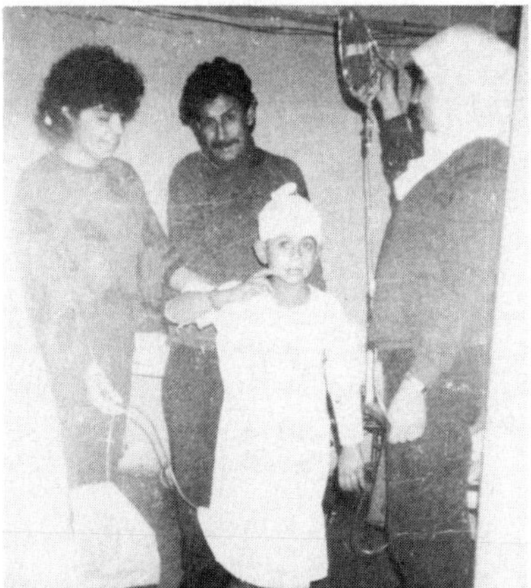

RÉGINE PONSON

Samir with nurses and his father while recovering from his head wound.

RÉGINE PONSON

In the ER, demonstrating a venous cutdown on a wounded infant to a Palestinian colleague.

The bomb shelter during the Six-Month Battle: people, pots and pans, mattresses and blankets, and more people.

RÉGINE PONSON

RÉGINE PONSON

Dancing in the same bomb shelter after the cease-fire, celebrating a wedding.

NASR ABU KHAROUB

A panoramic view of the destruction of the western sector and Shatila as seen from the sports stadium. Note the forest and high-rise buildings in the background – outside Shatila's boundaries.

AGENCE FRANCE PRESSE

Checkpoint entrance to Shatila after the cease-fire: Women on their way to fetch groceries await the exit of Red Cross ambulances evacuating wounded under the watchful eyes of Syrian soldiers.

UNWRA

Children of Shatila take a shortcut to school.

AGENCE FRANCE PRESSE

Leaving home, January 27, 1988: Amina is on my left.

Shatila, like all the refugee districts, needed much assistance. Its roads and alleyways were unpaved, and only two of them were wide enough to allow for the passage of cars. UNRWA had attempted to cover over the sewage system, and a series of cement-block sewer covers that could be easily lifted dotted the camp. A team of men had the continuous and thankless task of unblocking the pipes, using long flexible metal poles. Abu Said, a wiry man in his mid-forties whose mouthful of rotten teeth and craggy face made him look more as though he were in his sixties, was a familiar sight in his high rubber boots, hands and torso smeared with raw sewage. He kept the camp sewers unblocked – a very important task since flooding rainwater had to be regularly drained away from the area, and at times a difficult one, because the bodies of victims of the 1982 Massacre had clogged the main drainage system to the south of the camp.

The UNRWA had a small clinic in Shatila that functioned from 8:00 A.M. to 2:00 P.M., staffed by a general practitioner. During the first round of fighting in 1985, the Amal militia had bombed out the UNRWA clinic, and its staff, who all lived outside the camp, were never present during a siege. The transportation difficulties inherent in the security situation made it impossible for them to maintain a permanent medical presence in Shatila. We had very good working relations with the clinic, however, and it regularly accepted patients transferred from our hospital who might need specialized care in one of the major hospitals in West Beirut at UNRWA's expense. This applied to women, the elderly, and young men of the pro-Syrian factions, who usually had few security problems in entering or leaving Shatila.

In spite of help from the outside, most of the time our hospital provided the sole health services available to the 3,500 residents of the camp, as well as to the thousands of Lebanese and Palestinians entering and leaving Shatila on a daily basis when there was a cease-fire.

Oum Shakour plied me with yet another demitasse of coffee before telling me her tale. I had heard it before, from her and others. I had learned over many years that an important part of contemporary Palestinian folklore and the symbolism of Palestinian nationalism was the different battles that the people had lived through. Oum Shakour, her back curved by the weight of years of sorrow, was talking about the battle of the refugee camp of Tel el-Zaatar. "Our neighbours were all kinds of people – Palestinians, Lebanese Shi'ites, and Kurds. They were cheap workers for the nearby factories. The Phalangists besieged us for fifty-four days. We had enough food and weapons. What defeated us, what forced us to surrender, was the water supply. They cut the water pipes, and we had no wells inside Tel el-Zaatar. Snipers killed many women and children who tried to crawl up to the few spigots to fill a jerrycan with water." Palestinians considered Tel el-Zaatar a symbol and those killed before and after its surrender martyrs. Everyone knew the story. Everyone in Shatila was keenly aware of the critical nature of *our* water supply and the fact that this weak point would be crucial to our fate.

Water. A magic substance. A brain-racking, hand-wringing, sleep-losing problem. Water: for drinking, cooking, laundry, mopping up after an operation, sterilizing gauze for dressing changes. A series of large pipes from the municipal public water supply encircled the perimeter of Shatila. Two parallel systems existed, the larger and more consistent carrying ordinary tap water, and another, consisting of tenuous narrow-bore pipes, drinking water. From the larger system, smaller, three-inch-diameter pipes led into the camp at irregular intervals. Often in the past, UNRWA engineers had drawn up plans to place a series of large concrete water reservoirs, supplied by the municipal sources, at the four corners of the camp, and then to distribute the water to houses via underground pipes. They built a couple of reservoirs, which were destroyed, rebuilt, and then redestroyed in 1985. They never laid the water pipes underground; they wound along the alleyways and narrow streets of the camp, aboveground, in a cobweb-like network.

Maintenance and repair of the water-pipe system were constant tasks. War had damaged some, cars or people running over the others. Disconnected and no longer functioning, their useless carcasses still littered the alleyways. Since more than one three-inch-diameter feeding pipe led into the camp, many families attempted to pipe water to their homes from more than one source. Other families tried to piggyback pipes into their houses rather than lay whole new parallel lines. This was the subject of numerous family feuds, and the camp's plumbers constantly busied themselves undoing and redoing the water pipes. The Awaini warehouse provided the wherewithal. A large private warehouse, the Awaini abutted the last row of houses at the southeastern corner of the camp. It was full of water pipes, toilet and kitchen fixtures, and other plumbing supplies.

Because the engineers had never completed the system of reservoirs, they constructed a centralized water distribution complex, located beside our electric generators by the mosque. This consisted of one main pipe rising perpendicularly from the ground topped by a horizontal T-bar, from which sprouted eight half-inch pipes that snaked off in different directions through the camp. It looked like a Medusa's head, and so many of the plumbers had inserted new pipes and connections in various positions that the whole system appeared to be an irreparable mess.

It reminded me of the stories about the Cairo telephone exchange in the 1970s. Rumour had it that the Egyptian government had brought in a Swedish expert to examine the central telephone exchange and recommend improvements. The exchange circuitry apparently covered an entire wall, with myriad little cross-connecting wires sticking out helter-skelter in knots and tangles. It was a masterpiece of Middle Eastern *bricolage*. As people told the story, with one horrified look the expert said, "If this thing works, don't touch it!"

As precarious as the infrastructure seemed, the reality of it was even worse. The Amal militia occupied the area outside the camp, which included the mains controlling the municipal water supply, and could therefore shut them off. After the first round of the War of the Camps in the summer of '85, work crews piped a second source of public water into the camp, running down the hill from the area of the sports stadium through the western sector. The Lebanese in charge of building this pipeline and the accompanying pumping station were sympathetic towards the Palestinians in Shatila and placed the mains so that in the event of combat they could not be easily sabotaged by Amal.

During the Twenty-Day Battle, Amal cut off the main public water supply. The small, secret source coming from the sports stadium continued, but it supplied only part of the camp. Abu Moujahed came to me one evening at the hospital and asked for the aid of the hospital plumber, as well as any of the hospital workmen who were available, to help him replace the Medusa's head distribution complex and connect it to the one secret water source still running. Abu Moujahed, an officer of the PFLP and the head of the Popular Committee of Shatila, had married the daughter of a Guyanese government minister while a student in Cuba. He had a delicious sense of humour, and we developed a great camaraderie, co-operating on many projects, including sewerage, plumbing, electricity, food rationing, and burying the dead. We mixed the frustrations of dealing with sometimes unco-operative and selfish people in the camp, with the exhilaration of a task well done under difficult conditions. We were the same age and resembled each other, both physically and temperamentally. Neither of us was averse to getting our hands dirty, and we dug many a trench together. Abu Moujahed was wounded twice, and although his injuries proved not to be serious, the man was so widely respected and so selflessly active that the mere fact of his wounding threw all Shatila into an emotional turmoil.

And so, in the midst of the Twenty-Day Battle, between the intermittent shelling, several of us trudged off with Abu Moujahed towards the mosque. While some dismantled the distribution complex, others sawed new pipes to the required length and then fashioned the threads at each end to screw them together. We posted one of the group to listen for the whining whistle of incoming mortar shells to warn the others. It took us some four hours to complete our plumbing masterpiece, dodging under shelter from time to time. When we had finished, the camp's water supply was functioning again, and I had just received my first lesson in plumbing.

We had helped ourselves to whatever pipes and joints we needed from the Awaini warehouse. The PLO footed the bill of the Lebanese owner of the warehouse afterward. Since Abu Moujahed was a leading official of a faction of the National Salvation Front, he could not negotiate the funds for payment directly with Ali Abu Toq, who, as the head of Fatah, controlled the PLO budget. Syrian spies in the camp watched to see who received "Arafat money." I assumed the task of negotiating the payment between my two friends. As the responsible official of the Palestine Red Crescent Society, a civilian institution of the PLO, I knew no such constraints.

Both Abu Moujahed and Ali realized, however, that even the secret water supply was too precarious. The only long-term solution to our problem was an independent water supply. During the cease-fire, Abu Moujahed and Ali arranged to bring geologists into the refugee district from UNICEF, the American University, and the Lebanese Government Ministry of Hydraulics and Energy Resources. All agreed that there was no water table in the geographic area of Shatila capable of sustaining a well. The soil was simply too sandy, they said, and all we could expect was an ooze of unclean ground water. One "mad" fellow, however, the same one who had arranged our secret water source, continued to insist that there was water under Shatila, and that we could dig an artesian well. After the cease-fire putting an end to the Thirty-five-Day Battle, as part of the "humanitarian" measures allowed, he brought along a drill crew from the Lebanese ministry to forage test holes in three different locations of the camp and finally struck water at a depth of forty-two yards. Water: on the edge of the camp, in a vacant plot of land between the last row of houses and a large, solid four-storey building that had been the political headquarters of the PFLP. The building dominated the Amal positions just across the road and a large part of the refugee district, and so it constituted a military target. Shatila considered this building's defence crucial to the protection of the camp. The presence of water made it doubly crucial.

The crew dug two wells in that vacant lot – a small one that brought in 1,000 barrels of water per hour, and a larger one that supplied up to 5,000 barrels per hour. They then installed a system of pumps to distribute the water throughout the network of pipes in the camp. Two hours' functioning of the larger well sufficed to fill all the water reservoirs in all the homes of Shatila.

During every battle and siege, Amal severed electrical supplies to Shatila; the camp's generators provided the only electricity available.

Abu Moujahed and I consulted about setting up an electrical grid connecting the public current, the hospital generators, and the old 37-kva generator of the Popular Committee to the wells' pumps. We manufactured another panel of switches and laid new underground cables that bound together the different electricity sources and provided current to the hospital, the water pumps, and the bakery. We considered these latter three sites the essential services of the camp and common public property, but we always had problems with people cutting into the cables to steal electricity for their homes or for the offices of the political groups. The wireless sets for communications needed either a constant electric current or recharged car batteries. We repeatedly suffered heavy current loads that blew the fuses.

Abu Moujahed, the hospital workers, and I played electricity-policemen far too often, tracking down renegade electrical wiring snaking through alleyways and windows, regularly shouting ourselves hoarse admonishing people not to steal electricity. I couldn't believe some of the ingenuity involved in the attempts to filch electricity – disguising electrical wires as laundry lines, poking holes in walls to tack onto the inner surfaces of wall plugs and pilfer current from the outlet wiring.

The desire to live, and live normally, became an overriding consideration amidst the abnormalcy of life under siege. Water and electricity might help to overcome the desperate sense of abandonment and create a semblance of normal life, even if they had to be pilfered. During each battle and blockade of Shatila, no matter how short-lived, the psychological burden of the siege weighed more heavily on the inhabitants than anything else. The camp's population knew that they had to count on themselves alone to resist the onslaught of the opposing militiamen and soldiers. There was always a strange mixture of enthusiastic euphoria tempered by the obsession to break the siege and arrivc at a cease-fire as quickly as possible. The inhabitants of Shatila wanted to keep the road to the camp open and overlooked many provocations by the Amal militiamen in order to avoid a battle and the inevitable accompanying blockade. At times, when skirmishes or fighting first broke out, there were people on the main street on their way to and from the camp. Militiamen's sniper fire hit some; others, like Yasmine, were taken prisoner. Someone in the camp was always preoccupied with the safety of a family member or friend who had left the camp and might have been on their way back when hostilities broke out. Even if during a short blockade we lacked for nothing, a cease-fire always brought a collective sigh of relief. But the thought of giving in, of surrender, never occurred to anyone. Only resistance gave meaning to their lives. After all, this was Shatila!

5

Lessons in Ballistics and Matchmaking

AFTER THE TWENTY-DAY BATTLE IN APRIL 1986, SEVERAL factions' intelligence people warned me that Amal and their army support were preparing rockets and artillery for use against us. Basel, the head of the Military and Security Committee for the PNSF, approached me one day. He was the tallest man in Shatila, about six feet four inches, with a thick beard reaching half-way down his chest. I had known Basel since 1981, and we had had many meetings and encounters over the past months. For political reasons, he could not always meet with Ali Abu Toq, the Fatah-Arafat leader, even though they knew each other well. Too many Syrian *Moukhabarat* – the feared and hated secret police and intelligence agents dressed in civilian clothing – spies were watching the PNSF leadership in Shatila to see who was too cosy with the "deviationists." Like many of his colleagues from the Popular Struggle Front faction of the PNSF coalition, Basel disliked the Syrians deeply; only political considerations and expediency had led his group into the pro-Syrian coalition. He bristled at the thought and at the manoeuvres his position obliged him to perform.

Basel liked Ali personally and respected him as a leader, but regarded the pro-Arafat line of accepting negotiations with Israel as a betrayal of the Palestinian cause. In spite of political constraints, however, many security and military subjects had to be co-ordinated by the two men jointly in pursuit of their common goal of defending Shatila. They both had confidence in me, and so I became courier and intermediary for sensitive messages and delicate negotiations between them.

Basel explained that because of the military situation, we only had to fear mortar shelling, not heavy artillery. "Shatila is too small, and the front lines between Amal and us are too close. Heavy artillery is relatively inaccurate. Our sardine tin makes a bad target." My joking remark about Shatila's size had made the rounds. "Mortars are less destructive than heavy artillery shells, but they're more lethal as anti-personnel weapons. Nonetheless, 120-mm mortars can inflict heavy damage. We must take precautions."

The building construction in Shatila was rather flimsy, and the hospital was certainly no exception. The second storey above the emergency reception and pharmacy buildings provided some protection. Even better was Abu Mohammed Faramawi's building, with the underground shelter containing the operating theatre and four storeys aboveground. The middle building of the hospital, housing the kitchen and cafeteria, was a simple ground-floor edifice and, along with the three alleyways separating the four hospital buildings, the most exposed.

I thought it necessary to reinforce those relatively exposed walls of the buildings in which the staff performed vital functions, such as the emergency room. We lined several walls with sandbags, both inside and out. In other areas, we positioned barrels or aluminum water reservoirs filled with sand and debris to provide greater protection against shelling.

The alleyways still had their wrought-iron tubing scaffold, zinc sheeting, and sandbags. This provided ample cover for us to move about them during the first few minor skirmishes and battles. Mortar shelling, however, would cause problems. Ali Abu Toq ambled up to me one day and, stroking his beard, as was his way when he thought out loud, said it would be a good idea to replace the overhead scaffolding and sandbags with reinforced concrete. He organized one of his volunteer groups to remove the sandbags and iron tubing and set up wooden scaffolding, and then another to pour an eight-inch-thick layer of reinforced concrete, from the stockpiled cement supplies in Shatila, to cover over the alleyways, thus transforming the four buildings into one enclosed complex. Standing in the concrete-covered alleyway was now truly like being indoors.

I had overheard some engineers discussing how large rubber tires could be used, under the foundations, to reinforce bomb shelters. The idea of using rubber tires with their enclosed air pockets to dissipate the pressure wave of an explosion seemed logical, so I arranged to have one of the pro-Syrian factions deliver a couple of truckloads of old rubber tires. The men told the Syrians and militiamen at the checkpoint entry that they were going to burn them for heat and light.

We covered the reinforced concrete of the alleyways and half the roof of the middle, one-storey building with a layer of used rubber tires; we followed this with zinc sheeting and then several layers of sandbags. The sandbags would take the shrapnel of exploding shells, and the rubber tires would dissipate the pressure. The zinc sheeting prevented the seepage and accumulation of rainwater in between the rubber tires and served as a continuous plane upon which to lay the sandbags, and the reinforced concrete underneath constituted our final defence. We covered only one-half of the one-storey central building because we could not obtain enough rubber tires to cover it all.

This was typical of the constant searching, innovating, and discussing among various small groups, in attempts to draw on everyone's experience, curiosity, and imagination to keep finding better ways to defend

Shatila. We used several suggestions from other people with military experience to protect the hospital. Ali, Basel, Faramawi, engineers: all contributed ideas and opinions. If the leaders could not meet because of the political climate, as was usually the case, then we in the hospital would serve as a melting pot, a cauldron for the stew of fertile thoughts. Our little protective system resulted partly by applying engineering principles that had been worked out over years of war conditions in Lebanon, partly by improvisation, and partly by synthetic thinking.

Similar co-operative planning occurred time and again, whether concerning military questions, the water and electricity supplies, maintenance and repair, or even work in the hospital. I joked with Basel and Abu Mohammed Faramawi one day about setting up our own self-sufficient agricultural production – hen houses, goat stables, even planting spinach and other plants in the piles of sandbags scattered around the camp. Faramawi laughed, "The Shatila Commune, after your Women's Union barefoot doctors. Apparently, Ali Abu Toq was not the only one to go to China." Faramawi did buy several hens – a source of both eggs and meat – and put them in the vacant third floor of his building. I bought two goats and four sheep – for fresh milk as well as meat – from the hospital budget.

An old shepherd lived in Shatila, his family and three goats sharing their two-storey dwelling. He had been a shepherd in Palestine and saw no need to stop being one in exile, even in the urban slum of a refugee camp; it was his way of remembering. A short visit by "the Doctor," accepting his hospitality to sip Turkish coffee and smoke a water-pipe, and offering to pay for the grain and hay eaten by the animals I had bought, was enough to convince him to take on the responsibility of caring for them. There was no problem in getting the animals into Shatila. Many families in Lebanon slaughter sheep on religious feast days, and it is not uncommon to have an animal or two in the backyard, or on a balcony, for fattening up during the year.

The Lebanese buffer force established around Shatila after the Twenty-Day Battle solved nothing, of course, and skirmishes began again, often pitting the buffer troops from the secular militias against

Amal militiamen. Lebanese and Palestinians alike chafed at the heavy-handedness and brutishness of Amal militiamen and their Syrian masters – especially the Syrian *Moukhabarat*. Throughout the Arab world, every regime has one or more *Moukhabarat* agencies. They have achieved one of the rare instances of Arab unanimity – virtually all Arab citizens live in hatred and fear of them. Rabiha and Oum Mohammed Faramawi always kept me in touch with the most recent rumours, horror stories, and anecdotes current in West Beirut concerning Amal and the Syrian *Moukhabarat*. Apparently, the Khaldeh checkpoint at the main intersection leading to South Lebanon now had lists of pro-Arafat Palestinian and Lebanese activists, especially those from Shatila and Burj el-Barajneh. The trip to the torture-chamber prisons of the Beqa'a Valley and Damascus was a short one.

With the resumption of skirmishes in late June, another battle of thirty-five days' duration ensued during the summer of 1986. Amal imposed another blockade on the camp, cutting Shatila off from the outside world. In addition to small and heavy automatic weapons fire, irregular mortar and rocket fire slammed into the camp for four days. We buried another twenty-four dead.

Major Mohammed Hussein, the head of the pro-Iraqi Arab Liberation Front, and a calm and gentle man of impeccable personal discipline and manners, had just completed construction of the fourth storey of his building opposite the hospital when the Thirty-five-Day Battle broke out. When a mortar shell landed in the alleyway between his house and the Cabaret Giannou as he passed by, a large chunk of shrapnel entered his neck, severing the major blood vessels, before passing up into his skull. Mohammed died, but his work probably saved many of the hospital staff from a similar fate, as other mortar shells slammed into the upper storeys of his building rather than fall on us.

Abu Abdallah, a Lebanese, belonged to the anti-Arafat Fatah dissidents. He received a bullet to the abdomen that hit just about every possible major blood vessel. Two cardiac arrests, forty units of blood, and twelve hours of operating time later, he succumbed. Needless to say, the entire operating room staff – the Palestinian nurses, Kristen, Régine, and I – were heart-broken. Miracles were in short supply.

The four days of bombardment proved just how vulnerable the water source coming down through the western sector could be. Luckily for us, those four days were the final four days of the Thirty-five-Day Battle. The shells hit the pipeline and pumping station: no water. But for some unknown reason, the Amal militiamen had overlooked the narrow-bore pipe system providing Shatila with drinking water. We had a direct pipeline from it to the hospital. The trickle did not amount to much, but sufficed, thanks to strict rationing. Fully half the camp's families came to the hospital to fill plastic containers for their water needs. We had to police the pipe, however, to prevent anyone who did not appreciate waiting in line at the hospital from piggybacking onto it.

More diplomatic contacts resulted in the declaration of yet another cease-fire, and another buffer force, of Lebanese army troops under the command of a highly respected nationalist officer, supported by Syrian observers, occupied positions around Shatila.

As after the Twenty-Day Battle, we called on the services of the International Red Cross to arrange for the evacuation of those wounded who needed specialized care not available with our meagre means. I had become quite adept in organizing such evacuations with the ICRC, having done so for the wounded of Beirut in 1982, and Tripoli in 1983. We established a protocol for numbering the patients and preparing their dossiers, which greatly facilitated the task. Amal permitted such "humanitarian" measures as part and parcel of the propaganda war that the militia and the Palestinians waged against each other, parallel to the military conflict.

However, Amal and the Syrians imposed yet other measures at the end of the Thirty-five-Day Battle, even greater restrictions on Shatila: identity checks, searches of vehicles and packages going in and out of the camp. It was now almost impossible to smuggle in cement or iron bars, impossible even to bribe the militiamen at the checkpoint entrance to the camp.

We had spent much of 1986 organizing the camp and hospital, and preparing the inhabitants to face a series of onslaughts – the Four-, Twenty-, and Thirty-five-Day battles – and the final major one that we all knew, even if we didn't admit it, was to come. And we learned from each one of these "dress rehearsals," improving our logistics and services – water, electricity, food stores, spare parts. The work in Shatila continued feverishly with this sword of renewed fighting and blockade dangling over us.

The hospital played an especially important role. Everyone came there to visit. Knowing that by late evening, ten o'clock, I had completed my medical and administrative duties, many friends and political leaders of the camp passed by the kitchen-cum-administrative office of the hospital, transforming it into a sort of salon. They came to discuss various aches, pains, and allergies; to arrange medical treatment abroad for one of the wounded; or to have a midnight snack and cup of tea. The "hospital social-centre" seemed innocuous enough, even to spies and informers of the Syrian *Moukhabarat*, who often visited me themselves. They were always on the look-out for people who had contacts with the Fatah-Arafat "deviationists," and their agents in West Beirut applied pressure on the factions or individuals who made such contacts; the pressure could and often did include imprisonment. It did not appear suspicious to anyone if Ali Abu Toq, Basel, Abu Moujahed, Ali's adjutants, Abu Mohammed Faramawi, or whoever, pro- or anti-Arafat, all came to the hospital on the same night, as they often did whether they had business there or not.

Endless discussions about reconstruction projects, water supplies, electricity, garbage disposal, referral of medical cases, or the political and diplomatic situation continued well into the early hours of the morning over countless cups of coffee and tea, with participants sitting on sacks of rice or potatoes and large tins of cheese or olive oil.

"I got my hens," announced Abu Mohammed Faramawi as he came into the pantry one evening and made his way to a well-moulded sack of rice, his usual seat. Amina and her colleagues from the Union of Women, Nadia and Oum Nader, were already there. We had been discussing organizing regular doctors' visits to their kindergarten to check on the health of the children.

"Hens, Abu Mohammed?" asked Oum Nader. "What do you want with 'birds' when you have Oum Mohammed?" she asked wickedly.

"Oum Mohammed doesn't lay eggs," he dead-panned, and everyone, with the exception of Nadia, who blushed, burst out laughing. "Even the 'old man' [the affectionate code-word for Yassir Arafat; only Faramawi — though a member of the anti-Arafat PFLP, he knew Arafat personally — could continue to use the term affectionately in a time of increased political tension] lays eggs – diplomatic eggs, that is. Problem is, he keeps breaking them."

"You know what they say about omelettes?" retorted Amina.

"Sandwiches yes, omelettes no. Not at this time of night," put in Rabiha, popping her head into the doorway. She and a half-dozen staff were preparing the midnight meal for the night shift.

"None for me, thanks," said Faramawi.

"I'll have one, please. Good evening all." Abu Moujahed had arrived. "Nadia, I wanted to see you about the orphanage." Nadia, of the DFLP and Women's Union, was also involved in running the Palestinian orphanage in West Beirut. Abu Moujahed took a seat on a tin of something or other. It was starting to get crowded in the tiny pantry.

"Did you get the extra electrical cable today?" I asked Abu Moujahed. "The fellow from UNICEF said it was to arrive today."

"Yes, and the work crew has just about finished digging the trench from the Popular Committee's generator to the hospital. They reached Somaya's building today. We'll start laying the cable tomorrow."

"Good. Then we can finish the electrical panel in the switch box. I bought the 100-ampere switch yesterday."

Faramawi leaned forward and spoke with his tone of experience. "Soil first and then a layer of concrete to cover over the cable. It mustn't be too rigid or else any crack in the concrete from an explosion will cut the cable."

"How about shredded rubber tires" — I laughed — "to surround the cable? Or eggshells?" Faramawi smiled.

"I saw the 'scissionists' bringing in another load of tires today," said Amina, almost spitting out the words in talking about the Fatah dissidents.

"Now, now, Amina," scolded Abu Moujahed. "The Fatah-Uprising. They're helping protect the hospital." The Fatah dissidents were Abu Moujahed's and Faramawi's allies in the NSF coalition.

Abu Imad of the DFLP arrived. "Speaking of the devil. Hello, Scissionist," I burst out, referring to the split in Abu Moujahed's PFLP more than fifteen years earlier.

"Scissionist, and proud of it!" exclaimed Abu Imad, wedging himself between Faramawi and Abu Moujahed. "Besides, I'm still splitting the PFLP," he joked, referring to the sitting arrangement.

We then discussed at length the dynamics of political scissions in left-wing parties and national liberation movements; Rabiha arrived with sandwiches and tea. (Rabiha never took part in these discussions. I knew that she worked clandestinely for one of the factions and preferred not to speak.) We talked some more of electrical cables; Rabiha came back with Turkish coffee; and we finished off with the kindergarten and orphanage. Reeking of cigarette smoke and soggy with coffee, we went off for a few hours of sleep before the next day's activities. A short, traditional afternoon siesta allowed us to continue this train of eighteen-hour days for weeks on end.

As the year wore on, the hospital became the social heart of the camp, and everyone felt at home there. Everyone knew that the midnight snack for the night shift was open to all. Men going to their nightly guard duty, whatever their political allegiance, passed by and picked up a sandwich. This increased the hospital's influence in calming down passions among the factions whenever intra-Palestinian tensions were in danger of boiling over. At times, the political climate within the narrow, crowded confines of the camp was such that a minor feud or argument over anything from a chess match to the distribution of financial assistance could have degenerated into an open internal battle. My duties included cutting and patching up tempers as well as bodies.

I often joined my efforts in message-carrying, arranging, and refereeing with those of Abu Imad, the leader of the Democratic Front for the Liberation of Palestine (DFLP). Pragmatic and realistic, Abu Imad rivaled Ali Abu Toq in his ability to combine military prowess, administrative skill, and political acumen, and in his devotion to his people. The position of his DFLP, intermediate between the pro-Syrian PNSF coalition and Arafat's Fatah and PLO, made him a useful official political liaison among factions in the camp, parallel to the unofficial hospital one. He served often as conduit and arbitrator. The situation was not a comfortable one, and the extreme PNSF factions – Abu Musa's Fatah dissidents and the PFLP–General Command – often accused Abu Imad of being opportunistic. But convinced of the importance of his work, he just shrugged them off.

The notables of Shatila, harking back to a more traditional, peasant society, formed a third "independent" component. Some tacit, almost atavistic, reflex conferred on the twenty-odd assembled elder men a sense of moral power and suasion, and their opinions, judgements, and arbitration were sought out by all factions and carried a special weight. In distinction to this traditional and commonplace "institution" of the wise elders, there existed the *ad hoc* mobilization of the women – mothers, wives, and sisters – not officially a part of any one faction. Their tongues and judgements were trenchant, contrasting with the soft-toned compromising arbitration of us men. Another simple social reflex was at work; all the men, fighters or not, even while being belittled by them, respected and listened to the "mothers." Thus Shatila's inhabitants cooked up their self-sufficient social stew.

Preparations for the inevitable upcoming battle continued. Information from several factions based in Damascus indicated that the Syrians wanted to finish off Shatila as part of their ongoing rivalry with the Arafat leadership. I thought it obscenely brazen. "Finish off Shatila" – a small cog in the master plans of regional geopolitics, decided by faceless men sitting in the comfortable safety of far-off back rooms. In reality, it entailed the deaths of hundreds, if not thousands, of Shatila's inhabitants, the attacking militiamen – and me.

I bristled at the thought. So did Basel, of the Popular Struggle Front, and Abu Moujahed and Omar of the Popular Front (PFLP), all officers of the PNSF pro-Syrian coalition. They had their ideological differences with Fatah's Ali Abu Toq, but they were certainly no traitors and didn't appreciate serving as cannon fodder for the political goals of the Syrian regime. All the more since public and secret meetings of the leaders of the most important Palestinian groupings (Arafat's

Fatah, the PFLP, and DFLP), brokered by Algeria and the Soviet Union, were taking place, and with them the promise and hope of a reunited PLO and a failure of Syrian policies. Basel, Abu Moujahed, and Omar, all top officers of the supposedly pro-Syrian coalition, were nonetheless Palestinian nationalists foremost. They knew they had to meet with Ali Abu Toq to co-ordinate preparations. They asked me to arrange secret meetings at the hospital. Only the extremists, the Fatah dissidents of Abu Musa and the PFLP–General Command of Ahmed Jibril, who drew their strength almost entirely from Syrian support (they had little popular following), did not participate: no one trusted their close ties to the Syrian *Moukhabarat*. A reunited PLO under Arafat's leadership would forcibly demonstrate the bankruptcy of their politics.

My contacts, because of my daily responsibilities, included the leaders of the Abu Musa dissidents and Abdallah of the PFLP–General Command. Political discussions, inevitably, came up on the agenda.

These men talked blithely of Arafat's treason; continuing the armed struggle; liberating all of Palestine, from the Jordan River to the Mediterranean Sea. Their ideas were simplistic, theoretical, and juvenile in the extreme and often no more than chauvinism. The dissident leaders spoke of their "strategic alliance" with progressive, anti-imperialist Syria. I saw only hypocrisy in an ideologically bankrupt and corrupt regime, which didn't refuse "reactionary" Saudi pay-offs and whose policies seemed determined more by the petty self-interest of a small ruling clique than by any progressive rhetoric. Too many people in power in Syria's state-run economy profited through contraband from Lebanon's free-wheeling market economy and the narcotics and hashish trade. Their only legitimacy, as in all Arab regimes, came from the force of arms and the terror of the *Moukhabarat*.

My immediate impulse in these discussions with dissident leaders was one of impatience at what everybody knew was rhetorical posturing. Everyone understood the role of Syria in influencing political positions and policies and the tremendous pressure that the Syrians could bring to bear on those factions based in Damascus – and on the families of the factions' members there. Nonetheless, the fact that they supported Syrian political positions so vehemently among us in discussions never ceased to amaze me. It was almost as if they thought that by the energy expended they could overcome their sense of embarrassment at having to support policies with which they disagreed. Everyone saw them simply as quislings, lackeys for just another *Moukhabarat* agency of just another Arab regime.

Syria's policy of controlling the Lebanese and Palestinian cards in the Middle East poker game meant using a powerful proxy – Amal – to control the left-wing secular political parties and the Palestinian refugee camps, and bring to heel Syria's rival, Arafat. A divided and enfeebled Palestinian resistance movement also served Syrian interests. We understood all this only too well and the delicate political balancing act that some of the Palestinian factions had to perform. It was a difficult balancing act, a fine line. Some managed to walk it. Others, like the Abu Musa dissidents and Abdallah of the PFLP-GC, succumbed and became no more than agents of the policies of a repressive regime.

Exploiting the "hospital social-centre," I arranged meetings to coordinate plans and work far from the inquisitive ears and eyes of the *Moukhabarat* agents. Late one October evening, I was sitting as usual in the hospital pantry, poring over personnel schedules. Ali Abu Toq arrived first, accompanied by his adjutants, Amina and Baha. I went with them through the darkened, empty alleyway to the pharmacy, unused at such a late hour of the night, and let them in. The Popular Struggle Front's towering figure, Basel, chief military officer of the pro-Syrian Salvation Front coalition, came next, with Abu Imad of the DFLP: to the pharmacy again. The PFLP leader, Omar, and the PFLP head of the Popular Committee, Abu Moujahed, arrived last. These seven people were the real leaders of Shatila. Our fate, and that of the camp's 3,500 inhabitants, lay in their hands, and they knew it. It was the first time that they all had met together. The traditional preliminary greetings were awkward. They had spent so many months insulting each other to their followers and other listeners that they were now uncomfortable in each other's presence.

Ali began. His Fatah organization, he said, had stockpiled enough food supplies for six months. Abu Moujahed's Popular Committee, apart from the PFLP, had food for four months. All the factions had apparently learned the lessons of the Twenty- and Thirty-five-Day battles and had stored up on food, coffee, tobacco, spare parts. The next battle would surely last longer, thus the need for even more stores. "And what about the civilian population?" asked Abu Moujahed. "Who will provide food for the families?" He knew that Ali had the largest budget at his disposal.

"When I said six months, I meant six months' food stores for the entire camp, civilians and fighters," replied Ali. "Naturally, since I represent the PLO, I assume responsibility for the entire camp, all the people – even those politically opposed to me." All present smiled knowingly. Abu Imad snickered. Although each political faction was supposedly responsible for their own food and ammunition supplies, the truth of the matter was a poorly kept secret. During the two previous battles, the most vehemently anti-Arafat groups, the Abu Musa dissidents and the PFLP–General Command, had run out of ammunition, and during the Thirty-five Day Battle, the military wing of the PFLP-GC had no food left. Ali's Fatah had provided both with ammunition, and the PFLP-GC military, faced with starvation because of a personal conflict with its political leadership, ate from Arafat's Fatah kitchen. Ali's thinking was twofold. By feeding them and providing them with munitions, he could score political points against the people who called him and Arafat traitors. And, as an ardent nationalist, he could argue that anyone willing to sacrifice him- or herself to defend the camp was an ally, regardless of political differences. He won the moral high ground.

All the leaders present knew that each faction gained prestige from taking part in the defence of Shatila. Without ammunition or a role in the defence it was difficult to justify one's presence in the camp. Ali's largesse in providing his mortal enemies the wherewithal to participate in battle increased his influence and power.

Basel asked about Ali's ammunition stores, and Ali returned the question. He then queried Abu Moujahed and me about fuel supplies for the camp's electric generators. We took stock of what we had and what else would have to be bought and transported into Shatila. They all wanted to know the state of my preparations in the hospital. I could see the relief in their faces as I listed the number of staff on hand, our special schedules, the quantities of medicines, food, spare parts ...

The discussion went on until dawn.

A hospital is, in fact, medical services plus restaurant plus hotel. One has to provide food for patients and staff as well as laundry and cleaning services. Even without in-patients, the hospital cafeteria never emptied, feeding the large contingent of staff on duty and those living on the premises. All of this cooking, laundering, and cleaning consumed a tremendous amount of water. Because we couldn't always pump water from the wells, we required a series of reservoirs, scattered in every nook and cranny about the four hospital buildings. Some, of plastered-over concrete, we placed underground or on rooftops; others, of aluminum alloy, we cut and then welded into bizarre shapes to fit any available corner – under staircases, over doors or closets. Using a highly ingenious system of ordinary pipes, rubber hoses, and numerous small water pumps, the hospital workers filled the various reservoirs daily.

The pumps burned out regularly. This was usually the fault of Abu Abed, who was deaf and could never hear when the water was finished and the pumps ran dry. He had lost one child in the 1982 Massacre and a second in the first round of the War of the Camps in 1985. Another son was now a combatant, and Oum Abed, his wife, a pillar of the women's movement in the community. I eventually had to operate on Abu Abed's two youngest children: Samira, aged eleven, received shrapnel to the abdomen, and Samir, nine, had part of his brain splattered against a wall when a 120-mm mortar shell swept away a wall of their house. They both survived. It is incredible what horrendous injuries children can sustain and still live. The family home, with all their possessions including clothing, didn't survive. It burned down, for the third time.

In spite of his tragic history and deafness, Abu Abed was a tireless worker who performed any task asked of him. He even became an expert in roasting green coffee beans, which made him a vital member of the hospital staff. In the Middle East, one's daily dose of caffeine in the form of numerous cups of thick Turkish coffee with cardamom is considered essential. We bought and stored in the hospital great sacks of green coffee beans, which would keep for months without spoiling. During the Twenty- and Thirty-five-Day battles, the entire camp ran out of coffee, and Abu Abed had the chore of roasting the beans. The faction leaders, knowing we had a seemingly endless supply of coffee and hot meals, gathered in the hospital, to share our food and drink while visiting the wounded.

Apart from providing medical services, coffee, meals, refereeing, and a meeting place for faction leaders, the hospital also served as a venue for socializing. Many families had moved out of Shatila after the first round of fighting because of the destruction of their homes; only their young sons, fighters, remained. And the hospital provided the only place in the camp with an important concentration of young, unmarried women. Picking up a nightly sandwich while on the way to guard duty was often simply an excuse for a young man to discreetly visit one of the female nursing or cleaning staff. In Arabic, the narrow, tortuous alleyways are called *zeroub*. When a young couple attempted to surreptitiously hide away in one of the hospital alleyways, they were said to be *zeroubing*. I often surprised Fida, a young combatant whom I knew from Nabatieh days and on whom I had operated in Tripoli, with one of the nurses from Shatila in a *zeroub*. One day Fida asked me, as surgeon and hospital director – a much respected social position – to accompany him to visit his lover's family to request her hand in marriage. My presence, it was thought, lent weight to his offer – success, offer accepted. As word of this spread, it soon became another of my never-ending duties. Along with Amina and the Women's Union, I found myself acting as a matchmaker. Sometimes the circumstances were rooted in tragedy. There were quite a few seventeen-year-old widows in the camp, and their situation constituted a social catastrophe, not least because of the insistence of Middle Eastern society on virgin brides. It was often difficult for a man's family to accept a marriage to a widow. Not very different, I mused, from my own family, coming out of Greece, even if they lived in "modern"

North America. I laughed to myself about my social importance: divorced and not yet forty, I had assumed the role of village elder.

On October 22, 1986, about four months after the Thirty-five-Day Battle, fighting began around the Rashidieh camp in South Lebanon between the Amal militia and the camp's Palestinian inhabitants. This was the first time that Amal had subjected the very vulnerable Rashidieh to a siege. A large camp of about 17,000 people located on the Mediterranean coast, it was totally isolated from the nearby city of Tyre by open fields, orchards, and orange groves.

Palestinian forces attacked Amal lines just east of Sidon, the major city in southern Lebanon, hoping that the military engagement there would force Amal to lessen its pressure on Rashidieh. The strategy worked: Amal rushed militiamen back to reinforce the positions east of Sidon, thus effectively reducing the pressure on Rashidieh, though the camp remained, nonetheless, isolated and under siege. Arafat's forces continued their advance and eventually established a hold on the village of Maghdushah, the main site overlooking the refugee camps of Ain el-Hilweh and Mieh wa-Mieh, as well as the city of Sidon. Public opinion saw this as an important military victory for the Palestinians, and during the ensuing months of fighting it would provide an important pressure point in the negotiations between Palestinian, Lebanese, Syrian, and other Arab leaders.

The ever-expanding, see-saw battles to obtain that extra advantageous pressure point brought the fighting to Beirut. Amal responded to the Palestinian attack on Maghdushah by beginning rocket and artillery attacks on Burj el-Barajneh on October 29. Families fled the residential districts neighbouring Shatila, and visitors to the camp, as well as my traditional sources of information on the outside world – Rabiha and Oum Mohammed Faramawi – reported seeing military preparations and troop movements in the near vicinity. They also told of rumours rampant in West Beirut that the price for the Palestinian victory at Maghdushah was to be the loss of Shatila: Amal and Syria would not allow Arafat to use his capture of Maghdushah as an element of pressure in negotiations. In Shatila, we knew that the upcoming battle would be decisive, and that everyone outside expected the camp to fall.

Frantic activity ensued for a month following the outbreak of fighting around Burj el-Barajneh. I put the hospital staff on a special emergency schedule, and we piled up food, fuel, and medical supplies. Abu Moujahed passed by the hospital ten times a day, consulting on electricity and spare parts. I met with Ali and Basel every night, making certain of food stores. Abu Imad came nightly to the hospital "salon," leaving only at dawn. As the rumble and dull thud of exploding shells echoed in the distance, women, children, and men plied back and forth along S-S Street, carrying whatever supplies they could into the camp. A sense of exhilaration and expectancy mixed with dread lay heavily on us all. We knew that our turn would come soon.

On November 25, 1986, at 2:00 P.M., Basel, as head of the PNSF Security and Military Committee, approached me, his expression grim, eyes flashing. "Trucks are dumping sand by the eastern border of the camp, putting up ramparts behind which Amal can position tanks. Four truckloads have already arrived this morning. I complained about it to the Syrian observers and Amal leadership. Nothing! The bastards! If another truckload arrives," he told me in a half-whisper, "I'll order my men to shoot to destroy it." We were rapidly approaching zero hour. "Go tell Ali Abu Toq, quickly," he said.

Hurrying over to the Fatah offices, I gave Ali the news and called on the wireless telephone to the nearby house of our Lebanese anaesthetist-technician to tell her to get back to the camp quickly. Then, as calmly as possible, I returned to the hospital and made certain that all the necessary staff – general practitioners, nurses, technicians – were present. The hospital was a beehive of activity and rumours. Amal militiamen had picked up Palestinian civilians in West Beirut and the four hospital workers who had finished their round of duty were debating whether to leave the camp. I told them that fighting would probably break out that afternoon and, given the current security situation, there was obviously no guarantee that they could return safely to their families in the city. They decided to remain with us in Shatila.

I went into our administration office and sat at my desk, trying to appear as confident as I could. I waited for the tell-tale thud and explosion of a rocket-propelled grenade that, like a starter's gun, would announce the beginning of the fray. Outside, the narrow streets filled with people. It seemed that everyone in Shatila was in the alleyways, excitedly talking to everyone else; tension, nervous euphoria, and expectancy were in the air. In the distance, the dull echo of the fighting around Burj el-Barajneh resounded. Then – thud, whoosh, boom – sharper and clearer. Basel's men had fired an RPG, and an Amal truck carrying sand to the front had caught fire. A volley of small arms fire broke out and the streets quickly cleared. People scurried undercover or rushed to their positions at the fronts along the perimeter of the camp. A short time later, a herd of young men hurriedly brought a young fighter, the first of the wounded, to the hospital. There was to be no respite until April 7, 1987 – 134 days later.

6

Sunrise, Sunset . . . Sunrise

THE MID-WINTER'S EVENING DARKNESS FELL EARLY, AND with it, the small arms fire and grenade explosions gave way to a deluge of mortar and artillery shells. For hours, uninterrupted, shells rained down on Shatila, the reverberations of the explosions filling the narrow alleyways. The rickety tumbledown walls shook violently with the blasts of pressure. It was physically impossible to move about amidst the falling, crashing bombs and buildings. People holed up in their flimsy houses. No one came by the hospital to visit or see how we fared. No one dared.

Shortly after midnight, in the midst of the thundering roll of conflagrations, a particularly loud thud shook the hospital. Fifty of us huddled together in the ER building, occasionally chattering nervously between explosions. A shell had crashed through the ceiling of a nearby house, and I heard a great scurrying of feet in the covered alleyway leading to the hospital. The bodies of the first casualties arrived. The fighters who brought in the corpses looked on in stunned disbelief when they realized that only a little four-year-old boy, hidden under a bed, had survived. The exploding 120-mm mortar had wiped out an entire family – father, mother, and five of six children. The workers placed the bodies, wrapped in white bed-sheet funeral shrouds, in the hospital laundry room.

All I could do was register the deaths, the first of this battle. I turned to Dr. Khatib and asked, "What shall we name this battle? How long do you think it will last?" And then added to myself, silently, "And how many more dead before it's over?" Dr. Khatib looked at me, understanding, with sadness in his eyes. He was thinking the same thing. "The Battle to End All Battles?" A rhetorical answer to a rhetorical question. The shelling continued without respite, and in the early morning hours our work began.

November 26, 1986: second day of the battle; twenty-eight wounded, seven killed. A mixed lot: the casualties were mainly civilians, with only a few combatants – the latter knew better how to take cover – but all were victims of shrapnel from high-energy shells. The first patient had received shrapnel to the chest and abdomen. I had to repair his chest wall and diaphragm, take out his spleen, and repair a kidney and his pancreas. No sooner had we stitched him up than the nurses standing on the stairway leading down to the underground operating theatre announced the arrival of another casualty – another spleen to remove and liver to suture, as well as cleaning out major wounds of the thigh and forearm. The litany of mangled bodies continued. Day turned into night, and then into day again, though we didn't notice the difference. The gruelling hours of work in the operating theatre and hospital cut us off from all sense of time.

November 28: nineteen wounded, one dead. Another frantic day. We received two patients with shrapnel wounds to the abdomen and pelvis; loops of intestine and bared testes protruded. They were straightforward cases for laparotomy (an abdominal operation) and debridement of the scrotum to cut away injured and dirtied tissue. Traditional Middle Eastern society is patriarchal, and machismo a male cultural trait. Any injury to the testicles is a very grave matter and operating on the scrotum an exceedingly delicate undertaking. Relatives and friends crowded around me after the operations, more concerned about the injuries' effects on each patient's "manhood" than about the danger to his life. I was exasperated.

I tried to explain, according to my philosophy and in my manner. "His manhood is not in his balls!" I grabbed my crotch. "The brother was injured while destroying a tank, defending us all – sacrificing himself." I pointed to my head and heart. "His manhood, his humanity, is here, and here." The crowd stared at me through widened eyes. Some, but not all, were convinced.

In the meantime, we had other grave cases. Flying chunks of cinderblock and bricks had hit a young boy of five when the wall of his family's house had been blown away. His spleen was ruptured and I had to remove it in order to staunch the haemorrhage. This saved his life but left him slightly more susceptible to serious infections.

I wondered, as I often did during my years in Lebanon, at the irony of my surgical training. The Cancer Institute in Cairo had steeled my nerves and trained me to operate on just about any part of the body. But cancer surgery is radical, mutilating surgery. To overcome the disease, the surgeon must remove great amounts of normal healthy tissue; anatomical rules for eradicating the pathological process guide one's scalpel. In Lebanon, the philosophy determining my work was exactly the opposite. War surgery is essentially very conservative – one tries to save as much as possible. There is no underlying pathology or disease process to overcome, simply a hole in the wall of a viscus or a traumatically disorganized solid organ. One deals with the strict limits of trauma, retaining as much tissue as possible, trying never to add the doctor's insult to the bullet's injury.

At one point, Abu Mohammed Faramawi entered the passageway-dressing room where Régine and I sat resting between operations, savouring a cigarette and coffee. He had come to tell us the news, and I translated for Régine when she couldn't follow his descriptions. Soldiers of the Sixth Brigade of the Lebanese Army under the political control of Amal had joined the militiamen in their attack on Shatila. The Army First Brigade had come in from the Syrian-controlled Beqa'a Valley to further reinforce the Amal positions, and it was they who had provided the precision bombing of classically trained troops. Shatila was so small, and the front lines of the opposing forces so close, that only precision bombing was of any use. It was those several thousand troops of the two brigades, alongside the couple of thousand militiamen, that had us and our 1,000 active fighters pinned down inside our "sardine can" and accounted for the almost continuous barrage of shells that poured down on our heads. These army brigades, now unofficially under the control of "nationalist" Amal forces rather than the Phalangist-headed Ministry of Defence, had a hodgepodge of armaments: Soviet-manufactured and Syrian-provided 60-, 80-, and 160-mm mortars; North Korean 107-mm multiple rocket launchers; French 82-mm mortars; and 155-mm cannon and 120-mm mortars thanks to the U.S. Office of Military Cooperation, which had provided arms to the nominally united Lebanese Army in 1983 before they were returned in kind at the U.S. Marine Barracks bombing.

Geography determined the nature of the fighting. The proximity of the battle positions was ridiculous – the camp's defence lines and the soldiers' forward positions were within shouting distance of each other amidst the ramshackle buildings. Apart from the direct small arms fire of street fighting, mortars constituted the main weapons the soldiers used against the camp because they can be fired from the relatively short distance of several hundred yards. A mortar launcher is lightweight and can be carried and fired by a single man. The mortar shell can go almost straight up and then falls just about perpendicularly, passing between the buildings of a narrow alleyway. But such a trajectory limits the weight, and thus also the destructive power, of a mortar shell. Heavy artillery of an equivalent calibre is much more destructive but must be fired from a greater distance, and thus is much less precise. The shell from a piece of mechanized heavy artillery follows a sine curve and the shells therefore come slamming into the sides of buildings, bringing them down. At first, the soldiers used heavy artillery against Shatila, but for every shell that fell within the camp itself, five shells landed on their own troops. After several days, they stopped using them.

To add to this stunning array of hardware, as Faramawi explained it, Amal militiamen and First Brigade soldiers brought along a few Syrian-supplied Soviet T-54 tanks, and the Sixth Brigade their U.S. M-48 tanks. This explained the booming sounds we heard. Forty behemoths ringed Shatila, and a concerted tank attack along S-S Street and through the narrow streets of the neighbourhood was underway, the tanks' cannon bringing down the buildings at the periphery of the camp, exposing the defenders and forcing them to retreat. I wondered at the insanity of it all. I was certainly no stranger to war, but a concerted tank attack through the streets of the neighbouring slums boggled the mind.

The young Palestinians, students, and workers defending the refugee district had individual automatic rifles, AK-47s or M-16s, rocket-propelled grenade (RPG) launchers, and personal revolvers. There were four heavy machine guns in the camp, but only one could be used, because there was simply no hidden protected place to mount the other three. The camp's defenders also had three pieces of 60-mm mortars – for use sporadically and at great risk, again due to limited space. In all, it was not much as a defence against tank fire and dozens of artillery pieces and mortar launchers. The camp's fighters had managed to destroy several tanks with their RPGs, but at a terrible toll in destruction and death.

The bombing and shelling of Shatila went on. Day in and day out, dozens of wounded arrived. With day flowing into night and time losing all sense of purpose, we stopped trying to keep up the hospital routine and began to improvise. The staff – all ninety of them – sought various rooms, corners, and crannies where they could stretch out and catch a few hours of sleep while not on duty. The X-ray department housed twelve people sleeping on mattresses laid out on the floor, and two on the X-ray table. Another three people crowded into the darkroom. The laboratory was sleeping quarters for the four lab technicians and two administrators. The little room of reinforced concrete constructed as a passage to the operating-theatre stairway held six. Three others stretched out on mattresses on the stairway itself, and the operating theatre became a dormitory for twenty. I slept on the trolley that carried patients from the stairway to the operating table. The trolley was only twenty-three inches wide, but at least I could stretch out my full length after having to stand hunched over the operating table for hours on end because of the low ceiling. These conditions obviously did not allow for full sterile technique in the operating room, but there was simply not enough space elsewhere in the hospital for beds.

We set up a new protocol: every time a wounded patient arrived, we would wake the staff in serial order, those sleeping in the emergency room first, followed by the people in the X-ray department. They packed up their blankets and mattresses and moved out while X-rays were taken. The patient was then returned to the emergency room, and the nurses and doctors filed back into the X-ray department and went back to sleep. Next in turn to be awakened were the laboratory staff, and finally everyone sleeping in the reinforced concrete passageway, on the stairway, and in the theatre. After operating, the theatre personnel would mop up and then lay out their mattresses once again. The camp's wits began to call the hospital "Hotel Giannou-Sheraton."

The shelling and bombardment continued, hour after hour, day after day. The first few days and even weeks flowed together in one continuum. Few of us ever left the hospital itself, but we heard and felt the explosions around us. At times, it seemed as though the shelling engulfed the entire camp and western sector simultaneously. At other times, as though the region had been quartered off, the shelling concentrated on one small area. The hospital was not immune to this. The army soldiers had pin-pointed the hospital, and we received our daily dose of shelling, usually timed to coincide with the early-evening visiting hours.

After finishing operating one night, Régine left the Faramawi building carrying soiled surgical towelling and gowns to the laundry.

Five seconds later, a thunderous explosion rocked the hospital. A heavy artillery shell had scored a direct hit. I steadied myself against the pressure of the blast, which had thrown open the heavy metal door of the hospital building and shattered the glass in the windows, taped over to prevent the fragments from spraying onto the people inside. One thought rushed through my mind – Régine. I dashed out into the smoke- and dust-filled alleyway, dreading to find her body sprawled under the rubble. A gaping hole had opened over the alleyway between the central kitchen storehouse building and the pharmacy; the iron bars of the reinforced concrete hung down in strange, convoluted shapes, and the severed electrical cables dangled in a confused cobweb. I shouted for Régine – no answer. I made it to the emergency area, coughing and choking on the dust, and found Régine standing there, deadly pale and laughing nervously.

Even though our protective fortifications had not been intended to withstand heavy artillery of this type, our system of sandbags, rubber tires, and reinforced concrete had saved Régine's life. We quickly repaired the wiring, placed wooden doors over the hole in the alleyway ceiling, and then replaced our system of rubber tires and sandbags. Although heavy artillery was not used again, that five-yard stretch of the alley over the pharmacy building received about a hundred mortar shells over the next few weeks. We had to go up and repair the fortifications on five separate occasions during lulls in shelling, lugging into position the rubber tires and sandbags that had been scattered about.

The next day, after Régine's brush with death, as I was returning to the emergency room from the operating theatre, exhausted and dragging my feet, I was confronted by Abdallah, the head of the PFLP–General Command and chief political officer of the National Salvation Front. He was distraught, pleading with me to do something. I could barely understand what he was saying until I caught sight of the emergency trolley carrying a patient into the X-ray room. I rushed over to look at Leila, Abdallah's secretary. Livid, she was gasping, her pulse barely palpable. A large piece of shrapnel had lodged in her belly. In the emergency room, the doctors had managed to place one intravenous line and had then sent her for X-rays. I called for a stretcher immediately and told them to rush her down to the theatre. It was obvious that there was no time to lose – she would die while the X-rays were being taken. In the theatre, we first inserted another couple of intravenous lines. She went into cardiac arrest, and I did an external cardiac massage while the anaesthetist and nurses pumped her full of fluids, plasma, and blood. Her heart started beating again. After scrubbing quickly and slopping some iodine over her distended abdomen, we spread out the surgical sheets and I cut into her.

Her heart had stopped again. After placing a large vascular clamp across her aorta to prevent any further haemorrhage and keep whatever blood was left in her body circulating strictly between heart and brain, I now performed internal cardiac massage. The nurses clasped the plastic bags filled with blood, squeezing them firmly to increase the pressure and force the blood more quickly into her veins. I could feel the heart muscle start to quiver and vibrate again in the palm of my hand as I squeezed it slowly and regularly. She stabilized, and her heartbeat became full and regular. I could now turn my attention to the broth of mucus, faeces, and blood that filled her abdomen. I quickly cleaned away the debris that was once her intestines, mopping up with litres of sterile saline solution to see exactly the extent of her injuries. A large piece of shrapnel, two inches by one by one, had entered just above the navel, hit aorta and several other major vessels, and continued down through the pelvis into the buttock, stopping at the sciatic nerve. Her small gut had been minced into countless pieces. I began with the repair of the major blood vessels and finished with resection of at least two-thirds of her small intestine. After four hours' operating, the scrub nurse asked to be excused and was replaced by one of her colleagues. Another four hours and twenty-five units of blood later, we had finished and closed her up. Abdallah had waited patiently upstairs, and I went to tell him Leila was alive. He was overjoyed, but I warned him of all the possible complications; she was far from being out of danger. She remained in a coma for thirty-six hours; the two episodes of cardiac arrest and the severe haemorrhage had resulted in swelling of the brain. But Leila recovered consciousness and within a week was drinking and eating. Abdallah and her other friends and colleagues spent hours visiting her and keeping up her spirits. For the moment, we had cheated death once again.

The barrage of shelling continued, flattening buildings and entire sections of the camp and surrounding areas. Within the first few days of the battle, most families had abandoned their homes and taken refuge in one of the three underground bomb shelters, taking with them pots, pans, utensils, mattresses, blankets, and whatever food stores they could carry. But they left behind most of their worldly possessions, which, along with at least one-half of the food stocks in the camp, soon lay buried under the rubble of collapsed buildings. The communal bomb shelters constituted cramped quarters; 800 people teeming in a room thirty by twenty yards – the largest of the shelters. The toilets were soon overflowing, and the water reservoirs insufficient. But the families – all 492 of them – were safe, if uncomfortable.

As each day of that first week of relentless bombing wore on, less and less of the camp was habitable. The flattened buildings forced the defenders along the perimeter of Shatila to withdraw from position after position, moving closer to the centre of the camp. The noose around Shatila was being drawn tighter. Soon, there would be no camp left; not a building would remain standing. Where would the defenders go? What would they do? How could they continue to defend a mass of rubble?

Along the eastern border of the camp, a couple of men had dug, by the fourth day, a tunnel underneath one of the collapsed buildings, coming to surface beyond in a foxhole amidst the ruins. Ali Abu Toq, with his experience in the People's Republic of China and Vietnam, was acquainted with the practice of excavating a labyrinth of tunnels. Following the early example of the eastern front, and under Ali's guidance, the fighters in the camp spent ten days digging by hand with crude trowels and shovels, creating a network of interlocking underground passageways, tunnels, and even entire rooms. They excavated four miles of tunnels around the perimeter of the 200 yards by 200 yards of Shatila. The debris of shattered buildings overhead protected the men underground from any further shelling. After an artillery barrage to force back the defenders, the opposing militiamen and soldiers would attempt a frontal assault to occupy the terrain. But the foxhole exits of the tunnels and passages surfaced amidst the broken concrete slabs of collapsed walls, ceilings, and roofs at the original front lines. The camp's defenders could pop out of their foxholes to shoot down the oncoming militiamen. Thus, a handful of elusive gunmen, hiding amidst the jagged blocks of concrete, managed to cut down the great Iranian-style human waves of Amal militiamen and Lebanese soldiers.

The besiegers suffered enormous losses in these assaults, although there were minimal losses to the camp's defenders. The militiamen and soldiers believed they had wiped out any resistance by their devastation of the camp, and they were always surprised and angered by the stubbornness of the Shatila fighters, who seemed to appear from and disappear into nowhere. Intercepting CB frequency bands on the hospital receiver, we heard them vent their surprise and anger time and again. In West Beirut and among the militia, the bitter rumour had it that the Palestinians of Shatila lived in and used the sewers for their protection. For the attackers, it was bitterly frustrating; for the camp's defenders – even if we all eventually had to live underground – it meant that the camp could not be overcome militarily. We were jubilant.

Ali was an engineering genius, and his makeshift techniques using all sorts of everyday household materials were often brilliant. He had the men gather up all wooden doors, window-frames, and planks that could be salvaged from the houses and the one carpenter's shop in the camp and use them to strengthen the walls and ceilings of the tunnels. In some places, where the shelling had not yet quite levelled a building, the men dug trenches through its rooms and then covered them over with planks and soil – much less arduous work than tunnelling. When the building finally collapsed, the falling debris helped to fortify the roof of the underlying passageway.

At yet other points on the front, the young men excavated entire rooms, three yards square and two yards in height. These they also lined with doors and planks and outfitted with several mattresses and often a small television set powered by a car battery. A tunnel led into each room at one end and another led out at the opposite corner to a foxhole aboveground, where one man would be on guard duty watching out for any frontal assault. Underground, his comrades-in-arms played cards, watched television, or slept. Many of the young men would live in these bunkers for months on end, even after the eventual cease-fire; by then, there were few buildings left to house them.

Ali planned some of the tunnels to reach fifty yards beyond the camp, effectively placing the exits behind the Amal front lines. Small groups of commandos went out at night to wreak havoc among the opposing troops.

Each faction had positions or "fronts" as their responsibility; only a few, like the Awaini warehouse, were large enough to accommodate or require men from more than one faction. Political barriers between the fighters at the fronts fell – death was the common enemy.

Having ensured the safety of the families and non-combatants in the bomb shelters, and having positioned the defenders in their tunnels and rooms, Ali planned and started excavating a tunnel to join up with the main sewer system near the Sabra camp to the north. His idea was to create an underground path to West Beirut, effectively breaking the blockade of Shatila unbeknownst to the Amal militia.

All the while, the shelling went on relentlessly. After several days of fighting, the surrounding soldiers cut off the public electrical supply to Shatila. The hospital generator now functioned twenty-three hours a day (we interrupted it every twelve hours for a brief rest period). Under shelling, one of the workers would run out from the hospital, cross a narrow alleyway, and pass through two houses joined by a doorway knocked out in a shared wall to arrive at the generator. He would start it up after checking the water and fuel levels and finally pull the right lever on our special fuse-box-switchboard. The generator would growl and rumble into action, its voice lost in the cacophony of exploding shells. It was, at times, a terrifying experience; pumping fuel and water, flipping switches while shells landed overhead and in the alley just outside. But it had to be done.

One day one of the hospital workers, Menhal, had just returned from refuelling the electric generator, narrowly escaping a barrage of shelling. He took me aside. "Dr. Giannou, coming back I saw a stream of red tracer bullets going up from the corner of Faramawi's building. This isn't the first time I've seen them." He continued in a whisper, "And every time, just a few minutes later, the hospital is hit by shell fire. Do you know what that means?" Menhal's tone was conspiratorial, and with reason. "There's a spy in the camp, shooting tracer bullets to locate the hospital, to help the army units and Amal aim their shelling." There was no need to tell Menhal to keep quiet about this. He knew it was just the sort of news to create panic.

I got word to Basel, Omar, and Ali Abu Toq that I needed to see them urgently. Basel and Omar came first that evening; as leaders of the Popular Struggle Front and the Popular Front, they constituted, in Palestinian parlance, the "democratic" factions – a code word for left-wing, nationalistic, and independent-minded – within the pro-Syrian National Salvation Front alliance. I ushered them into the back of the pharmacy building, one of the few areas of the crowded hospital where we could talk quietly and discreetly. Basel told me that his men had reported tracer-bullet sightings as well. Omar said that several Syrian soldiers had taken refuge in Shatila when the fighting began; part of the observer buffer force stationed around the camp, they had had no chance to flee with the eruption of hostilities. To avoid being caught in the cross-fire, they had jumped for cover in the nearest house in the camp just as the opposing Amal militiamen hit their sandbagged position with a rocket-propelled grenade. One of the pro-Syrian factions in Shatila had taken them in, providing food, shelter, and cigarettes. But, although they made obvious suspects, we all agreed they could not be the culprits behind the tracer bullets – too dangerous, and politically compromising, for uniformed soldiers who didn't know the camp's alleyways well enough to move around undetected.

We formulated a plan to trap whoever was responsible, and I said I'd relay it to Fatah's Ali Abu Toq when he managed to make his way to the hospital. Before Basel and Omar left, however, I told them something that Ali had requested I remain silent about; I now felt I had to tell them. A week before the outbreak of fighting, Ali was coming to the hospital one night when somebody took a shot at him. Ali suspected an officer of Saiqa – the Palestinian wing of the Syrian Ba'athist Party in power in Damascus. Saiqa had only five members in Shatila. Their chief officer was from Shatila itself, his wife held a position of responsibility in the Democratic Front, and his son was a fighter with Ali Abu Toq's Fatah – in sum, the normal sort of political mix one encounters in families in a Palestinian refugee camp. But others in Saiqa were not from Shatila, were not even Palestinian. Two had arrived only a couple of months before. They were Syrians and made no secret of being operatives for the *Moukhabarat*. Ali suspected one of these Syrian agents–Saiqa members to be the would-be assassin.

Basel and Omar looked at me wide-eyed, stunned. They had their political differences with Ali Abu Toq's Fatah, but did not question Ali's patriotism and were vehemently opposed to the political assassination of a fellow Palestinian, especially by agents of an Arab government. With several million Palestinian refugees living in a diaspora, scattered among half a dozen Arab countries, political assassination was just the sort of intrusion by Arab regimes in internal Palestinian affairs that every nationalist Palestinian feared and dreaded. Basel and Omar knew too well the sword of Damocles hanging over their own heads and those of their factions' leaders, the sort of pressure that had already caused them to enter into an anti-Arafat pro-Syrian alliance with trepidation and foreboding. A round of reciprocal assassinations would be suicidal to the Palestinians and their aspirations. Not stopping foreign agents in the camp, shooting tracer bullets to locate vital installations, could also be suicidal – for us.

I relayed the information and plan to Ali and told him that I had spoken to Basel and Omar about the assassination attempt. He appreciated their reaction. Within twenty-four hours, the plan bore fruit; two of Basel's men, furious, entered the hospital, pushing ahead of them one of the Saiqa officers. They had hidden near the hospital generator, and when they had seen the tracer bullets, had opened fire at the source, wounding the Saiqa officer in both legs. Basel, Omar, and Ali all responded to the tracer bullets, for which everyone was now on the lookout, and soon arrived at the hospital. Ali took one look at the Syrian, spoke a few words to Basel, and left. Basel and

Omar had trouble controlling Basel's men, who wanted to simply finish off their quarry. The Syrian spy, contrite and frightened out of his mind, hid under one of the examination couches in the emergency reception. Politically, this constituted a difficult situation: a supposedly pro-Syrian Palestinian guerrilla leader does not execute a Syrian intelligence agent, notwithstanding his feelings and immediate reflexive reaction. Ali, the pro-Arafat Fatah leader, left Basel and Omar to ponder their quandary and solve it in spite of their conflicting nationalism and patriotism versus their sense of *realpolitik*.

They decided to turn the spy over to the other more avowedly pro-Syrian factions of the National Salvation Front and hold them responsible for anything he might do. Omar waited for Abdallah of the PFLP–General Command to come visit Leila that evening. The pain and embarrassed confusion in Abdallah's face spoke eloquent volumes. Before sheepishly returning to Leila's bedside, he told his bodyguards to quickly take the spy away to his compound. It was difficult to claim to be anti-deviationist Arafat and pro-Syrian, have one's own head on the block in the Shatila sardine tin, and be held responsible for the care of a Syrian spy who had helped to pin-point the location of the very hospital where one's own beloved assistant now lay, the victim of bombing by the Syrian-backed Amal militia. Such is the politics of the Middle East.

I took care of the spy's leg wounds. Young, twenty-five years old at most, and frightened, he pleaded with me, "Dr. Giannou, you know me." (I did. Before the battle, he constantly passed by the hospital, amused to hear me speak Arabic, asking my opinion on various delicate questions of Middle Eastern politics.) "Please, don't let them hurt me." I assured him that, as long as he was in the hospital, no harm would come to him. I kept my word; neither Basel's men nor anyone else would dare touch him in my presence. When I had finished his dressings, I turned him over to Abdallah's bodyguards. He was kept with the Syrian soldiers who had taken refuge in Shatila; all survived and eventually left the camp, ignominiously, after the cease-fire.

December 2: nineteen wounded, four dead. Another endless day in the operating theatre. A couple of straightforward cases moved along very quickly. The theatre staff was getting its routine down very well, with little loss of time between operations for cleaning, resterilizing, and moving the patients in and out. Just when everything seemed to be going smoothly, another difficult multiple-trauma case arrived: injury to the chest; a major vessel in the thigh; and lacerations of the liver, stomach, and pancreas, requiring the equivalent of three separate operations all at once.

Having finished, I wearily climbed the stairs from the operating theatre to find out what was happening. The nursing staff informed me that other wounded had arrived, one of whom needed my attention. I rushed over to the emergency room to find an eight-year-old boy with a piece of shrapnel lodged in the middle of his head. Part of the bone from the right side of his skull was missing, exposing the brain. I peered into his eyes with a flashlight; his pupils reacted. Experience had taught me that there was still hope to save him. I am a general surgeon by training and have not had formal instruction in neurosurgery, but more than once in Lebanon, I was faced with the situation of being the only surgeon present, with no possibility of evacuating the wounded.

In 1983, during the fighting in northern Lebanon, I had had to operate on fifteen such cases. It was a choice of either sitting back and watching a patient die, or intervening to try to do something. By applying the classic principles of trauma surgery (cleaning out the wound – debridement; tying off or cauterizing blood vessels – haemostasis; and covering over sensitive or delicate tissue such as the brain, attempting to prevent infection), I was able to help my patients more than harm them. In Shatila, during the series of minor battles, I had already performed twenty-odd craniotomies. This youngster was the first of thirty-five such cases that we would treat during this round of fighting. More improvisation, out of desperation; but then, miracles seemed to abound in Shatila.

Again, I trudged upstairs from the operating theatre and was making my way towards the emergency room when I heard a great noise coming from the pharmacy building. I went in and found thirty of the hospital staff crowded into one of the small rooms eagerly awaiting the beginning of the evening newscast on television. I had not heard the news for a week now and knew nothing apart from the fact that the camp still existed, and what Faramawi had told me of the amplitude of the military onslaught against us. The announcer's voice began, "Shatila has not fallen yet!" A great cry and laughter went up from all of us.

My colleagues and friends, sitting there in the pharmacy, watching the news, filled me in on the happenings. The outside world had expected Shatila to fall; the Amal leadership had for days been making announcements that the overrunning of Shatila was "imminent," and "just a matter of a few hours"; they were saying, "Part of the camp is in our control." The previous day, Dr. Khatib told me, the radio had apparently announced "the fall of Shatila." The shelling continued, but although life in the camp was paralysed except for the hospital, none of us felt that we were in any immediate danger.

We applauded even more the next day when we heard the news that 100 men of the Sixth Brigade ringing Burj el-Barajneh had left their positions, refusing to fight, refusing to participate in what they called a "diabolical, fratricidal war."

By the end of the first week of fighting, the destruction of the camp was massive, the men were tunnelling, and the families were hidden away in the shelters; we in the hospital were the only ones in the entire camp working and living aboveground. The situation on the military fronts, and in organizing food distribution to the families and the defenders was critical. A co-ordinated effort on the part of all the factions was imperative. Forgetting their rivalries, the various leaders met in one of the offices. There were, among others, Ali, Baha, and Amina of the pro-Arafat Fatah; Abu Moujahed and Omar of the PFLP; the DFLP's Abu Imad; Basel of the Popular Struggle Front; Abdallah of the General Command, and Abu Firas of the Fatah dissidents, looking somewhat constipated, reluctantly participating in this meeting with the much-hated "Arafat deviationists." But then Ali Abu Toq not only had the most fighters in the camp, he also controlled more food and ammunition stores than all the other groups put together. And he had the only support services – repair and maintenance of weapons and electric generators.

They set up seven committees involving all the factions and covering every aspect of life in Shatila under siege and under the bombs. There was a joint military operations command to co-ordinate the defences; a committee to oversee building fortifications and ramparts and continue the tunnelling; another to take care of the shelters and needs of families; and yet another to help with the wounded – clean pyjamas, a tooth-brush and razor, moral support, and companionship. Other committees dealt with general utilities – water, fuel, electricity; the preparation and distribution of food; and the bread bakery. The bakery held a special place in the minds of the people and deserved its own committee. This is the culture of peasants and poverty. Bread is *the* staple food and is eaten with everything; even linguistically, the round loaf of pita bread – *ghif* – popularly denotes a helping of food. (The heavy eater consumes two and even three *ghif*, the anorexic "a half-*ghif*" – the meagre quantity represented by placing the upright right hand over the open left palm, "cutting" away the fingers.)

The hospital, with its large electric generator and network of switches and fuses, food supplies, workmen trained in maintenance, plumbing, and electricity, and – above all – as social centre and heart of the camp, played a central role in the functioning of these co-operative committees. Those of us who realized the need for unity were ecstatic, but others co-operated only grudgingly. Still, they had no choice: their survival also depended on it.

7

Crossing the Champs Elysées

AND THE SHELLING CONTINUED. GREAT BLOCKS OF THE camp were being literally flattened. One evening, six of Basel's men from the Popular Struggle Front overran and occupied a building formerly held by Amal militiamen just across the street from the camp. A horrendous artillery barrage poured onto the building, levelling it. The men were trapped under the rubble, but we could hear shouts; at least some of them were still alive. The position was difficult. Sniper fire raked the street separating the building from the camp. Basel, Abdallah, Omar, and Abu Imad gathered with their military leaders to figure out what to do to save the men. Ali Abu Toq arrived at the scene, took one look at the situation, and spontaneously assumed command and responsibility, even though the men belonged to a rival, pro-Syrian faction. He motioned to several men to position themselves with RPGs and automatic rifles. Upon his signal, they started shooting furiously at the source of sniper fire. Ali jumped into the centre of the street, shooting all the while. The other officers crossed over under cover, and Ali followed them into the rubble of the collapsed building. The shooting ceased. They dug frantically and pulled out two survivors. Covering fire shielded their return and, carrying the two wounded survivors, they crossed back into the camp. Months later, after the cease-fire, when workers were clearing the rubble, we recovered the four remaining bodies, some of them piece by piece.

The heavy artillery fire had ceased after the first few days, but the deluge of mortar shells continued. The tanks proved more devastating still. The soldiers placed them at strategic locations around the entire periphery of Shatila, particularly in the fortifications of the sports stadium complex. A heavy machine gun on a tank could be fired against any RPG sniper who might have it in mind to shoot. After thirty seconds of raking gunfire, the large cannon would blast away. Apart from ordinary tank shells, they used another type that I could only deduce to be of an armour-piercing variety. Basel brought one to the hospital to show us – a bullet-shaped solid hunk of metal, about eighteen inches long and weighing about seventy-five pounds, that did not explode but pierced fifteen or sixteen of the flimsy dwelling walls before coming to a stop. One such shell could punch its way through four or five buildings, and a barrage could level several at once. I marvelled at the fiendish military imagination behind the inert metal hulk.

December 10: twenty-eight wounded, two dead. The dead were from the *Masheikh* Battalion, a group of about twenty young men, mostly students and all inhabitants of Shatila. They were the Islamic fundamentalists of the camp, few in number and not very aggressive ideologically, but the camp dwellers respected them for their good manners, strong discipline, and gentleness, even though most snickered in private about their religious fervour. Palestinian refugee camp society is decidedly secular. Two of Abu Mohammed Faramawi's children belonged to the *Masheikh*, although he himself was a hard-core Marxist-Leninist, executive committee member of the General Union of Workers. I had met the *Masheikh* in Faramawi's home on the second floor of the hospital building where I usually went in peacetime to watch the nightly news broadcast. Refusing salaries from any of the factions, they had worked after school and with their money bought AK-47 Kalashnikov rifles on the widespread Lebanese arms market. They were defending their homes and families and did not want to be "tainted" by any money from a secular political group.

A piercing tank shell had passed through the barracks where some of the *Masheikh* had been sleeping and struck them at the level of the pelvis as they lay side by side. Two mangled bodies arrived at the emergency room. The tank shell had literally cut the first body in two. The second had an almost identical injury, but somehow was still alive. I took a quick look at him – a great, gaping hole where his hip bones should be stared up at me, half his intestines lay on the table beside him, and he had received a blow to the head as well. An impossible case.

I never got over the sight of young bodies so disfigured. We took the one who was still alive down to the operating theatre. It would be bad for the morale of the camp, as well as of the hospital personnel, to leave him to die in the emergency room without treatment, especially since there were no other cases at the time. Besides, in spite of his horrendous wounds, he refused to die a quick death. We worked feverishly to resuscitate him and stem the haemorrhage. I removed a leg with half the pelvis and half his intestine before dealing with his brain injury. I felt as though I were back performing mutilating cancer surgery again. But nothing could be done to save him.

The tanks continued their work, focusing on our water reservoirs. Raised on pillars, these were four yards cubed, with walls of reinforced concrete ten inches thick. Two such reservoirs remained, one each at the northeastern and southeastern entrances to the camp. The tank shells blew away the pillars and the reservoirs fell into the streets below, effectively blocking them and cutting off sniper fire that had previously reached deep into the bowels of the camp. When the men filled them with sand and rubble, they made excellent fortifications.

One of the reservoirs had not been placed directly on pillars. Instead, there was a square frame, also of reinforced concrete, sitting atop the pillars and creating a foundation for the reservoir. When this reservoir came crashing down, it created an empty space two feet in height between it and the ground. There had been a sandbag rampart just below, and when the reservoir fell it trapped four men underneath. Their comrades frantically dug a tunnel under the framework resting on the ground to allow the four men to escape. They were badly bruised and dehydrated by the time of rescue, but they were alive. One had severe contusions and crushing of the muscles of one leg, and I incised the skin, cut away bits here and there, and placed him under medication and observation. At least there would be no more amputations that day.

Our need for sandbags was unlimited. During the slowly tightening siege around Shatila in the months prior to this outbreak of fighting, we had been unable to smuggle into the camp more than several thousand burlap bags. Amina organized the women of her co-operative committee to gather sheets and blankets. During lulls in the shelling, they searched the destroyed and abandoned buildings in the camp and went to the families in the underground bomb shelters, convincing them to give up any extra blankets. The women cut them up and, with electricity provided by the hospital generator for a couple of sewing machines, stitched the pieces of material together to form sacks. We thus had a new supply of sandbags, limited in number only by the quantity of bedding in the camp. The fortifications inside the emergency room were a multi-coloured mosaic of stripes and paisley patterns.

For the first weeks of fighting, I was in the OR eighteen or twenty hours per day, sometimes more, getting by on only two or three hours of sleep, sometimes none. Between operations, while Régine and her team mopped up, I made rounds of the patients, wrote out prescriptions or rested in the transformed kitchen-laboratory. The administrative staff and lab technicians often hunkered down there with our wireless CB transmitter-receiver to maintain radio contact with Mar

Elias PRCS headquarters and the Haifa Hospital in Burj el-Barajneh, also under bombardment and siege, and to listen in on the radio banter of the Amal militiamen, speaking on their wireless CB transmitters as they specifically targeted the hospital. Sometimes, we intercepted the tell-tale words of their military co-ordinator: "Rice on Giannou's square." Within minutes, dozens of rounds would come smashing into the upper storeys of the hospital buildings. The dark humour of survivors immediately came into play again. "What kind of sauce are you serving with the rice today, Dr. Giannou?" railed the technicians and nurses. "Someone go tell the cooks right away that today's sauce is 60-mm, with green peas!"

The hospital was functioning – at least the medical facilities were. But the massive shelling rendered unsafe the exposed central building where food was prepared and laundry normally done. We were eating tinned food; the laundry of soiled sheets, surgical gowns, and towelling was piling up in a bloody mountain. Something had to be done, or we would shortly be without drape sheets and gowns for the operating theatre. Régine had already broken out packs of disposable sterile paper towels for relatively minor procedures. We commandeered a deserted house protected by a second storey next to the emergency room. Its door gave onto the protected alleyway of the hospital complex, and the cleaning staff of the hospital relocated the laundry in this building and started in to take care of the huge backlog, boiling the sheets over a wood fire to save our supply of butane gas. The cooks also used the wood fires to prepare food. We were eating hot meals again.

Inside Faramawi's sturdily constructed building, we knew we were as safe as possible, but we had to make an effort to overcome our natural fear. Most of us had been through shellings and bombings many times before, but one never really escapes the fear. One can only attempt to overcome the paralysis that fear may provoke. All the while the shells fell directly overhead, the more experienced personnel kept busily moving about, giving comfort, reinforcing morale, encouraging where courage might flag, trying to make an abstraction of the deathly reality that hung over us. At times, when I was trying to sleep on my trolley in the OR, I would be awakened by the vibrations from nearby explosions. Feeling guilty that I was in the underground shelter while the nursing staff was in the more exposed ground floor, I'd climb down from the trolley and go upstairs. Here, I sat with the nursing staff or moved among the patients as nonchalantly as possible, hoping that my presence would help them to forget the rattle of the window panes and the heavy thud of falling shells. We made half-hearted jokes to give each other courage. When the shelling moved off to concentrate on another sector of the camp, I would make some excuse and go back downstairs to my trolley to get some sleep.

We were not surprised that the hospital was targeted in particular. The militiamen and soldiers understood its important role in the resistance of the camp. In 1985, during the first battle of the War of the Camps, the ghastly spectacle of the slowly dying wounded had sapped the morale of Shatila's inhabitants and brought the refugee district to the brink of collapse and surrender. During several subsequent minor skirmishes, without medical services, a case of even one severely wounded person obliged the camp's leaders to submit to political concessions in order to obtain a cease-fire and permission to evacuate the wounded to a West Beirut hospital. Added to the horror and agony of watching a friend or relative slowly bleed to death for lack of medical care was the raging frustration and despair of negotiating a cease-fire over the CB transmitter through the political leadership in Mar Elias, the cynical tactical manoeuvring of proposal and counter-proposal.

The establishment of the hospital changed all that. Through the Four-, Twenty-, and Thirty-five-Day battles, whenever Amal negotiators, seeking a weak spot and a tactical advantage, brought up the question of evacuating the wounded from Shatila, the camp replied, "We have no wounded in need of evacuation." It was not entirely true. Some cases needed specialized treatment that we could not provide – a piece of shrapnel in the eye, for instance. But then, the shrapnel had already wreaked its damage; we could at least take measures to prevent complications. However, never did we face the predicament of evacuation or death. No one would bleed to death.

The hospital's reputation had grown, even in West Beirut, and popular gossip credited us with performing miracles. The "miracle hospital" of Shatila enhanced the camp dwellers' and defenders' morale. We became a pillar of Shatila's resistance. We knew it, and the enemy knew it. All the more reason for them to destroy the hospital.

We had divided the doctors and nursing staff into groups so that they were on twelve-hour shifts. The laboratory and X-ray personnel were on call day and night, but because of the nature of their work, they really only had about four hours' duty per day. The six pharmacists, cleaning staff, and workers responsible for the water and electricity supplies sufficed to cover six-hour shifts. In the operating theatre, on the other hand, the seven scrub nurses, one anaesthetist technician and her assistant, an assistant surgeon, and myself were occupied twenty hours per day. The burden of wounded was such during the first several weeks that we had no respite. As case flowed into case, we lost track of time, date, hunger, and fatigue. We ceased to feel ourselves or our bodies. A scrub nurse would, like an automaton, circulate for two hours during an operation, fetching compresses, instruments, and suture material, and then curl up in a corner to snooze for a few hours, relieved in her duties by a colleague. Then she would awake and sterilize or pack gowns and towelling before going off to sleep another couple of hours; reawakened, she would assist at an operation for several hours and then return to her corner to sleep. And on, and on. Everyone in turn. This became the routine of the operating theatre for weeks on end.

In previous battles, one of the general practitioners had assisted me. Now, I had two assistants – one in general surgery and another in orthopaedics – and although this was the first real battle that either had been in and their war surgery experience was limited, they could take care of post-op work and dressings and could scrub up for an operation: a luxury for me.

What were shells surely intended for Faramawi's building were also making a shambles of my "villa." Mortar fire regularly slammed into the one-room, second-storey apartment just across the alleyway from the laboratory. The group ensconced in the laboratory mockingly talked about the military significance of the "villa." "Why should the 'villa' be a target for such intense bombardment?" Menhal asked.

"What, Dr. Giannou, could you possibly have hidden under the reed mat or in your clothes rack?" (I had managed to salvage some of my clothing and books and was to spend many a long hour at night during the battle rereading a few old texts. They had survived numerous battles and air raids in Beirut, and a friend brought them to me on my arrival in Shatila. It was interesting to reread, say, Maxim Rodinson's historical and social observations on the Arab world – *Le Marxisme et l'Islam* – while we were being bombed and starved in Shatila.) My companions took great delight in ridiculing Amal's massive destruction of the camp by using my meagre dwelling as an example of the futility of such an endeavour and as a symbol of Shatila's will to resist. But when a shell jolted the building opposite, the tinkling of broken glass would scatter our taunts as great clouds of dust billowed through the tiny laboratory window, choking off our laughter. We crouched nervously; more shells crashed just outside the window. "Damn that villa!" someone exclaimed. "If they want it so badly, why not just give it to them – in pieces?"

"No, no! It's the 'cabaret' they're after. They didn't like the last show." Another round of laughter relieved the tension and fear.

With dozens of wounded arriving on a daily basis, we had opened the "cabaret" on the second day of hostilities. It was an annex located just across the street from the hospital and "villa," and we had equipped it with forty beds and an impromptu nursing station. Menhal and the other workers had strung electrical wiring from a laboratory outlet, through the window, around a drain pipe, across the street, and into the "cabaret." I transferred patients there from the hospital when their clinical status allowed. For four or five weeks, we had a daily average of fifty in-patients in the hospital and annex. The kitchen and cleaning staff were kept busy, cooking for patients and hospital personnel – 150 people – and washing daily at least 120 sheets soiled with blood, urine, faeces, and vomitus. Our personal laundry and bathing had to wait.

The dingy and squalid cabaret, bare light bulbs dangling here and there from the naked concrete ceiling, gave a macabre comfort to its inhabitants. After the first ten days, when we were without kitchen or laundry facilities, the wounded ate hot meals, slept on clean sheets, and received the "tender loving care" of the nursing staff – a far cry from the cramped, wet, cold tunnels and trenches of their comrades on the fronts, making do with pita bread and tins of sardines or hashed beef. But the cabaret was also the only space available for two custom-made refrigerators – portable morgues set on small chassis with wheels and equipped with sliding shelves to hold three cadavers each. I thought that six places would be sufficient. In the past, we had never had that many dead at any one time, and in keeping with Muslim tradition, the dead were buried either before nightfall or prior to noon the day after death. But during the long siege, the six shelves soon contained nine corpses.

Under the deluge of shells, it was impossible to reach the mosque burial ground to inter them. Abu Moujahed's Popular Committee crew and the hospital workers literally could not safely walk the thirty yards to the mosque. The bodies lay in the refrigerators blocking the entrance to the cabaret, protecting even in death the patients within from any stray shrapnel. We piled other corpses in the laundry and administration rooms of the hospital's central building. By the seventeenth day of the battle, December 12, we had forty-six cadavers on our hands. The stench, even in the cold weather, began to infiltrate the hospital.

When Abu Moujahed passed by for a hot meal, I told him of our predicament. That evening, during a brief calm in the shelling, he organized a group of elderly men from the bomb shelters to help the hospital workers carry the corpses to the mosque, dig a large mass grave, and bury the bodies in layers, one group laid upon another. From then on, during lulls in the bombardment, they carried out and buried the new dead. They never sealed the large holes immediately, but left them open to the air until filled to capacity with cadavers.

The macabre abounded in Shatila. During the very first battle, Dr. Khatib had gathered the wounded on the ground floor of the mosque; if they died, he buried them where they lay. The real cemetery was well outside the camp's boundaries, impossible to reach during a siege, so Shatila's inhabitants converted the mosque into a cemetery. Normally, the dead are never buried in a mosque, and there are separate burial areas for men and women. In Shatila, the dead – men, women, elderly, young, Muslims and Christians, Palestinians and Lebanese – were buried on top of one another in the mosque. In the narrow limits of the camp, facing the ultimate common denominator of violent death, such distinctions as sex, political affiliation, nationality, and religion meant little.

Eventually, the inhabitants interred more than 500 corpses, and expropriated a house just next door when the number of dead spilled out over the confines of the mosque building. On feast days when there was no fighting, Oum Shakour, Abu and Oum Abed, and countless others visited their dead children. Families and friends garlanded the tombs and interior of the mosque with wreaths, flowers, and palm leaves and lined the walls with photographs of the dead, considered martyrs by one and all. The transformation of the mosque – a religious and living social institution – into a mass grave was symbolic of what had happened to Shatila, just as the large Palestinian Martyrs Cemetery in West Beirut was symbolic of what had befallen an entire people: it was the only cemetery in the Middle East where Jews, Christians, and Muslims were buried together.

December 16: ten wounded, one dead. The shelling increased in intensity. All hell seemed to break loose. The furor of this new onslaught stunned us all; little was left of the camp after three weeks of continuous bombardment, and I wondered how much more we could take. As it turned out, this was a final gasp by Amal and the army to cover a massive frontal assault on three different fronts of the tiny camp's perimeter. The charging militiamen and soldiers threw themselves in human waves against our defences, just as Iranian troops – those other Shi'ite Muslims – did in the Gulf War. They hoped to overwhelm the defenders popping out of their tunnel foxholes amidst the rubble. For hours the attack went on; but Shatila's young men repulsed every assault. Amal suffered enormous losses, and as every wave broke fruitlessly on the camp's ramshackle ramparts, a little more of the militiamen's morale was broken. After eighteen continuous hours of shelling and close combat, the attack exhausted itself. It was a turning point. Our losses seemed light; one dead, and nine of the ten wounded were only superficial cases.

The tenth was horrific, in both the extent and the manner of his injuries. Khaled was the first cousin of Hanan, one of the hospital nurses. He had destroyed a tank, and the comrades who carried him back to the hospital bleeding profusely were in a state of near exaltation as they excitedly described to anyone within earshot in the overcrowded cramped ER what had happened. "A tank had been blasting away at our position on the eastern border of the camp. Khaled timed himself, and between shots from the tank's cannon, while the heavy machine gun beside the turret was firing at the far end of its arc, he jumped out into the open, an RPG launcher on his shoulder. He fired as the turret moved back into position, then he jumped for cover. Just as his grenade hit the tank, the cannon fired and caught him still exposed. But he got the mother-fucker! You should've seen that tank explode. What a sight!"

I turned my attention to Khaled. The exploding tank shell had chopped great chunks of flesh out of both thighs, an arm, and his belly. He was in shock but we easily resuscitated him. In the theatre, I covered his wounds with moistened towels and then examined his abdomen – the site of the haemorrhage. I tied off the bleeding vessels, removed several parts of his small gut, and made a colostomy where a piece of shrapnel had perforated the colon. He would live with this artificial anus for the next few months. Then I cleaned and debrided his other wounds. Khaled had a muscular athlete's body, and I calculated that the tank shell had removed at least ten pounds of flesh. A cruel bargain: ten pounds of flesh versus thirty tons of steel! But, after six hours' operating, I could tell Hanan that her cousin would survive.

At two in the morning, just after I had finished my last rounds, Rabiha and Régine brought the night shift's meal. Abu Imad, Baha, Basel, and Omar showed up on their joint nightly patrol of the different fronts and sectors. They knew it was time for the night meal and helped themselves to hot cups of tea and sandwiches. They said that by their and the offices' in Mar Elias calculation, more than 250,000 shells – heavy artillery, mortar, tank – had been fired against Shatila in just over three weeks. "Thank you, comrades! Have another cup of tea."

The tank and mortar fire was methodically levelling the camp and taking its toll on the hospital as well. Every barrage of shells landing on the hospital blew away part of a wall, dishevelled our sandbag piles, or riddled the ceiling of the residence just above the emergency room. Flying chunks of cement injured two of the hospital workers. We placed new fortifications and repaired the old, time and time again. Nonetheless, if the destruction continued, it would become impossible to work in the hospital. We started excavating under the central building; the hospital, like the rest of the camp, would have to go underground.

In the meantime, in case of further damage, we put into effect what Régine called my *plan catastrophe*. I told the pharmacists to divide up all medicines, dressings, and surgical supplies and distribute them among the cupboards and crannies of the hospital buildings. Régine took all the critical goods – suture material, anaesthesia, analgesics – and stored them in the safest location, the underground operating theatre. Now, if the ER or pharmacy building were destroyed, we would lose only one-third of our antibiotics, dressings, and other supplies. The destruction of even one of those buildings would mean the death or injury of many of the hospital staff, but we had to remain functional no matter what, and I had to look with a cold clinical eye on any eventuality and plan for it.

Ali Abu Toq was everywhere, from the military fronts to the shelters, helping organize, cajoling, keeping up people's morale. Rounding up a few elderly men sitting quietly in the shelters, too old for the battlefield but still capable of wielding a shovel, he sent one group to help Abu Moujahed in constructing fortifications and ramparts, and another to the hospital to help with the excavations. Fortunately, that last massive bombardment and assault seemed to have been Amal's and the army brigades' last burst of energy. Although the shelling continued fitfully over the next three weeks, it was no longer mortar and artillery fire but simply the tanks, with their piercing shells, that continued to knock down building after building. Once again, as when they targeted the water reservoirs, I marvelled at the military stupidity of the militiamen and soldiers. The tanks shot head on from very close range; the mounds of rubble from collapsed buildings now blocked their view and aim and they were too close to lob their tank shells over the mountains of debris and rubble into the camp. The streets and alleyways constituted the only weak points left in our defences: a piercing tank shell could pass through them into the heart of the camp, but a few well-placed ramparts, several yards thick, blocked that access.

A four-yard-wide street – named the Champs Elysées in deference to Régine – separated the hospital from the cabaret, with its forty hospital beds. It was one of the main thoroughfares of the camp and exposed to sniper fire from a tall building some 600 yards from Shatila. In previous rounds of fighting, we had hung up blankets between the buildings to cut off the snipers' view; now, we dug a trench two yards deep across the Champs Elysées, joining Faramawi's alleyway to the cabaret. We then took the bookshelves and filing cabinets from the hospital administration office and, laying them flat on the exposed side of the trench, filled them with sand and piled one on top of another. Our *ad hoc* fortifications would protect hospital workers and nurses carrying a patient on a stretcher from the hospital to the annex through the trench.

One afternoon, I stepped out into the alleyway and looked across the Champs Elysées, the air saturated with brown-grey dust, smoke, and the tangy odour of cordite explosive. The hospital sign dangled precariously from a single nail over the trench at the exit from the alleyway. "PRCS" was written boldly in English and Arabic and remained intact, but "Shatila Hospital" was perforated with shrapnel, the word "Shatila" almost illegible. It spoke eloquently of our situation: Shatila might be reduced to rubble, but its institutions still held strong.

8

The Culture of Struggle, The Literature of Resistance

WITH A DECREASE IN THE INTENSITY OF FIGHTING AND the number of patients, hospital work fell into a simpler routine. Many of the wounded were now superficial cases, and the ER staff well practised in the protocol of receiving patients. The general practitioners, under the authority of Dr. Khatib, took care of many cases on their own, cleaning out wounds under local anaesthesia and calling on me for consultation only with more difficult ones. After the blur of the first few weeks, I could now turn my attention to individual patients.

In the central building, our cooks – Saadou and his brother – were back at work in the kitchen. The roof over the food store-room, kitchen, and cafeteria had the rubber-tire and sandbag fortifications. A 120-mm shell that landed on an unprotected part of the roof left a hole a yard and a half in diameter and would have been fatal to anyone standing underneath. When a similar shell fell on the protected kitchen roof, however, it resulted in a hole only six inches in diameter; the staff preparing food were covered by a fine shower of concrete dust, but escaped unhurt. The washerwomen were still in the neighbour's house because the hospital laundry was unprotected.

Six weeks into the fighting, we had used up just about all our butane gas stores, and we now took to cannibalizing the hospital furniture to provide fuel for the wood fires for cooking and laundry. Smoke from the fire went up through the holes in the ceiling left by mortar shells. We had grimy, sooty walls and meals, but we were still eating, at least for the moment.

Saadou, a gentle and kind-hearted man, had a sixteen-year-old son at the front. Mohammed had been injured in 1985 and again during the Twenty-Day Battle. On December 26, 1986, a sniper's bullet found its mark, entering the left side of his head and exiting above his right eye. Saadou was crushed; he waited quietly and patiently at the hospital nursing station while I operated.

The bullet had passed through the frontal sinuses, causing damage requiring a difficult operation. There is always a danger in such cases of infection reaching the brain through the open connection to the nasal passages. But Mohammed recovered consciousness after a couple of days, and within a week he was taking fluids. Saadou, his wife, and brother quietly came to the ward three times a day to look in on the boy and then patiently spoon-feed him. Both Saadou and I were delighted that he was doing so well.

In the other ward room of the hospital was Abu Ahmed, another young man hit by a sniper's bullet that had followed almost the exact same trajectory, passing through the frontal lobe of the brain, taking out an eye. Both Abu Ahmed and Mohammed were conscious, drinking and eating, and seemed well on the way to recovery – with one exception. Mohammed developed a strange fascination with his faeces. Every time Saadou now came to feed or look in on him, the boy would have a small clump of faecal matter in his hand, slowly squeezing and shaping it into a ball. This, he would either throw across the room or smear on the wall. In one of those eerie coincidences in medicine, Abu Ahmed began to do the same, showing identical regressive social behaviour. Normally, one would have to wait years to see a similar case, but here were two boys with like injuries, wounded within days of each other, and both suffering the same syndrome. I had never come across anything like this and was hard put to explain the phenomenon.

The nursing staff also had difficulty dealing with it; the hilarity of the tragedy was stunning. We explained to the two that this was naughty, and that they should not play with their caca. If they felt like going to the toilet, then they should tell one of us, and we would do what was necessary.

Over several weeks, Abu Ahmed's toilet training went on successfully. But Mohammed was recalcitrant. After long and detailed explanations of why he should not play with the clump, he would agree and promise not to begin again. A couple of hours later, blankly staring at the opposite wall, he would again move his hand to his anus, and we would have to repeat our routine yet again.

Saadou was overjoyed that his son was still alive, but the behaviour he considered to be improper and uncouth left him crestfallen. It affected his sense of his son's, and his own, virility. Mohammed was a hero, at the age of sixteen wounded for a third time in defending his people and home. After I explained the situation many times, Saadou finally began to understand his son's condition, I believe, even though he could not accept it. After a few weeks of improvement, however, the boy was at it again, and Saadou was so overcome that he lost his temper, shouting and screaming, and slapped his son's face sharply. I had difficulty controlling myself; my own nerves were quite frayed by then. I almost tore the man apart. After that, the boy's condition started to deteriorate. The concussion of the blow had perhaps ruptured some delicate balance, and he became totally uncooperative. He refused to eat or drink, and we had to force feed him, in a manner of speaking. I would extend his head back and pinch his nose. When he opened his mouth to breathe, I'd quickly pour in food or drink;

either he swallowed in order to clear his mouth and take a breath, or he would suffocate. The natural reflex to survive caused him to swallow, and he could not spit out the food with his head thrown back.

Then Mohammed started to develop a fever. A leak in the meninges developed, and cerebral-spinal fluid started to drip from one nostril. It was exactly what I had feared. I operated two more times, trying to close off the leak, but this was real neurosurgery, and beyond my means and experience.

Almost the entire frontal area of Mohammed's brain had been transformed into a sack of crystal-clear fluid. In effect, he had suffered a traumatic frontal lobotomy, and the personality and behavioural changes were to be expected. I never really managed to repair the leak, and the boy slowly withered away. Two and a half months after being wounded, he had a convulsive fit and died. We didn't always cheat death in Shatila. Saadou was inconsolable. He thought that he had killed his own son. Of course, the war had killed Mohammed, and he had died a hero to his people, notwithstanding the humiliating behaviour of his last days. I, like his father and our hospital colleagues, wept in sorrow at the loss. I was feeling an ever increasing identification with my patients, with their friends and relatives, and it started to weigh heavily upon me. Unlike others in Shatila, as the only surgeon I was a part of every surgical patient's story, of every death.

Abu Ahmed survived, Mohammed died, and I remembered only too clearly the Malian hospital where I had once been a patient and which admitted another Westerner, by coincidence also a Canadian and a teacher, and also suffering from infectious hepatitis. She had only the slightest tinge of yellow in her eyes. I had been admitted in a near coma and was by then well on my way to recovery. Within ten days, however, her condition deteriorated and they evacuated her to Canada. The young woman died en route. This had stunned me. What resistance and strength had I had that this young woman had not? Why was I still alive? What was the fine line between life and death? How easy it was to cross over and back! Now, as a war surgeon, I saw in flashes, time and again, that fine, that ridiculously but imperiously fine line.

Leila continued to receive daily visits from Abdallah of the General Command (who was also Mohammed's leader) and from her other friends and colleagues. Amina, though a political rival, spent many hours visiting Leila and keeping up her spirits. But the complications that I had expected soon made their appearance. Leila developed an intestinal fistula – liquid faeces drained from her abdominal wound and continuously soiled her garments and sheets. It closed, then opened again, then closed once more. Leila's fragile, finely chiselled features showed her disgust with herself, and her frustration. She wanted only to get off her back and return to work. But her weight loss and poor general condition meant there was little we could do except wait and hope.

Hossam had been one of the young workmen in the hospital, until the second day of fighting, when he disappeared. Several days later I saw him wearing military fatigues and carrying a rifle, running through the hospital alleyway. I stopped him to ask what he was doing and why he had left the hospital. He replied that he was at the front. Some time later I saw Hossam again, definitely staggering as he made his way through the alley. I inquired about his whereabouts "at the front"; no one there had seen him. The next time I caught sight of him, I pulled him aside. A quick examination revealed dilated, sluggish pupils, and heavily slurred speech. I was furious. People were dying and being mutilated, all hell was raining down on our heads – and Hossam was hiding somewhere, dropping pills. Disarming him, I pushed him into a chair and told Menhal to fetch Basel, who as senior Security Committee officer could imprison him. A few days later, Basel brought back a very sober and contrite Hossam, who pleaded with me to take him back onto the hospital staff, promising that he would never take drugs again.

In the stressful living conditions of civil–strife–torn Lebanon, there was much abuse of narcotics, tranquillizers, hashish, and alcohol – probably less than in New York City, but in Lebanon everyone was armed and carried their weapons openly in the streets. The relatively rigorous social strictures and taboos of Middle Eastern society had given way to escapism, escape from the terrors and anxiety of torture or violent death through the oblivion of addictive drugs. Black markets existed in Beirut for anything from Parisian *haute couture* and perfume to weapons, appliances, or supposedly prescription-only medications. Drugstores openly sold antibiotics, tranquillizers, and analgesic narcotics (morphine and pethidine) over the counter. In Shatila, the pharmacists and I tried to keep a tight rein on tranquillizers and narcotics in the hospital, but between sieges anyone who wanted could easily get a supply from private pharmacies in the city. We were always on our guard, especially in a war or siege situation. Young men would quickly finish their reserves and then exploit a personal friendship with one of the pharmacists or nurses to obtain more pills at the hospital, trying to convince the staff to take pity on them.

We did suffer one leak of tranquillizers, and months later, just prior to the cease-fire, I was obliged to reincarcerate Hossam and send a young woman pharmacist to prison. It was one thing to be compassionate, another to indulge in stupidity. Her supplying Hossam with a powerful sedative almost cost him his life when, in a senseless stupor, he stepped out onto a roof in full view of snipers.

Radio and television news broadcasts and our wireless CB receivers constituted our sole contact with the outside world. In Lebanon, many factions and political parties have their own private radio stations; coincidentally, but more likely by tacit agreement, each broadcasts its version of the news at a different time, spaced at quarter-hour intervals. Over a couple of hours, by regularly flipping the station selector, one could listen to seven or eight different news broadcasts. In addition, there were also the BBC World Service, Radio France International, the Voice of America, Israeli Arabic-language broadcasts, Egyptian radio, and Radio Monte Carlo – the latter emitting only in Arabic and widely listened to in the Middle East.

We continued to receive news of frantic diplomatic and political activity in Beirut, Damascus, Tunis, and other Arab capitals, in an attempt to arrange for a cease-fire. The political manoeuvring became very intricate and esoteric. Iranian, Algerian, Libyan, and Soviet emissaries travelled to Damascus to influence the Syrians. Any party that could conceivably obtain some political advantage from playing the role of intermediary and negotiator seemed to get involved. An Iranian cleric entered Rashidieh and refused to leave, saying that it was his "Muslim duty to remain and starve with the besieged women and children in the camp." Saying it was God's will, he called upon Amal to lift the siege of the refugee camps and put an end to the fighting, knowing full well how that would play in the Shi'ite community. Hizbollah organized demonstrations against the War of the Camps; the Shi'ite community was divided. All to no avail – Syrian will was stronger than God's. And, of course, political rivalry among the factions in Shatila had not ceased.

Each faction, as well as the hospital, had its own wireless set to communicate with its central leadership in West Beirut or Ain el-Hilweh, to obtain information not divulged on the public air waves. The Fatah – always the privileged Yuppies among the revolutionaries – had a cellular telephone with a base antenna hidden somewhere out in the city. In addition, Ali Abu Toq had bought and brought into the camp a fax machine as early as December 1985. He received directly from Yassir Arafat documents dealing with the ongoing Palestinian negotiations. The leaders of the most important groups outside the PLO – the PFLP and the DFLP – openly criticized the Syrian role in the War of the Camps and met with Arafat people abroad. The defence of Shatila, Burj el-Barajneh, and Rashidieh and the resistance to Syrian tutelage of the Palestinian national movement was forging a new national unity. But, this created friction within the ranks of the National Salvation Front. The hard-line pro-Syrians – PFLP–General Command, Saiqa, and Fatah dissidents – reacted vehemently to these discussions with the Arafat-deviationists, criticizing the Popular and Democratic fronts. The Salvation Front was breaking up, and Ali earnestly and eagerly awaited news of reconciliation and the reunification of the factions within the PLO.

The political manoeuvring abroad only served to exacerbate the rivalries in Shatila. The hard-core dissidents decided that they no longer had to "taint" themselves by co-operating directly with the Fatah-Arafat people and withdrew from the joint committees. The factions were now obliged to establish parallel committees. As a consequence, three newsletters were published in the camp. The first came from the Fatah-Arafat group – Ali Abu Toq wrote the political analyses himself – and the second from the pro-Syrian National Salvation Front. When the three hard-line pro-Syrian factions left the regular joint meetings, they often also had important political differences with their nominal allies. Thus, the PFLP–General Command, Saiqa, and Fatah dissidents began to publish a third newsletter, leaving the original in the hands of Omar's and Abu Moujahed's Popular Front, Basel's Popular Struggle Front, and the Palestine Liberation Front. The titles of all three were based on variations of the word *samoud*, Arabic for resistance, tenacity, or steadfastness, and indicative of everyone's state of mind.

These stenciled newsletters, comprising four or five pages, were at first published every two or three days, and then, due to a shortage of paper, weekly. They usually included an article giving the group's particular interpretation of political developments and diplomatic negotiations; other articles were intended to raise the morale of the people, or organize life and discipline in the camps.

> The revolutionary carries a weapon only as a continuation of the political struggle. Weapons are to be used to defend the people, not for pompous parading or to frighten and terrorize the common people.
>
> We are certain that everyone wishes to go to the hospital out of a sense of duty, love, kindness, and charity to comfort and be reassured of the health of a wounded brother or sister, father or mother, or child. This is an understandable human emotion and reaction; however, we are reminded of the expression "the love that kills." And this saying applies to all who visit the hospital. The wounded need rest more than discussion, quiet more than words. Make your visit brief and quiet, and give the others the chance to visit as well.

Still other pieces dealt with rationing of essential supplies or items concerning personal hygiene, preventive medical measures, and first aid were written by members of the hospital staff. This was especially necessary considering the difficult and overcrowded conditions in the underground bomb shelters. Other articles described to the camp defenders – basically a popular militia – military techniques and tactics.

The RPG

This is an effective weapon against armoured vehicles, ramparts, and personnel, yet is easy to use. The grenade is capable of penetrating 12 cm of steel or 30 cm of concrete if fired properly. One must observe the following points.

1. Reconnoitre well the firing location and the target, so as not to give away your position before shooting ans expose yourself to enemy fire.
2. Judge the distance of the target well.
3. Aim for the target's weak spot. For a tank, this is the juncture between turret and body. The tank will be immobilized if you hit its track, but will still be capable of shooting its cannon. The most protected parts are the tank's turret and front.
4. The angle of impact of the grenade should not be less than 70°, or else it will ricochet off.
5. Keep your mouth open at the time of firing, to prevent rupture of the eardrum.

And a final note, brother combatant ...

Keep your weapon and grenades clean and secure, and use them only when absolutely necessary.

And finally, there was always a poem or two. Among others, Dr. Khatib, the hospital's poet-in-residence, kept himself busy in between rounds of receiving wounded by putting his thoughts and feelings down on paper.

To the steadfast on the front of resistance,
your finger wrapped tight on the trigger,
to the brave in the trench of honour,
your head held high,

your lover and beloved await your return
to wrap their eager hands around you
and bestow kisses on your eyes and lips.

I suppose that in any situation of danger or stress, there will always be sensitive, artistic souls who will respond by writing poetry. Shatila was no exception to this, and the people in Shatila avidly read these poems. The newsletters were distributed in the shelters, at the fronts, and in the hospital. People would read every single word and recite the poetry out loud. I often walked into the emergency reception area late at night to find Dr. Khatib surrounded by a group of acolytes, their Kalashnikov rifles resting haphazardly on their knees, spellbound as he declaimed his latest creation. The culture and values that struggle engenders, and that were so obvious in the genius of improvisation and adaptation of the inhabitants of Shatila, were complemented by this literature of resistance. An underground literature, quite literally.

Our wireless set in the laboratory enabled us to communicate with the PRCS administrative offices in the Mar Elias camp and with the Haifa Hospital in Burj el-Barajneh. The director of the Burj hospital and I regularly exchanged statistics on the number of dead and wounded, since we were the source of such information for the political groups and the press. We also talked about medical supplies and how much we were using and what remained. Many of the staff in the hospital had friends and relatives among the personnel in both the Haifa and Mar Elias medical centres, and they often kept up a constant chatter of gossip and questions about the well-being of loved ones.

Many people in Lebanon apart from militias have such wireless sets. There are those who find it amusing to listen in and then interrupt important business, often using crude language and insults. We often kept under surveillance the Amal broadcasts, and they attempted to do the same with us. This meant developing a special code language and a programme of broadcast frequencies that we regularly changed and made known only to insiders. I eventually had to put severe limitations on the use of the wireless set; a long period of jabbering over useless affairs could easily give away our frequencies. This was one of the prerogatives and responsibilities of the hospital director, even if it angered some of the more gossipy personnel.

January 1, 1987: three wounded, none dead. Nabih Berri, the leader of Amal, had announced a cease-fire for New Year's Eve, but the tank fire and sniping continued, with a brief outburst of mortar shelling at midnight – a cynical celebration of the cease-fire.

It was no longer a question of overrunning the camp, but simply reducing it to rubble; close to ninety percent of Shatila already lay in ruins. With the tanks methodically pounding away, Burj el-Barajneh, large enough to hold several mortar launchers, often came to our aid. Palestinian fighters there regularly shelled Amal positions encircling us, effectively helping to relieve the pressure on Shatila. Palestinian artillery positions in the Socialist Party–controlled Shouf Mountains also entered the fray, devastating areas in the southern suburbs of Beirut and hitting Amal and Lebanese army military targets especially in the sports complex. Ali faxed precise locations to Tunis HQ through Cyprus, which faxed back instructions to their artillery in the mountains.

In Lebanon, one very quickly becomes an expert in the sounds of war. One notes the difference among shots fired from a revolver, a Kalashnikov AK-47 or an M-16 rifle, incoming versus outgoing mortars and artillery. This is the cacophony of destruction and death: the distinctive sound of each calibre of mortar shell, the boom of the tank cannon, the deep rumble of heavy artillery and Grad rockets.

A salvo of artillery fire or Grad rockets crashing into the Amal neighbourhood, the pressure waves of which would shake the entire hospital, was sufficient punishment to stop momentarily the bombardment of Shatila. The nurses and patients would explode in a shout of joy with each pressure wave; then a sigh of relief, echoing the blast more quietly. It meant that we were not alone, not forsaken, in spite of the hermetic siege.

With the tanks and their piercing shells still firing on us, Abu Moujahed and one of the seven joint committees continued to build sand fortifications in the camp's alleyways. They piled oil drums and house water reservoirs filled with sand and debris on top of one another to erect the ramparts. Dheeba was a twenty-year-old member of one of the committee's contingents. She was busy at work with Abu Moujahed when a sniper opened fire at them. A bullet hit a second-storey wall and ricocheted downward, hitting her just at the eyebrow, then, like a needle threading its way, passing through the upper eyelid, into the eyeball, out again at the edge of the lower eyelid, and down into her cheek. Her eye was totally destroyed and I had to remove what was left of it. She never removed the patch over the empty eye socket, and at first seemed embarrassed by her injury. There had been so many dead and gravely injured that she felt her wound to be a mockery. Abu Moujahed held her in his arms, calming her, explaining to her. "You were wounded while performing a dangerous and vital task. Consider yourself fortunate that it was not worse." He wiped away her tears before continuing. "You should be proud of your injury. It's a badge of courage. Wear it with pride!" The culture of hope and dignity was pervasive.

The battle in Shatila was now six weeks old. The hard-line pro-Syrian groups had at first believed that this was simply another round in the War of the Camps, another attempt at Syrian pressure on Arafat, and that a cease-fire would intervene rapidly. They had consumed their food, fuel, and ammunition stores without much consideration. Others, however, had realized that this was the decisive battle and that the siege of the camp would last a minimum of three months. The pressure from the continuing siege and the potential for conflict within the camp would become more critical as the probability of intra-Palestinian reconciliation increased. The dissidents' need provided a new impetus for the activities of the joint committees, since the main food stores were with the Fatah and the Popular Committee.

Abu Moujahed, head of the latter and affiliated with the Popular Front, refused to countenance the idea of distributing food to the military factions before the civilian population. Thus, Fatah and the Popular Committee pooled their food stores, now consisting of tinned and dry goods, and established the principle that all goods would be distributed among all residents of the camp equally. Priority was given to the wounded and ill, pregnant and lactating women, and children.

There were 492 families in the camp, and 834 children under the age of fifteen, half of them younger than six years of age. The hospital, with its ninety staff members and ten volunteers, outnumbered all but three of the political groups, and therefore counted as a unit on an equal footing with all the factions. The joint committee took into account not only food but also the special needs of the hospital for soap, bleach, and other cleaning items.

I met repeatedly with Abu Moujahed on the one hand, and Ali on the other, to organize the distribution of necessary items. We decided to start rationing everything in the camp. We thought that the siege would last at least three months, and we had to take into consideration that it might last even longer. Food, fuel, soap, water, cigarettes, and ammunition were to be strictly controlled. As the battle and siege continued, interminably, Shatila faced an administrative challenge. How to organize a harsh self-imposed discipline? manage drastic restrictions on everyday life? oversee a slow starvation?

In the hospital, we rationed more than food; laundry for the personnel was to be taken in by the washerwomen only once a week. I allowed each person one change of trousers or skirt, shirt, and undergarments. We still had between forty and fifty patients hospitalized and were laundering 100 sheets on a daily basis. Soap, water, wood for the fires, and even the washerwomen's energy, all had to be saved. Régine and the nurses from the OR stopped using the electricity-devouring dry-heat oven for sterilization. They used a non-electrical autoclave, a large pressure cooker that they placed on a wood fire. A special apparatus to provide distilled water for the laboratory produced a large quantity of boiling hot water run-off, and Régine delivered it to the kitchen or laundry for further use, to save on wood. To help create new habits and attitudes, we put up signs and posters throughout the hospital buildings: "Ration." "Save." "Fight waste."

We devoted all our energies to finding new methods and ways to cut down on the expenditure of vital goods. Only I could prescribe certain drugs and those I restricted to severe post-operative cases. Strict criteria regulated the use of certain antibiotics and analgesics. The nurses never threw away elastic bandages; soiled ones were gathered after wound dressings and were washed and sterilized for reuse. To save on gauze compresses, we cut them into smaller pieces. We still had relatively plentiful supplies in Shatila, but we wanted to be prepared for the worst.

The General Command and Fatah dissidents ate from the stores of Fatah, their political enemy. Their participation in the defence of the camp depended on ammunition, also supplied by Fatah. Once again, as in the Twenty- and Thirty-five-Day battles, they received food, cigarettes, and ammunition from their arch rivals. Ali Abu Toq knew that the defence of Shatila depended on every able-bodied man and woman doing his or her duty. For him, it was only natural that he supply his enemies from his own stores in the pursuit of a common goal. He also knew that it was politically astute.

In a series of bad days, some seem even worse than others. Another liver injury, then a sixty-year-old woman who had left her shelter for some unknown reason and was thrown against a wall by the pressure of an exploding shell, fracturing her skull and resulting in a concussion. Next came little Rana, a winsome girl of nine who had gone out to fetch some water. A mortar shell had turned her leg to pulp. I had to amputate.

With trepidation, I climbed the stairs of the underground operating theatre. I went slowly, half from sheer exhaustion, half from anxiety at having to face Rana's family. I was dealing with sudden death on a daily and even hourly basis, yet as I had noticed before on other battlefields, it was often easier to announce a death to friends and relatives than a mutilation, above all when dealing with a child. In the ill-equipped Third World, many handicapped persons can look forward only to a life of begging, and a mutilated female child makes for the best of beggars. At the least, the handicapped become a heavy burden on family and society. Announcing a mutilation to family and loved ones can therefore often be a pronouncement "worse" than death. "*Al-hamdulillah* – thank God – Rana is alive, but I could not save her leg." Rana's mother broke down in near-hysterical wailing and sobbing. Her father turned away, his eyes filled with tears, and whispered, "She's alive. *Al-hamdulillah*." But there is always hope. A year later, Rana would find herself in a Parisian hospital, being fitted for an artificial limb, thanks to the generosity of the French Ministry of Foreign Affairs.

Some tragedies came to feel like blessings. Dr. Khatib and his wife were first cousins, a common enough practice in the Middle East. But some gene was at work, afflicting them with several miscarriages and their two live-born children with congenital kidney disease – Fanconi syndrome. Saamer was one of those human tragedies who makes one wonder about the meaning of it all. Barely four years of age, he had the body of a two-year-old and the wizened, wrinkled face of an octogenarian. But he had a precocious maturity and intellect in a body racked by the ravages of an insidious disease. Belly bloated, skull and limbs emaciated, he drank huge quantities of fluids and ate little more than boiled potatoes. Every few months, he or his two-year-old sister, Fatima, suffered a new crisis — the quick, shallow, panting breath of acidosis; glazing over and rolling upwards of the normally overly bright eyes. The American University Hospital in Beirut had the necessary laboratory and expertise to handle them, but this was Shatila under siege, surrounded, bombarded. No one could enter or exit. We dared not even show our faces at the camp's periphery for fear of snipers, shelling, or tank fire. First Fatima and then shortly thereafter, mercifully, Saamer slipped into a coma and succumbed. Their torment was over, as was that of Dr. Khatib and his wife, who, knowing full well what to expect, had lovingly watched over and cared for their children.

After Saamer's death, I went straight to the ER from the hospital ward. Dr. Khatib looked at me, reading my face, my eyes. "It's over, isn't it?" he said.

"Their torment, your torment is over," I told him as we fell into each other's arms, tears streaming uncontrollably down our faces. Another burden lifted. Our common burden, though, one that was to drive us to our limits, was just at its beginning.

9

The Ironies of War

THE PALESTINE COMMUNIST PARTY WAS NOT AN OFFICIAL member of the PLO. It had never accepted the necessity of "armed struggle" – guerrilla warfare – as the only or even the most important way to liberate Palestine, and Palestinian Communists had accepted the existence of the state of Israel many years earlier. Most of its members were in the occupied territories, not in the Palestinian diaspora, as was the case with the guerrilla groups. In consequence, the PCP had only three members in Shatila: the leader, his wife, and one fighter. The fighter, Ali, was wounded and had lost a leg, had the other fractured and half his body burned. We spent weeks doing daily dressings for him, hours and hours of tedious, back-breaking work, trying to keep him clean and comfortable. Like Leila, he was slowly melting away. There was simply not enough high-protein food available to overcome his body's tissue breakdown. Ali then became frankly schizophrenic, hallucinating, hearing voices, and shouting at his grade school teacher, dead for at least ten years.

His schizophrenia made him very uncooperative and the job of caring for him that much more difficult. Once again, my colleagues and I found ourselves in an unfamiliar situation, frantically looking up in our medical texts the doses of heavy sedatives and psycholeptics necessary to treat him. We were tired and not really emotionally equipped to cope with psychiatric work. Moving between the mangled bodies in the operating theatre and the mangled psyche of Ali, I think that I probably started to hallucinate too. After a month and a half battling his burns, amputation, fracture, and infection, he died one night at midnight. While Ali was in his death throes, his leader's wife was in labour in the emergency reception. She gave birth to a child two hours after Ali's death, and the morbid humour of the camp had it that there were still three communists in Shatila.

The ironies of war are never-ending. Several days later, on January 27, 1987, Baha's wife came to the hospital at noon, in labour. Baha was Ali Abu Toq's second-in-command, more than ten years younger than Ali, less experienced and much less serious a leader, but he was kind-hearted and had been in Shatila since before the first round of fighting in 1985. He had been a hero of the resistance in that first battle and had never dared step outside the camp since for fear of the Syrian *Moukhabarat* and their repression of Arafat loyalists.

Even amidst carnage and death, there was new life. Ali Abu Toq and Baha sat in the waiting room outside the ER awaiting the news of the birth of Baha's child. We chatted and had a demitasse of our dwindling supply of coffee. Ali had passed by the hospital with Basel the previous night, and we had discussed plans for storing dried figs, dates, and nuts – non-perishable food stores – for the next battle, after this round was over. Basel, the military and security commander of the Salvation Front, and Ali Abu Toq, the Fatah and PLO leader, together — doing night rounds of the military fronts together, co-ordinating and planning together, visiting the hospital for a midnight meal and cup of tea together. We talked, as usual, about political and other developments. "What fools! What idiots!" Ali was beside himself. He raged on, "Did you see what these 'agents' did? Bombing the airports in Rome and Vienna. Listen, we are all in favour of the armed struggle, but *this* has nothing to do with the armed struggle." Everyone in the hospital agreed. Indeed, their anger at the actions of the terrorists created a certain uneasiness among the handful of members of the Abu Nidal faction present in the camp, whose group was held responsible for the airport attacks.

A squeal from the next room, a nurse popping her head out the door: "It's a boy!" A round of embraces and congratulations followed, and Ali, with Baha in tow, went off to do the rounds of the military fronts. A half-hour later an explosion resounded in the distance, and within minutes Baha and another fighter were brought back to the hospital, covered with blood and in a great state of confusion. Baha threw a sickly glance at me and said, "Giannou, brother Ali! Brother Ali has been wounded."

Within seconds, four men carrying a stretcher rushed into the ER and laid down their burden. I shoved them all out and locked the door behind them, leaving two nurses and me alone with Ali. I was afraid to look at the body. I knew, from having seen too many cases, that the limp arm hanging over the edge of the stretcher and the head thrown back at an irregular angle meant that Ali was dead. The two nurses with me moved away from the body, and I went over and mechanically examined him. There was a large, gaping hole in his neck and blood coming from his mouth. I called for an endotracheal tube and intubated him, fully realizing that he was dead and my actions useless. I went on anyway, trying not to think, not to feel, examining his pupils and checking his pulse. Finally, giving myself up to the cold clinical reality before me, I left the room and told the nurses to lock the door behind me.

Hearing that Ali Abu Toq had been injured, political leaders, ordinary fighters, women, the elderly, children had quickly filled the hospital. They stared at me standing in front of the ER door. I burst into tears, and all hell broke loose.

Ali Abu Toq was dead. People wailed and shrieked their anguish. Pandemonium: everyone wanted to see the body, touch it, if only just to convince themselves that this most selfless and beloved of men really was dead. It was impossible to clear the area. People pushed and shoved; some shouted for everyone to get outside, for the men to return to their posts on the fronts; others shouted that they wanted to get inside to see. Shots were fired into the air in the hospital alleyway and at the entrance to the emergency area in an attempt to clear out the people. Tempers flared. I clasped one of the men in my arms to stop him from shooting and disarmed him as we sobbed in each other's embrace.

Sobbing, weeping, shrieking crowds massed in the hospital alleyways. They finally cleared out after what seemed like interminable hours of pleading and cajoling. The men returned to the fronts on double alert, fearing that the news of Ali's death would reach Amal and provoke a sudden attack on the camp. The Amal militiamen might hope that the morale of the grieving defenders was broken, and they could thus gain a strategic advantage.

We buried Ali in the mosque – the seventy-fourth martyr of this round of fighting. And so we wept at the ironies of war. New life follows and precedes death; Ali Abu Toq is dead; long live Baha's son, Ali Ibn Baha.

We held many meetings to decide what to do next and how to organize things now that this pillar exemplifying the tenacity and resistance of Shatila was gone. Everyone, including his political enemies, praised him for his courage and honesty and his political, military, and administrative genius.

Witnesses said that a mortar shell had fallen directly into a trench that Ali, Baha, and two companions were passing through at the southern outskirts of the camp. Ali and another man had been killed, their bodies riddled with shrapnel travelling upwards. Baha had received only one shrapnel wound to the thigh and had been thrown up into the air by the explosion, as had the two dead men. The fourth man had escaped injury. The distribution of shrapnel and its entry into the bodies disturbed me, as well as the fact that the explosion had excavated a hole in the depths of the trench. This was not the work of a falling mortar shell. Something was wrong, terribly wrong.

The shell had been placed in the trench, buried, and set off by a wireless detonator. Months later, after much investigating and questioning, four men confessed to having planted an 82-mm mortar shell in the trench. They knew that Ali visited the men at all the fronts every day to inspect the fortifications, offer advice, hear their complaints, and keep up morale. This trench was the only passage to the southern front, and Ali had to use it, so they had hidden themselves and set off the shell just as Ali passed. The conspirators were members of the Fatah dissidents; in their videotaped confessions, they admitted that the military head of the dissidents in Shatila, Abu Firas, had given the orders for the assassination of Ali Abu Toq. Treason!

When we learned of this, the War of the Camps was not yet over, and the men of Shatila were still under siege. We did not make the information public, for fear that it would provoke internal fighting among the factions. It wasn't until much later that the facts became public, and by then it was too late to save Shatila.

10

Raw Goat's Liver: Breakfast, Anyone?

THE LOSS OF ALI WAS KEENLY FELT. BAHA AND AMINA, head of the Women's Union, member of the Palestine National Council and now the highest-ranking Fatah officer in Shatila, attempted to take charge of the many duties that had been Ali's. They divided between them his administrative, organizational, financial, political, and military responsibilities. Amina had always been very active and a good organizer, warm, kind-hearted, and honest. The children, women, and most men of Shatila loved and respected her. The Syrians and dissidents detested her, especially her efficiency and organizing capabilities. Despite many disagreements, we developed a good working relationship, speaking openly and frankly about political and social issues. A well-educated, broad-minded, and tolerant woman, with family living in Philadelphia, she understood Western society well. In our discussions – planning food distribution, care for the convalescent, social welfare services – we did not have to use the elaborate code language of usual Palestinian discourse, concealing difficult and embarrassing social and political realities behind a verbal screen of hypocrisy, modesty, and obfuscation; we could get down to the nitty-gritty immediately.

Ali's death had affected Amina deeply, and it took a while for her to overcome her grief and anguish. Ali's death had affected me as well. I had known him for years, worked with him in Nabatieh and Tripoli. He had confided in me, told me more than one political and administrative secret – the Palestinians, like everyone else, have their share of skeletons in various closets. It was he who, shortly after his arrival in 1985, had asked specifically that I be sent to Shatila to set up the hospital there. Amina was well aware of the special friendship and mutual respect that Ali and I had had. She asked me through her tears, almost reproachfully, "You've saved so many, Giannou. Couldn't you have saved brother Ali as well? Couldn't you save your friend?" How to explain to her, to myself? "Amina," I replied, "I couldn't save my own father and he died of cancer while I was doing my training in cancer surgery. I can't save myself. If there had been anything, *anything*, I could have done for brother Ali, you know that I would have done it. *It was written.*" The stereotypical fatalism of the Middle East – unacceptable in Shatila, which refused stubbornly to submit to a seemingly inevitable fate. This refusal of and resistance to fatalism was what empowered us, kept up our spirits, gave meaning to our sacrifice. Ali's death was part of that sacrifice. Unsuitable, incomplete as it was, fatalism was all that I could come up with in my sorrow and my struggle to comprehend. *It was written.*

Shaking off her sorrow, Amina assumed ever greater responsibilities in political leadership and administrative tasks, organizing distribution of food to the families and powdered milk to the children, raising the morale of the people and fighters. She was constantly moving about the camp, visiting the men at the fronts and the families in the shelters. But, as with all of us, fatigue and lack of sleep and food began to take their toll. People were almost literally melting away, and once plump friends now appeared with ribs sticking out and sunken eyes in darkened sockets. These conditions and the ongoing battle made us feel Ali's absence all the more acutely. As the siege continued, we would mutter to each other, "Where is Ali now that we really need him?"

Visiting any of the bomb shelters was an unforgettable adventure. One day in February 1987, for the first time since the fighting had begun, I went with Amina and Régine on their regular tour. We picked our way through the narrow alleyways clogged with rubble, climbed over the debris, dodged sniper fire, ever on the alert for a salvo of mortar shells that would catch us exposed. Rushing down a darkened stairway, we ran into a wall of human stench in the stagnant atmosphere of the poorly ventilated room. Eight hundred people – children, women, the elderly – had been living for months now in a room thirty by twenty yards, 600 square yards. Pepsi bottles filled with kerosene and then stuffed with a cloth wick provided a dim light barely strong enough to make it possible to make one's way through the jumbled crazy-quilt amalgam of bodies, mattresses, blankets, pots, pans, and rubbish strewn on the bare concrete floor. The smoke from the kerosene lamps stung the eyes and covered everything and everyone with a greasy, black soot. Horrendous living conditions, but the people had nowhere else to go. Even if there was a calm in the fighting, most of their homes had been destroyed or damaged and would not provide any shelter from the elements.

This was the largest of the three bomb shelters, and the newest. Ali Abu Toq had overseen its building during reconstruction of the camp early in 1986. Planned to accommodate 250 people comfortably, the crowding of 800 into its confines severely taxed the series of wash basins and four toilets, and the drainage system and water reservoirs underneath its floor. The hospital generator provided electricity several hours each day to run the ventilation fans and water and sump pumps. The other underground shelters, as well as the Awaini warehouse, were not nearly as large, or as well outfitted; the living conditions there were even more crowded and horrendous. The methodic shelling of the camp by tank fire had rendered the warehouse unsafe; those who had taken refuge there had been forced to join the others in the shelters, making worse an already overcrowded situation.

With one of the joint committees, the people in the shelters organized local committees themselves to deal with the basic needs of daily life. One dealt with water, the toilets, cleaning the rubbish, laundry. Another committee distributed food, soap, and kerosene from the pooled stores of the Popular Committee and Fatah, and organized "kneading sessions" to help prepare pita bread dough for the oven since the bakery machinery never seemed to finish on time due to the rationing of electricity.

As the battle wore on, less electricity, and therefore less water, was supplied to the shelters. Such a large number of people gathered in so small an area with very limited facilities for regular bathing and laundry meant that it was virtually impossible to maintain hygienic conditions. No matter how hard the committees and GPs who visited the shelters tried, after a couple of months of such overcrowded living, an epidemic of lice, scabies, gastroenteritis, and upper respiratory tract infections ravaged all the families. Without fresh air, fresh fruit and vegetables, and better living conditions, there was little that we could do.

The children especially suffered from the confining life underground. Virtually all the fathers were at the fronts or busy with repairs or fortification-building. The mothers had more than enough problems on their hands, trying to suppress the normal penchant of children for running around, playing, and making noise, without taking into account the tedious hours of unproductive talk that ultimately led to nothing but depression and frustration. There was simply not enough space, and everyone's nerves were on edge after weeks of listening to the continuous cacophony of war and the radio news broadcasts of cynical political manoeuvring.

Stopping the kids from leaving the shelter, a very dangerous thing to do, was very difficult. The committee in charge of the underground population set up classes for the children. Sometimes, they read stories to the children, who would then enact them as plays. There were also sessions of singing and joke- or story-telling. But, all too often, the only sounds emanating from the shelters were the screams and cries of sobbing children and the pleading voices of the mothers, whatever the political affiliation of their menfolk, imploring Arab, Muslim, and world public opinion to "not forget the victims of Shatila."

Many of these women had lived through the Massacre of 1982 and had lost loved ones then or in other rounds of the War of the Camps. Their sons, brothers, and husbands were in the trenches now. Who would return? Who would not? These questions troubled their waking and sleeping hours, and so they pleaded that the world not forget Shatila. The women did not suffer from factionalism, however. Their anxiety and pain were the shared emotions of the stereotype of "women during war" throughout history. "The men," whatever their political affiliation, were defending them all and were considered sons and brothers of them all. The better-educated women knew about the heroic resistance of the Warsaw Ghetto or Stalingrad during the Second World War and saw the parallels between those sieges and battles and what was now happening in Shatila. They knew, along with the men of Shatila, that their only salvation lay in their own capacity for sacrifice, resilience, and resistance.

Only sporadic barrages of shelling and tank fire interrupted the eerie silence of the alleyways, their walls blackened by explosions, blocked by ramparts – man-made or otherwise – of debris, rubble, and sand, and inundated with raw sewage and rainwater. Most military activity was confined to sniping that reached into the depths of the camp. The bombardments had levelled so many buildings on the periphery of the camp that snipers positioned in tall edifices up to a mile away could see into the bowels and central alleyways of Shatila. The people fled the shelters whenever possible, hoping to get away from the stench and cramped quarters and breathe a bit of fresh air, if only for a short while, and a few tried to return to the shambles of their former dwellings to salvage whatever they could from underneath the rubble. Naturally, they became targets for the snipers.

The weather had turned very cold; snow blocked the mountain roads of Lebanon at an altitude of less than 2,400 feet, and a freezing rain fell on the coast. The deluge of water cascaded down the hillsides of West Beirut, pooling in the Shatila gully. This created havoc, flooding our system of tunnels and trenches. The men took the few small portable electric generators to the fronts to run simple water pumps to drain the water and save the labyrinth of tunnels upon which depended the defence and survival of the camp.

The winter cold and rains added a bitter edge to our deprivation in the trenches, shelters, and hospital. We were numbed by the cold. Rain poured through the yawning holes in the roofs of the hospital buildings, pooling on top of the ceilings and slowly oozing through. The pressure of exploding shells had fissured the buildings, and water trickled down the walls of the emergency room and the patient ward. The staff in the cabaret spent many a cold and wet night as water cascaded down the walls. Mildew and fungus swept across the hospital walls in a slowly advancing blue-green sheet. The damp entered every nook and cranny, every bone. The men at the fronts broke up and burned whatever wood was not used to shore up the tunnel walls. Shatila was burning so that its inhabitants could keep warm.

Our generator provided the hospital with a few hours of electricity in the evenings. Visiting hours, from 5:00 to 8:00 P.M., deliberately limited as much as possible, saw the hospital invaded by an army of friends, relatives, and comrades-in-arms of the wounded. Visitors came to see the patients, or visit the visitors, or simply remind themselves what electric lighting looked like. For several hours every evening, a bustling, talkative humanity took possession of the cramped hospital quarters and turned them again into the social centre of the camp.

Abu Abed kept busy roasting his green coffee beans and then grinding them. According to the traditions of Middle Eastern hospitality, it would have been rude to distribute coffee only to the hospital staff, so I ordered that it also be served to any visitors present. I had received a barrage of requests from various friends and political leaders in the camp for coffee beans, and distributing coffee to the visitors seemed the best way to finish our supplies as quickly as possible. We would then have no coffee left, and our inability to hand it out would not offend anyone. It would relieve me of at least one headache.

The visitors engaged in long, detailed discussions of the military and political situations and the probable evolution of events; analyses poured forth. In spite of acute political differences and rivalries, everyone respected the neutral position of the hospital, and these discussions were all carried out in a polite and good-natured manner. Every day different political and military leaders made a round of the patients. They visited and gave encouragement not only to their own wounded, but to all the patients, including those of rival factions; the wounded, and the dead, belonged to everyone. Leila, by now emaciated from infection and her intestinal fistula, was a favourite of all, her bed surrounded by a horde of young men and women every day. Everyone admired her courage.

I allowed no weapons into the hospital among the visitors; all guns were checked at the door. I wanted no "accidents" to happen on the hospital premises. I had seen too many over the years in weapon-laden Lebanon and had read how in any "classical army" there was a certain attrition rate due to "accidents" – someone shooting himself in the foot, or shooting a friend in the head ... "by accident." A number of young men objected to giving up their weapons, but my reputation in the camp for imposing strict military-type discipline, and my withering stare and sharp tongue, were well known. The young fighters feared me more than any perceived affront to their machismo when obliged to check their weapons.

We were rationing everything by this time and the smokers received only ten cigarettes per day. It was known that I had bought a large private stock of cigarettes just before the battle had broken out. I smoke strong unfiltered Gitanes, and the men believed that one of my French cigarettes was equivalent to several of theirs. It was also well known that I quite liberally offered them to any smoker present, in spite of the rationing. I discovered this was a good and easy way to placate any young fighter with a ruffled ego.

Anyone now going around the camp confronted a transformed Shatila. Lakes of stagnant water and mountains of debris and rubbish filled the narrow crooked alleys, along with hordes of rats – the only beings that seemed to thrive under the circumstances. Dust-filled air and burnt-out buildings gave everything a dull grey-ochre tinge. The central square garbage dump overflowed. After shells had landed amidst the rubbish, soiled dressings, broken syringes, and rotting, fermenting food spewed over the ground. The rains continued, and it was impossible to incinerate the refuse. The camp had become one soggy mass.

Shrapnel had riddled the water pipes and direct mortar hits twisted them into mangled heaps resembling works of abstract sculpture. Water spewed forth and added to the wet and stench of the camp whenever the water pump functioned. Abu Moujahed and his crew were constantly closing off mains to prevent the loss of water and redirect the flow through a new network of pipes that they constructed time and time again. The well water inside the camp remained clean, and although it had a heavy mineral content, was drinkable. Across the main street, in the western sector under the Amal ramparts in the sports stadium, this was not the case. The water supply that came from the municipality was tainted by the sewers.

In mid-February, Ra'id, a nineteen-year-old fighter from the western sector, made the journey via the tunnels under S-S Street and came to the hospital. He presented all the classic signs of a ruptured appendix and localized peritonitis. He had a mild fever that he said he had developed three weeks previously. This did not square with the diagnosis, but his tender and rigid abdomen necessitated an immediate operation, nonetheless. The appendix was healthy, but there was a small linear perforation about one foot up the small gut. I closed up the hole and cleaned out the pus. I thought back to my tropical pathology – central to medical training in Egypt – and recognized a typhoid ulcer. Perforation of the small intestine is one of the classical complications of typhoid fever. Now we were faced with a new menace that could easily decimate Shatila more readily than bullets or bombs – typhoid fever.

Over a period of about ten days, another seven young men from the military front in the western sector complained of fever, lassitude, loss of appetite, and irregular bowel movements or constipation. The cases stank of typhoid. Our laboratory could not perform the necessary serological tests to confirm the diagnosis, but I nonetheless placed all the suspected cases on the standard antibiotic regimen.

We had to mobilize, and quickly. The feared contamination of the water supply from damaged sewers and pipes had taken place, at least in the western sector. The mingling of sewage and water can be deadly, leading not only to typhoid, but also to hepatitis and a score of other diseases. Treatment and quarantine were readily taken care of. I called Abu Moujahed and asked him to prepare one of the joint committees. It would be their responsibility to educate the most exposed young fighters in adapting measures of personal hygiene to the conditions of the trenches and tunnels. How to filter, boil and chlorinate water while shells landed all around, or snipers' bullets whizzed by: the logistics were by no means easy.

The fighting continued in a more subdued but nonetheless deadly manner. Massive shelling no longer resulted in great masses of wounded and four to five major operations per day. But snipers' high-velocity bullets could wound seriously, and we fell into a routine of one or two major cases, day in and day out. Exhaustion, boredom, and frustration made the young men at the fronts negligent, and the people who came out of the shelters to fetch water or simply to stretch their legs were all too often easy prey. One spot by a water faucet became particularly lethal: three women were killed and eight wounded, on separate occasions, while filling water cans there. The human toll, too often the result of carelessness and negligence, angered me no end. I was constantly splattered with blood, regularly wakened from a fitful sleep to operate, because someone was fed up with going through a tunnel or trench.

I had operated on Fida during the 1983 fighting in Tripoli – a head wound. When he arrived in Shatila he came by the hospital to visit me regularly. So regularly, in fact, that he soon developed a romantic relationship with one of our nurses. His visits to me as his former doctor became more frequent, if shorter in duration, and served as an excellent pretext to see his sweetheart. Finally, he asked me to serve as his wedding guarantor. One day, while moving from a trench to a tunnel, he tarried too long. The last time he came to the hospital, he had a bullet through the heart.

The work of the doctors in the emergency room had improved enormously. Once, the nurses called me frantically to the ER, where I found Dr. Khatib covered with blood – which had also hit the ceiling – calmly standing beside a patient with his stubby index finger stuck in a hole in the man's neck, quietly giving orders to the nursing staff to set up the intravenous lines and take blood samples. He had recognized from the leaping spurt of bright red blood an injury to the carotid artery in the neck and had inserted his finger in the wound, effectively closing off the laceration in the vessel and stopping the haemorrhage. I told him to stay exactly as he was, which he did all the way over to Faramawi's building, walking beside the stretcher down the staircase to the operating table, while we scrubbed up and draped the patient. I sterilized his hand and the patient's neck with iodine and cut with the scalpel around his finger, which he removed only after I had placed vascular clamps on the vessel. A ricocheting sniper's bullet had struck the edge of the carotid, which was easily repaired with a vein patch graft. The patient had lost very little blood, in fact, and owed his life to Dr. Khatib's finger.

The fighting ground on through the bitter cold and rains of February 1987, with no end in sight, and we decided to ration our food and supplies even more drastically. We stopped using fuel oil for the hearth of the bread-baking oven and burned wood instead. We reserved all fuel oil for the large generators that supplied electricity to the water pumps and hospital, but our main generator was using far too much fuel per hour. To cut down on electricity consumption, we used our series of switches in the hospital to provide current only for those areas and tasks that were absolutely necessary.

It occurred to me that we did not really need the amount of electricity produced by our generator. Eissa, an electrical engineer who worked with the repair committee, and I sat down and, instrument by instrument, appliance by appliance, light bulb by lamp, we calculated the minimal electrical expenditure we absolutely needed to receive and treat a wounded patient. The culture of resistance, from poetry to physics.

"Eureka!" We discovered that it was possible to turn switches and equipment on serially as a patient went from one room to another on the way to the operating theatre while using a small gasoline-run 5-kva generator. Furthermore, by strict control of the serial distribution of electric current through the hospital by means of our network of fuses and switches, we could operate on one patient in the OR and receive another in the ER at the same time. We set up a new protocol. With each patient the hospital workmen would run about, throwing switches, breaking fuses, turning lights on and off. The electric current followed the wounded patient as his or her trolley meandered from ER to X-ray room; the blood samples to the laboratory; finally to the operating theatre. More ingenious improvisation: the culture of resistance, from poetry to physics to administration.

This little 5-kva generator provided less than one-tenth the energy of our large diesel one, but used less than one-tenth the fuel. I had been terrified at the thought that hospital work would grind to a halt because of a lack of electricity – now I knew we could go on. I was jubilant, but anger mixed with my joy when I realized the waste. We had used the large diesel generator for months, wasting enormous amounts of fuel. I cried and laughed, laughed and cried, slapped my forehead and pulled at my hair. Eissa watched me in bemused bewilderment and just smiled quietly.

Saving on our electrical needs meant that we could use all the diesel fuel remaining to run our large generator for the water pump alone. Two hours per day sufficed to fill what was left of the water reservoirs in the camp. In the bakery, the committee would have to arrange their machine-kneading within those two hours; the women in the shelters and even the hospital would do the rest. We could cut our fuel consumption enormously, but we also had to cut our water consumption.

We had several large freezers in the hospital, and during the month before the battle Rabiha and Oum Mohammed Faramawi had loaded them with frozen chickens, fish, and meat. Whereas at the beginning of the siege, the hospital staff and patients each ate a quarter chicken per meal – meaning some thirty or forty chickens in all – two months into the battle, we were preparing ten chickens for 120 people. In another couple of weeks, we stopped serving chicken to the hospital staff and reserved the remainder for the patients alone, as we did with all the cheese and most of the powdered milk. From the very beginning, I had decided that our ample supply of eggs should go only to the wounded.

Faramawi's hens provided an extra ten eggs per day, a pittance for forty patients, but they helped to stretch our supply, as did the goats and sheep for milk. We were rationing drastically; every few days, we decreased the quantities of everything – water, soap, bread, rice, dried beans and lentils, canned goods, cooking oil, sugar, and cigarettes.

As the siege continued, we slaughtered the goats and sheep one by one, providing fresh meat for the patients. We were quite hungry though not yet starving, when we slaughtered our last goat. We served up a Middle Eastern delicacy: raw goat's liver for breakfast. Of course, the amounts involved were not very great, but the event raised the morale of the fighters and families immeasurably. Shatila was besieged and ninety percent destroyed, cold and damp. Hunger stalked the inhabitants – the men at the fronts had a tin of sardines and one piece of pita bread each as an entire meal – but the people of Shatila cheered and laughed when they heard the news that the hospital patients had received a gourmet meal of raw goat's liver. They joked about whether or not it was accompanied by the traditional glass of *araq* – a Lebanese anisette. The fighters visiting the hospital also joked about getting wounded in order to exchange their sardines for raw liver.

Rationing in the hospital extended to medical supplies as well as water, fuel, and food. We invented all sorts of little tricks to economize on medicines, dressings, and suture materials. We also learned the importance of working rapidly, as there was only one operating theatre available, and several wounded could easily arrive while the theatre was occupied. After more than two months of operating, we had finished our supplies of oxygen and anaesthesia gas. News got out, and not a few people passed by the hospital, consternation etched into their gaunt features, wondering if we could continue to function. I reassured them, telling them that even without oxygen and gas, we still did not lack for anaesthesia. "The hospital," I told the more incredulous and suspicious, "can hold out longer than the military defences."

We had fortunately had the foresight to stock a sufficient supply of Ketalar (ketamine), a wonder drug in war surgery. Given by intramuscular or intravenous injection, or better yet as a continuous IV drip mixed in a litre of ordinary physiological saline, it induces a type of anaesthesia called "sensorial dissociation." Add a little bit of Valium, pethidine, and a muscle relaxant, intubate the patient, ventilate, and cut away. This little cocktail permits the performance of major surgery without canned oxygen, using ordinary air with its normal twenty percent oxygen content. It was both simple and safe.

All the euphoria and jubilation about goat's liver, electricity, and operating without oxygen and gas were tempered by stark reality. We were all hungry and rapidly losing weight; there was little available in the way of protein dietary supplement, one gourmet meal notwithstanding. An emaciated, beleaguered Leila, with an intestine that simply refused to heal, developed another infection that burrowed its way into her repaired blood vessels. Another couple of operations were useless in attempting to save her, and she died with a sudden gush of bright red blood mixed with the pus and liquid faeces of her fistula. Her friends and the nursing staff were heart-broken. Over the last two and a half months, they had spent countless hours of gentle care and difficult nursing work keeping her clean, alive, and in high spirits. When Leila had first recovered, we had been euphoric in the midst of death and suffering. Now we were despondent. In Shatila, sometimes we managed to cheat death; sometimes it only appeared for a while as though we had.

By the beginning of February 1987, we were down to two meagre meals a day; by mid-February, we had no bread; and by the end of February, we had only four hours of electricity and were eating fewer than 1,000 calories per day. Supplies were dwindling rapidly, and starvation loomed in the not too distant future.

11

The Pangs of Hunger Gnaw at the Belly

LIFE GOES ON, EVEN UNDER SIEGE. A TOTAL OF THIRTY-five women brought forth new life amidst the death and devastation of Shatila. A couple of general practitioners who had previously served as gynaecology-obstetrics residents, and three midwives, who did most of the work – apart from the mothers, of course – performed the normal deliveries. I intervened only if there was a complication and performed one Caesarian during the siege. Children born at the beginning of the Six-Month Battle were a full five months old by the time of the cease-fire, and there were another eighty-three infants less than one year of age in the camp. With this number of newborn and small infants, we deemed it necessary to immunize them, even during the battle. Part of the routine of our preventive medicine services in peacetime was to provide vaccinations, so we had the necessary vaccines available. With the "barefoot doctors" of the Women's Union, the two obstetrics doctors organized three rounds of vaccinations. The Women's Union committee went around to the shelters, making up lists of infants in need of inoculation, and informed the mothers of the timetable for the shots at the hospital.

The periodic shelling and tank fire were becoming more and more irregular. Amal and the Lebanese army brigades had turned Shatila into rubble, pounded it to dust. Any further attempts at heavy shelling were met with salvos from Palestinian artillery positions in the mountains falling on the Shi'ite-inhabited southern suburbs of Beirut and Amal positions. With the exception of sniper fire, the military pressure eased. The hunger increased, and it was obvious by now that, unable to overcome the refugee camps militarily, Amal was trying to starve us into submission. The news from Rashidieh was alarming. They had finished all their food stores and had resorted to eating grass. Many paid with their lives in attempts to sneak out of the camp and gather fruit from the surrounding orchards to take back into Rashidieh; in spite of this, they managed to provide a steady supply of oranges and bananas to sustain the camp's inhabitants. In Burj el-Barajneh, they had apparently waited too long to institute radical rationing, had eaten too much, and now were lacking; the situation there was also critical.

In early February 1987, the team of foreign volunteers working in Burj el-Barajneh – sent by Medical Aid for Palestinians–U.K. and led by Dr. Pauline Cutting, an English surgeon, and Susan Whighton, a Scottish nurse – published a desperate press release, which the PRCS offices in Mar Elias distributed to journalists in West Beirut. It told of the dire conditions prevailing in Burj el-Barajneh, the imminent starvation of the inhabitants who had even asked religious leaders for a dispensation to allow them to eat human flesh. A couple of mules, along with the cats and dogs of Burj el-Barajneh, had already gone the way of our goats and sheep. The news we received from Haifa

Hospital over our wireless set and from the political factions described the situation there as threatening and borderline. The camp was in danger of falling.

I had met Pauline Cutting when she first arrived in Lebanon the previous year. Sol-Britt, the Swedish co-ordinator of the foreign volunteers, had come to me one day to announce that a British surgeon would be arriving. We planned to send her to Burj el-Barajneh, so that both camps in Beirut would then have a surgeon permanently present. But before sending her off to Burj, I told Sol-Britt to bring Pauline into Shatila for a week of orientation. Pauline was thin and pale-looking and was to become much thinner. Although enthusiastic about the work she was about to undertake, she appeared to have some misgivings, not knowing if she would be able to function well in the primitive conditions – compared to British hospitals – or if she would fit in. But function she did, and brilliantly.

Pauline and Susie were now issuing appeals through the press to lift the siege on the refugee camps. They described the horrendous conditions in the bombed Haifa Hospital and Burj in many interviews over the wireless set. They and their foreign volunteer colleagues categorically rejected the possibility of leaving the camp, preferring to starve with these refugee people and only relieving their own hunger when that of the camp's residents was similarly assuaged. I was surprised that the situation in Burj el-Barajneh had become so extreme. This other camp in Beirut did have a larger population than Shatila, but it also had larger food stores. Also, many of our supplies had been buried and lost under the rubble of destroyed buildings. The extent of destruction in Burj el-Barajneh was great, but still far less than in Shatila. The inhabitants had been under siege almost a month longer than we had, but apparently administration of the camp was less well-organized, and the rationing less strict. We had also had Ali Abu Toq.

Although the situation in Shatila was not yet as dire as in Burj el-Barajneh, we were hungry and had spent two and one-half months hungry, severely rationing our food supplies by eating 1,000 calories or fewer per day. There was no end in sight to the siege and fighting, but we never felt desperate. Some of the men did, however, slaughter and roast a few cats (there were no dogs or mules in Shatila); the only problem was that there were not enough cats to go around.

If Burj el-Barajneh were to succumb out of starvation, then the Amal militia would double the pressure on Shatila. We prepared plans to outstrip any such eventuality. I met with Omar, Basel and Baha. They asked me how many medical supplies remained and what our capacity for receiving wounded was. I understood that they were planning a military initiative. There were residential areas not far from Shatila, the population of which had fled at the beginning of the battle. We knew that in those abandoned houses there would be food supplies – sacks of rice, sugar, dried legumes, and canned goods. The strategy was to make a sortie, attack and occupy this residential area for a brief period – twelve hours would do – gather up what food we could find in the houses and bring it back into the camp. We would have to count on the element of surprise to succeed in this venture. We planned with the knowledge that it might cost us fifty to a hundred dead: the price to pay to save the more than 3,000 people from starvation.

By mid-February 1987, the camp had suffered 95 dead and 650 wounded, and we had performed more than 150 major operations in the theatre. I told Omar, Basel, and Baha that we had enough supplies to perform another 100 major operations entailing at least 500 wounded, with one exception: our supply of blood bags was running low. If we could somehow solve this problem, then the medical facilities would not have to limit any military action they were contemplating.

In modern medical practice, transfusion sacks consist of sterile plastic bags for single use; they contain a special mixture that prevents donated blood from coagulating and provides nourishment for the red blood cells. In this way, blood banks can store donated blood for up to three or four weeks. We had started the battle with 450 bags; we were now down to about 60.

Omar's PFLP in West Beirut had contacted several of the Lebanese soldiers involved in the siege and bribed them to throw satchels of various medical supplies from their positions across one of the roads into the camp. Late at night, the soldiers tossed the satchels, which never seemed to land in the right place. Powerful searchlights swept the rubble-strewn street on the camp's periphery. The PFLP men crawled stealthily out from their positions to retrieve these vital supplies, keeping their bodies close to the ground to avoid being seen by snipers. In this way, we received another forty blood bags, but it did not solve our problem; one severely injured patient could use as many as thirty units of blood, and should our military plan ever be carried out, the available blood bags would not be nearly enough for the expected number of wounded. We had to find another way.

The head of the laboratory and I had already discussed alternative methods. We ruled out direct blood transfusions from donor to recipient using a large syringe – Dr. Norman Bethune's mobile, on-the-battlefield transfusion technique during the Spanish Civil War – as being too unwieldy. Eventually we came up with two solutions – recycling bags through an unorthodox but effective method, and using glass bottles – another return to an old-fashioned technology, out of use in the West for more than twenty years – which were easier to resterilize.

Our blood supply, of course, came from Shatila's inhabitants. The women and non-combatants constituted the first source. We tried to avoid having the men at the front donate blood, since we didn't really need them. There were always great numbers of people, more than necessary, ready and willing to give their blood. Everyone on the hospital staff donated, and many gave twice during the battle. More than once we gave a pint and then immediately went down to the theatre to operate.

Slowly, more and more problems arose, exacerbating the predicament of the people in the besieged camp. A one-month-old child developed meningitis. A young woman with rheumatic valvular disease, who a year previously had been advised to have heart surgery, succumbed, drowning in the froth of her soggy, overburdened lungs. Several of the elderly suffered from the usual gamut of geriatric ailments – hypertension, diabetes, emphysema, asthma, and cardiac conditions. The overcrowded living conditions and intense humidity of the shelters were throwing the more frail into outright heart failure. We had two children, aged five and nine, who possibly had cancer, and few means at our disposal for making a proper diagnosis, let alone treating them. The five-year-old probably had an abdominal lymphoma with involvement of the kidneys and nephrotic syndrome, and kept pissing away the proteins of his body. His belly bloated, and there was not enough high-protein food left in the camp to compensate for his losses. The other child had a possible brain tumour; we put him on steroids to control his headaches, vomiting, and dizziness. But what could I say to the parents? How to alleviate their concern, anguish, and sense of helplessness? We would have to wait for an eventual cease-fire and lifting of the siege; the children could be dead by then. Our meagre means in the Shatila field hospital were sorely stretched. Performing surgery on wounded but otherwise healthy young adults was one thing; dealing with complex cases of internal medicine was another. How to alleviate *my* concern, anguish, and sense of helplessness? We could invent and improvise, but there was a limit to what we could do, and that limit tore me apart.

Outside the besieged camps, in the real world, negotiations continued at a desperate pace to reach some solution before mass death through starvation overcame the inhabitants of Shatila, Rashidieh, and Burj el-Barajneh. Under the pressure of the War of the Camps, contacts among Palestinian leaders were rapidly approaching a reconciliation and reunification of the major groups in the PLO. An Islamic Summit Conference was held at the end of January 1987; thanks to the press releases from Burj el-Barajneh and others that I began issuing from Shatila describing the horrendous conditions, the War of the Camps was a prime topic of discussion. On January 30, Palestinian fighters in the town of Maghdushah turned over their positions to the Hizbollah and troops of the principal Lebanese militia of Sidon. An Iranian delegation was busy in the south supporting the role of the cleric who was starving with the people in Rashidieh (Iranian influence with the Lebanese Shi'ite population was extensive). The delegation arranged a cease-fire around Rashidieh and the entry of food into the camp, then rushed off to Sidon, where they negotiated an end to the fighting there. The Iranian initiative then shifted to Beirut. A convoy from the Iranian embassy, with ambulances and UN food trucks, attempted to enter Burj el-Barajneh on

February 13. Amal militiamen opened fire and killed an embassy bodyguard. A tremendous outcry arose; Amal was quickly losing its political support within the Lebanese Shi'ite community. The Iranian Shi'ite clergy were calling the siege of the Palestinian refugee camps "unholy, inhumane, and contrary to Muslim principles." They demanded that Amal end the fighting. As for Amal itself, its losses had been great during the hostilities, and militiamen were abandoning the pro-Syrian movement in droves to join the pro-Iranian Hizbollah.

On February 17, 1987, calm reigned around Shatila, but war raged in the streets of the city. Ever since the West Beirut uprising of 1984, the sectarian leadership of the Shi'ite Muslim community – Amal – had tried to impose its hegemony and become the representatives of "Nationalist Lebanon," and thus the privileged interlocutors of the right-wing Phalangists in East Beirut. However, Amal militiamen had been harassing the civilian population of West Beirut – Sunni and Shi'ite Muslims, Christians still living there, and Palestinians – outclassing anything that had happened previously. Rampaging through the streets of the city, the militiamen used politics as an excuse for simple gangsterism. The two main Lebanese political parties sharing control of West Beirut with Amal, the Socialists and Communists, considered Amal's actions to have gone beyond the limits of the tolerable and also considered Amal to have been weakened by the latest round of the War of the Camps, entering its fifth month without respite. The left-wing coalition now waged battle with the militiamen of the Amal Movement.

Civilians disappeared from the city streets, which were taken over by ragtag militiamen – experts in street fighting in built-up urban areas after more than a decade of civil strife. Mortar fire, rocket-propelled grenades, heavy machine guns, and tanks echoed throughout the divided city. The coalition of Socialist and Communist parties was pushing back Amal at strategic points everywhere in the city. Their front lines were approaching Shatila, where we listened intently to the radio and our CB receivers, twenty-four hours a day, following the developing battle. Would the left-wing coalition, the remnant of the Lebanese National Movement, lift the siege of the

Palestinian refugee camps? Would they break the back of the much detested Amal Movement? Should the camp become involved in this intra-Lebanese fighting among Syrian allies; enact the planned sortie and attack Amal positions from the rear; aid the left wing in breaking Amal and the siege? We listened to the news, and waited.

Some Lebanese, right- and left-wing, had criticized the Palestinians before for entering the fray of intra-Lebanese fighting during the civil war, while others had specifically sought Palestinian military support. Now, after 1982, the evacuation of PLO cadres, the Massacre, the years of repression and siege, the Palestinian refugee districts had one overriding and preponderant goal: survival.

The anti-Palestinian Amal and the pro-Palestinian left-wing parties, fighting it out for control of West Beirut, were both allies of Syria. Lebanese rules of engagement: Who are the friends of my friends? friends of my enemies? enemies of my enemies? In this four-cornered labyrinth with intertwining two-way passages, interests rather than principles governed action. The new battle between the rival Syrian allies, paralysing the city and frightening the inhabitants, was like quicksand to the Palestinians; they had to either stay out or sink.

Fighting in the streets of West Beirut ravaged the city for five days. The civilian population complained of the ferocity of the hostilities and of being isolated in their homes, taking refuge in basement shelters and stairwells without water or electricity. (Five days: we had been at it for months!) Prominent Lebanese politicians and religious leaders requested that Syrian troops positioned in the eastern Beqa'a valley be redeployed to West Beirut to put an end to the fighting and assume security responsibilities alongside the official Lebanese army.

On February 22, 1987, 7,000 Syrian troops entered West Beirut for the first time since their evacuation in 1982 during the Israeli invasion. The fighting ended between its nominal allies, the Communist and Socialist coalition, and its cherished ally Amal. Syria was the guarantor, the "big brother." The Palestinians had not entered the quicksand; they had not become involved. But our problems were not yet over. The camps remained under siege and the Iranian initiative, which had gained results in the south, was dead.

Syrian motives greatly influence much of what happens in Middle Eastern, Lebanese, and Palestinian circles. Syria has vital historical ties to and interests in Lebanon. More important, the regime wishes to ensure its role as the most important Arab party, a position of leadership, in any international negotiations on the Middle East. A priori, however, Syria cannot claim this position; Egypt, Saudi Arabia, Iraq, all have better substantiated claims. Syria's will to political supremacy depends, in its view, on the ability to control Lebanon, the abscess of the region, and the PLO. Syria believes that it, and only it, must hold the Lebanese and Palestinian cards in any Middle East peace game, if it is to play the leadership role to which it aspires. The fighting in West Beirut, the return of Syrian troops to the city, the siege of the refugee camps, were all part of that strategy.

The Syrian army was a classical army with the authority and responsibility of the state. (The *Moukhabarat* were, as ever, in the city, but acted surreptitiously.) The army could be held legally and politically responsible and could not engage in the covert operations of the intelligence service. The Syrians were in Beirut ostensibly to put an end to the street fighting – all fighting – at the request of legal Lebanese authorities. But Shatila was at the juncture of West Beirut and the southern suburbs, Burj el-Barajneh deep within the suburbs. Did Syrian deployment include the area around the refugee camps which would put an end to the siege legally and officially? Yes, but not quite yet.

Still, Amal and the Lebanese army units could no longer use their positions in West Beirut or in the sporting stadium to shell us. They could not fire off their mortars in front of Syrian soldiers who were supposed to control the streets and prevent firing; and any mortar fire from Amal positions would provoke a Palestinian response. Shells could fall on the Syrians. With Syrian troops less than a mile from Shatila, bombardment of the camp ceased; it was no longer politically permissible. But sniper fire from the tall buildings surrounding Shatila, where Syrian troops were not deployed, could continue. The rules of war, Lebanese style.

Members of the hard-line pro-Syrian factions in Shatila literally danced when they heard of the entry of Syrian soldiers into Beirut.

Many of them were from and had families living in the Yarmouk refugee camp in Damascus, and they were delighted at the thought that the Syrian presence in West Beirut would not only save the camp from starvation, but would also give them strategic leverage in their rivalry with Arafat's Fatah. They preferred to forget that many Palestinians in the Yarmouk camp, their kinsmen if not cousins, had demonstrated in the streets, condemning Syrian responsibility and complicity in the War of the Camps and had been brutally and bloodily repressed by those same Syrian troops.

The battle was not over. Sniper fire continued even if the mortars had stopped. The siege and hunger raged on.

12

The Pangs of Hunger Gnaw at the Spirit

AFTER SYRIAN TROOPS HAD ENTERED WEST BEIRUT, THE oppressive weight of the physical deprivations of everyday life under siege took over from the awesome destruction and fear of violent death from shelling. The rains had more or less ended. People moved out of the shelters and into the few remaining buildings of the camp, houses with half a wall missing or with huge holes in the ceilings – anything to get out of the stench of the cramped underground quarters. But this did not put an end to the overcrowding. Now people lived twenty to a two-room, half-destroyed house. Still, they were aboveground and had some fresh air and sunlight. They scavenged for wood and broke up pieces of furniture to build fires for cooking and simply to keep warm. We strictly reserved all fuel for the few functioning generators and the vital services that they made possible.

The hospital staff continued to adapt and improvise to keep things going. We were down to four, then two hours of electricity per day. The large diesel generator that also worked the water pumps provided for half the allotted time; the other half came from the small gasoline-powered generator. There were always problems with the water supply, with pipes breaking or falling apart; and as the people came out of the shelters, lice- and scabies-infested, there was an ever greater demand for water for doing laundry and bathing. Soap was in short supply. Sometimes we did not have enough water in the hospital and had to scrub up for an operation using sterile physiological saline, sparingly poured over our hands and forearms. Fortunately, we had rather large stores. Still, we invented an economizing ritual for hand-washing.

Boiling in water is a sterilizing method that cannot be used for dry supplies such as gauze compresses, towels, or surgical gowns. These are sterilized in the pressure-cooker autoclave. Régine and her operating theatre troops were kept busy stooping over the hearths, cooking up endless batches in their wood-fire autoclaves.

With momentous political developments abroad, and a new and precarious situation in West Beirut, we needed to keep in touch with the outside world. All the political factions maintained contact with their political leaderships outside the camp by means of CB radios that ran on electricity – either the AC supply from a generator (which now functioned only in the hospital), or DC from a charged car battery. The room next to the hospital kitchen, where we kept the small generator, now became the centre for recharging the camp's batteries.

Our rolls of extra wire came out of the store room, and the camp's electricians changed the wiring of the hospital's fluorescent lights and the laboratory's centrifuges to allow them to function on car batteries as well. The nursing staff could continue to take patients' observations and give medications by the light of the neon lamps. And for routine blood tests, the lab technicians used the Sahlé technique – based on the naked eye and a standard colour chart – described in the historical medical literature and the first known method for haemoglobin estimation.

We had long since finished our stores of candles. Some men had manufactured candles from sand, ash, and lard, but by now we had eaten the last of the lard. Looking through the meagre remaining stores in the warehouses, we came upon several camping lamps and two cartons of propane cartridges. One cartridge provided six hours of bright light. These I had Régine hide away in the OR, for the day we had no electricity left whatsoever. I tried not to, but was obliged to think about what we would do if the siege continued to the point where we no longer had fuel for the generators or propane cartridges for the camping lamps. Operate by sunlight in an alleyway? And at night – build a bonfire?

With ever stricter rationing of water, food, and electricity, we adapted our equipment and routines to keep on working, but hunger and exhaustion were taking their toll, and we wondered how long we could keep on working. At about this time, Abu Mohammed Faramawi came to me one evening with a naughty gleam in his eye. He asked to see me in private, inquiring if there were any scraps of dry bread available. A rocket had hit the wall of his second-storey home in the hospital building some months before, and the family's entire stock of flour, rice, sugar, beans, oil, olives, and pickled peppers had been tossed about by the explosion and lay scattered on the kitchen floor. It had been impossible to sift through the mess to salvage anything, with the exception of one intact jar of black Russian caviar that Faramawi now slipped out of his pocket. Abu Mohammed Faramawi, who had become like an elder brother to me, was here to share this treasure. We scrounged about the hospital pantry and managed to come up with a few crusty bits of bread. We laughed at our caviar feast, regretting only that there was no vodka with which to wash it down. We laughed, the only thing left to do, for we knew very well just how quickly we were all losing weight and beginning to look like scarecrows in our baggy, threadbare clothes.

Starvation was proving to be as debilitating as the siege itself. The local and international press were full of reports, pleas, and communiqués emanating from the besieged camps, telling of the plight of the people in Shatila, Burj el-Barajneh, and Rashidieh. The foreign volunteers in Burj el-Barajneh, and Régine and I in Shatila, spoke daily to journalists in Mar Elias and abroad over the CB wireless sets and cellular telephone. The hospital had been a social-centre not just for Shatila's inhabitants; international press correspondents had come regularly to the refugee district, especially just after a cease-fire ending one of the many battles, and always passed by the hospital. Many came specifically for the hospital, and I had formed close friendships with many of them over the years in Lebanon.

I had learned early on that the enormity of the truth of events in Lebanon and the Palestinian refugee camps spoke for itself. These journalists seemed to appreciate anyone who respected them enough to tell the unembellished truth and did not take them for idiots or propaganda pawns, to whom one could easily lie. They provided a contact with the outside world and a good source of information for political and diplomatic developments. Now they related the story of Shatila and Burj el-Barajneh to the outside world. Even if we were under a military siege, there was no information blockade. International and Arab public opinion mobilized to put an end to the inhuman conditions prevailing in the besieged camps.

However, Syrian plans for Shatila had not yet been accomplished; the Palestinians were still in control. And the pro-Arafatists were still too powerful, had too much prestige and popular support, even after, and especially due to, the death of their heroic leader, Ali Abu Toq. The Syrians devised a new and insidious plan to break the spirit if not the body of Shatila. Starvation yes; but also a fifth column of the most extremist, anti-Arafat, pro-Syrian people within the refugee camp. Playing on people's fear, a campaign of intellectual and moral terrorism broke out.

Shortly after the arrival of Syrian troops in West Beirut, Amal proclaimed a two-day cease-fire in the War of the Camps, and two truckloads of food and supplies, one belonging to UNRWA and the other to the National Salvation Front, were allowed to enter the camp. "A delegation of the Palestine National Salvation Front" accompanied the two trucks. Three men from the three hard-line pro-Syrian factions – PFLP–General Command, Saiqa, and Fatah dissidents – composed the delegation. It was extremely unusual for a National Salvation Front delegation to be so constituted. Normally there would be only one or two people from the fanatic pro-Syrians, and one or two from the other three factions in the NSF coalition. Above all, such a delegation would almost invariably include a member of Omar's and Abu Moujahed's Popular Front – by far the most important group in the NSF.

We were surprised at their arrival. I looked at Omar and Basel with an obvious question in my eyes. Their blank stares were eloquent. They could not say anything in public. The "delegation" said that they came "carrying a message." The message was simple: "Either the Fatah Arafat loyalists disband and end their organizational, military, and political existence, or the siege will continue and Shatila will slowly starve to death or face the wrath of the T-62 Syrian tanks that have replaced the T-54s of Amal and the Lebanese army. The Syrian T-62s will leave the camp in blood up to your knees, if necessary." A hungry, emaciated, and exhausted camp looked at these three fat fellows preaching political extremism and reacted with deep-seated disgust and revulsion. Those who could not speak in public poured forth in private. "The Syrians want to control the Palestinians and the PLO. They want to stop any reunification of the PLO and recognition of Arafat's leadership."

We were flabbergasted at this brutal audacity and bare-faced attempt to create political *faits accomplis*, and so influence the ongoing negotiations for Palestinian political unity. The cruelty of the challenge was unconscionable, especially since the most important of the pro-Syrian factions, the PFLP and DFLP, were engaged in fervent negotiations with Arafat to reunify the PLO. The Syrian ploy was an obvious attempt to use Shatila's inhabitants as a political pawn in a pressure-politics game to sabotage any reunification of Palestinian ranks around the Syrians' nemesis, Arafat.

The "delegation" left Shatila, and the local leadership of the three hard-line factions began a campaign of denigration, insults, and exploitation of the fear of repression. They approached the Arafat loyalists one by one, men and women, sometimes cajoling them, sometimes threatening them with what could be expected now that several thousand Syrian troops were stationed in West Beirut. Syria's allies tried to convince the loyalists to commit political suicide. They used the food, coffee, and cigarettes that were brought in on the NSF truck as bait to bribe the loyalists to break with Fatah.

The supplies had been brought in under the name of the National Salvation Front, and the three hard-line groups wanted to distribute them only to the NSF coalition members. News of this got out and increased the disdain and disgust felt towards the dissidents. The Popular Committee, led by Abu Moujahed of the PFLP, received the UNRWA supplies of powdered skim milk, flour, and cracked wheat. The Committee distributed them to everyone in the camp equally; families first, hospital next, military last, with extra rations for the wounded, and pregnant and lactating women.

I walked over to the PFLP offices late one night; it was only recently, with a cessation of the shelling, that I had been able to leave the thirty-by-twenty-five-yard enclosure of the hospital compound. Everyone in the camp, including all the political leaders, had given me strict orders, impassioned pleas, not to leave the shelter of the hospital. I was the only surgeon in Shatila, a strategic asset as far as everyone was concerned. If anything happened to me, who would operate on the wounded? I entered the offices and came upon a meeting of the three "democratic" factions in the NSF – Popular Front, People's Struggle Front, and Palestine Liberation Front – led by Omar, Abu Moujahed, Basel and Mohsen, a Lebanese Shi'ite married to a Palestinian woman and head of a small Palestinian guerrilla group in Shatila. Amal wanted his skin – a Lebanese Shi'ite in a position of responsibility in a Palestinian refugee camp!

Cartons, crates, and sacks were piled in the corner — their quota of the NSF supplies. I greeted everyone present and took a seat.

The anger of those assembled was palpable. "They think they can buy us off with a few cigarettes and some apples! The Apple Political Programme, bah!" Abu Moujahed was scathing in his irony. "Who do they take us for – Adam?"

I laughed. "Abu Moujahed, you're a Marxist and you use biblical and Koranic anecdotes?"

Basel added, "Giannou's right. As a Marxist, you don't understand. Apple, yes; cigarette, no!" We shrieked with laughter.

"In any case," added Mohsen, "they can take their apple and cigarette – one fat and round, the other long and thin – and shove them." We shook and fell off our seats. Hunger and weakness were making us giddy.

Omar restored order. "The camp is still under siege, the battle continues. As far as I'm concerned, there is no question of applying political pressure on anyone until the end of hostilities." He spoke for all of those present. "And we will not be a part of this campaign. We refuse our quota of the NSF supplies. All foodstuffs should have been given over to the Popular Committee for distribution, equally to everyone in the camp."

"Those bastards!" Mohsen's language was always as crude as mine. "They've been eating from Fatah stores for months. And now that they've been saved from starvation because of the policies of the martyr Ali Abu Toq, they want to starve Fatah into submission. The bastards!"

"And if starvation doesn't work, they think that fear will." Basel knew what he was talking about. "Shatila is already up to its knees in blood. These people didn't surrender to the Phalangists, or the Israelis, or Amal. They have already been through how many massacres? There are over 500 martyrs buried in the mosque." Basel paused, controlling his anger. "If the inhabitants of Shatila were afraid of blood and sacrifice, we wouldn't be here now. Shatila has been up to its knees in blood for years. Do they think that all of a sudden, Shatila is going to fear the nationalist Arab army of Syria? What political stupidity!"

"We have our political differences with Arafat, but we also have our principles," added Omar. "We believe in a democratic dialogue to overcome those differences: not fear, blackmail, extortion. And certainly not internal fighting!"

Omar had mentioned the magic and dreaded words: internal fighting. The three hard-line pro-Syrian factions were thinking the unthinkable. It would be a horror story. Shooting from window to window and doorway to doorway through the narrow alleyways of what remained of the camp would be a nightmare and a catastrophe.

Whatever their differences with the Fatah Arafat leadership, these men knew that negotiations taking place in Algeria would probably result in Palestinian reconciliation, and that the Fatah people in Shatila were every bit as patriotic as they, had sacrificed and bled and died, were the essential pillar, in numbers, finance, and means, of the resistance of the camp. And they knew that the Syrian army would never directly attack the refugee camps. Syrian troops were ostensibly in Beirut to put an end to hostilities, and their return after the 1982 evacuation meant – in the code language of Middle Eastern politics – that there was tacit Soviet, U.S., and Israeli approval. They were not there to foment new hostilities and certainly did not want Arafat's representatives before the UN Security Council complaining that the Syrian army was attacking refugee camps.

The leaders of the three "democratic" factions of the National Salvation Front knew these political realities very well. They told their hard-line pro-Syrian allies that they had been eating from Fatah stores for weeks on end, and that what ammunition they had to defend the camp also came from Fatah. Either all of the supplies that had been delivered on the two trucks would be distributed to everyone in the camp on an equal basis, or they and their men would refuse their portion from the NSF supplies. Hungry and exhausted, they took a courageous position of principle and gained the respect of everyone in the camp. They also made known their opposition to any internal fighting: they would take up arms against anyone who attacked, would defend anyone under attack, whatever the faction.

At the same time, everyone knew that any internecine fighting might weaken Shatila's defences and provide the pretext for Syrian intervention. Syrian troops were there to stop fighting, after all – between Lebanese militias or between Palestinian factions, it could be argued. The prospect of more carnage mobilized the camp's elders and women and the hospital staff. Our moral authority carried great weight. We had saved many among the members of all the groups. They had all eaten at the hospital, drunk our coffee, smoked our cigarettes. Using all our accumulated moral prestige and powers of persuasion, delving into the deep recesses of what was left of our convictions and courage, my companions and I undertook a round of meetings with the leaders of all the factions. The hospital personnel, the notables, the women and families, made it known beyond a doubt that internecine fighting in the debris-strewn alleyways was a taboo, a red line that could not be crossed. The people would hold responsible anyone who instigated the nightmare of internal fighting, whatever the political reasons. We would not stand for it. Shatila was still under siege and the battle continued. Anyone who did not want to defend the camp was free to leave.

The continuing allegiance of the vast majority of Arafat loyalists with their ammunition stores, the principled position of the three "democratic" NSF factions, and the activity of the Democratic Front, hospital staff, women, and notables put an end to the most dangerous part of the conspiracy. We managed to mobilize all the political factions, some whole-heartedly, others half so, still others hypocritically, to denounce officially any attempt at internal fighting. Our press campaign was stepped up and pressure built to end the War of the Camps and lift the siege.

The UNRWA food that had entered Shatila and was now distributed equally throughout the camp gave us some respite, as did the exhaustion of the contending forces. Some men had managed to siphon off several gallons of gasoline from the food trucks' reservoirs, and they brought it to the hospital. Others picked through the rubble and went out into exposed areas at night to scavenge whatever wood they could find for cooking, laundry, and sterilization at the hospital.

I met daily with the hospital cooks, Saadou and his brother, Rabiha, and Oum Mohammed Faramawi, to decide on our menu. I thought back to all the greasy-spoon Greek restaurants where I had worked in Toronto during my youth, calculating portions and making up daily menus. This was simpler, because we had so little left. Breakfast: a glass of skim milk per person. Lunch: a cup of yogurt. Dinner: a small plate of rice with canned-vegetable sauce and half a loaf of pita bread. The next day's menu might consist of a cup of yogurt for breakfast, a handful of lentils for lunch, and a similarly meagre quantity of cracked wheat with a tomato-paste sauce and half a loaf of pita bread for dinner. For variety, the day after that, we would share a tin of sardines among three people with half a *ghif* each. And so on – for five weeks.

The supply of powdered milk allowed Saadou and his brother to make yogurt–and–sour cream paste – *labneh* – on a regular basis. When Rabiha made cheese, we drank the whey. I tried to take into consideration our nutritional needs in making up the menu, which was why we depended so much on dairy products. They provided a balanced diet of proteins and carbohydrates, with little in the way of fats; we had no butter, and very little oil; even the powdered milk was skimmed. No fruits, nor fresh vegetables. Even if we could balance protein and carbohydrate intake, the caloric value left something to be desired.

Normally, we prepared twelve kilograms (26.4 pounds) of rice and thirty tins of canned vegetables for the 100 people of the hospital staff per meal. We were now down to four kilograms (8.8 pounds) of rice and six cans of vegetables per meal. Of the three cups of tea per person per day (we had finished our coffee beans), only one had sugar — this for drinkers accustomed to very sweet tea. We were rapidly reaching the last of our frozen chickens, and ten wounded patients had to share one chicken daily. We had to serve them chicken every day because there was not enough electricity to keep the chickens fully frozen.

The rationing became ever more severe, and some items started to run out. This was deleterious to morale, and especially so when it concerned cigarettes. A package per person per day had been distributed during the first part of the battle to every smoker – and most men, and an appreciable number of women, smoked. This became ten cigarettes per day, then seven, and finally four. Many of the men took up smoking sawdust or tea leaves – after brewing the tea, of course. Wild rumours spread about the hallucinogenic qualities of tea leaves. The smoking had helped to cut our appetites and ease the pangs of hunger. We were already overwrought and our nerves frayed; we thought that smoking helped to soothe them.

I still had my supply of Gitanes and gave away numerous packets to colleagues, as well as hospital visitors. I refused to ration myself and decided that I would continue to smoke normally until my supply was finished, when I would no longer smoke. Near the end of March, I reached the end of my fifty cartons of Gitanes. It seemed to me that the question of smoking, like food and comfort, was a simple matter of will-power. I watched the hospital personnel – technicians, nurses, workers, doctors – as they lined up for the evening meal, or gathered around the fire, waiting for the large pot of tea to boil. Philosophical musings: the mundane details of daily life – eating, sleeping, smoking, washing – while under conditions of siege and deprivation are the best test of the mentality that drives people. The class attitudes that motivate individuals are best observed in the queue before the stew-pot. We had tried over the past year and a half to create an egalitarianism in the Shatila hospital cafeteria and sleeping quarters: the democracy of risk, suffering, death. If we could overcome the fear of death by bombardment, the hardships of deprivation and hunger, and the threat of political repression, then we were not going to surrender to a lack of cigarettes. This was simply another challenge that had to be met. The litany of challenges seemed never-ending, and it was a testimony to the psychological preparation of the people that, one after another, the challenges were met. There was never any discussion of giving in, although grousing and complaining became commonplace.

In Burj el-Barajneh, while we were in the throes of the anti-Arafat campaign, the Amal militiamen allowed women and children to leave the camp through a special trail, and then sniped at them when they returned with food: "the passage of death." A group of women, out of desperation, tried to march out of the camp to obtain food supplies. Amal fighters shot at them, and demonstrations broke out in West Beirut.

By mid-March 1987, political pressure was building, fed by the daily press releases from Burj and Shatila, and the public pronouncements of Lebanese religious and political leaders. The United Nations negotiated an agreement; UNRWA was given permission to bring food and medical supplies to the besieged camps. For every truckload of goods that arrived in Shatila or Burj el-Barajneh, an equal quantity was to be handed over to Amal. Several trucks got into Burj el-Barajneh.

At Shatila, the trucks came down S-S Street, past Gaza Hospital, manoeuvred around the sand ramparts that blocked the street, and arrived at the camp entrance, in full view of Amal snipers and Syrian observers in the sports stadium. As the trucks came to a stop, the drivers jumped out and dashed for cover into the camp, joining the besieged. A volley of rifle fire and RPGs rang out, and the trucks burst into flames and exploded. The half-starved faces of Shatila watched as the food melted before their eyes and went up in smoke.

Time and again, a food convoy was negotiated and the trucks arrived, only to be destroyed. The frustration at seeing the food convoys appear, only to go up in flames, gnawed at our guts even more than did our hunger. Somaya and her two children, waiting with a crowd for the food trucks, were victims of this frustration. It could go on forever, I thought. Our supplies were rapidly dwindling, and there was as yet no cease-fire in view. We asked ourselves, seriously, "Are we in Shatila damned?"

Hungry, angry, frustrated, and disgusted, we knew no rest. Sniper fire, tolerated by the Syrian "peace force," continued, creating a steady stream of wounded and dead. Young boys gathering wood in an area exposed to sniper fire were carried lifeless to the hospital. Alleyways and first-storey roof-tops were discovered to be newly accessible to the snipers' range of vision. The siege ground on relentlessly. My clothing hung on my bones, and I grew sick at the sight of more blood.

The inhabitants of the camp were at their wits' end. The hunger, deprivation, and steadily increasing number of dead were taking their toll. Arguments broke out regularly among families. They directed their anger towards anyone who carried any responsibility, direct or indirect, for the plight of the people of Shatila – Amal, Lebanese political and religious figures, the Syrians, the Palestinian leadership.

One day a crowd had gathered in the *zeroub* between Faramawi's and Somaya's houses, just around the corner from the hospital. The voices of women and men, children, and passing fighters in tattered camouflage uniforms rose in a crescendo. I stopped and stood in Faramawi's doorway. "What do they want from us?" screamed one woman.

"And they call themselves Arabs, Muslims!" shouted another.

"It's inhuman to allow us to die like this, slowly from hunger. And the children? What have the children done to deserve this?"

An old man on crutches said, "The Israelis were better. Even the Jews didn't treat us like this."

"Yeah, they bombed us, mercifully. And then sent the Phalangists. *Ya Allah*!" shouted a younger fellow in return. "Oh God! It's all Arafat's fault. He's too stubborn. He should get his troops out of the villages east of Ain el-Hilweh."

"Hafez el-Assad of Syria should get out of Lebanon," retorted another. "An *assad* [lion] in Lebanon, but an *arnab* [rabbit] in the Golan Heights [facing Israeli troops]."

"But Arafat provoked this! And the Saudis just let it go on. They like to see Palestinians die, and then send money – blood money."

"With this apple," sang a Fatah-dissident soldier, chomping into the fruit as he passed the group, "I'll get laid by the most beautiful girl in Shatila."

When a frail child of five looked up dolefully at her mother and said, "I want an apple too, Mama," I left and went back to the hospital.

On March 26, 1987, hundreds of Lebanese and Palestinian women gathered in West Beirut and tried to march to Burj el-Barajneh to force open the road and lift the siege. At least six were killed when Amal snipers attacked them. Two days later, a group of women in Shatila organized themselves spontaneously into a demonstration to protest the continuing siege. Convinced that the Lebanese soldiers and Amal militiamen would not fire on a group of unarmed women marching in the open, they wanted to break the blockade by simply marching out of the camp to bring back food.

The fighters at the periphery of the camp turned them back once. The second time, they managed to make it out onto S-S Street, separating the camp proper from the western sector, and walked past the gutted food trucks. Shots rang out and chaos descended upon the scene as the women scrambled back under cover of the rubble and debris. It took an hour-long firefight to provide the necessary protection to pull the bodies in off the street. Five women were dead, one of them eight months' pregnant, and nine were wounded.

We walked about the camp in a daze, not knowing how long this stalemate was to continue, nor how long we could contend with it. I was still functioning on twenty-hour days. During the first few weeks of the battle I had spent the majority of my time in the operating theatre. Now I had to contend with administering the rationing of food and medicines; continuing the press campaign to make known to the world the inhumane conditions that the people of Shatila faced; and as always being a part of the political discussions and trying to keep the camp together physically and psychologically. From time to time I curled up in some corner, wrapped in my woollen *burnoose* to catch a bit of sleep. After a couple of hours, I would awake with a start; too much stress, adrenaline levels too high. Though exhausted and hungry, I could not rest.

The staff in the emergency room slogged on, changing dressings on wounds that were three and four weeks old. After five months without fresh fruit or vegetables, vitamin deficiencies were beginning to manifest themselves in delayed wound healing: minor superficial wounds that should have closed up within a week or ten days still showed a bright red granulating surface more than a month later. Pregnant women started aborting spontaneously or delivering before term. The diet of rice, cracked wheat, and tinned sardines lacking in roughage and fibre had made most inhabitants constipated. Although our pharmacy still contained plentiful amounts of antibiotics and other crucial medicines, we had long since gone through our stock of laxatives. We had prepared for so many things – vaccines, antibiotics, anaesthesia, steroids, intravenous fluids, dressings, cough syrup. We even distributed iron tablets to supplement the meagre diet. Who would have thought that we would face an epidemic of constipation? We prescribed copious amounts of water as the only possible remedy available to keep bowels open.

Radio broadcasts regularly carried news that another food convoy was on its way and the siege was to be lifted, but the trucks were always fired upon as they arrived. And snipers were always ready to pick off anyone attempting to reach the burning trucks to salvage a carton of food. Another head trauma: I recognized the patient. I had operated on him in the first month of fighting, removing his spleen, left kidney, and part of his gut. The man had recovered and returned to the front. Now, he was back at the hospital again with a bullet in his head. There seemed to be no end.

In Tunis, at the headquarters of the Arab League, foreign ministers met, and the sessions were rowdy. Soviet pressure came into play. Algeria held Syria responsible for the continuing siege of the camps – after all, its troops were nearby. The assembly delegated the Saudi (the influence of money) and Algerian (Soviet influence) ministers to go to Damascus for discussions. Syria was being shamed into lifting the siege.

The sniper fire was becoming ever more lethal and indiscriminate. A frail skeletal woman, her age estimated at somewhere over ninety-five, had been standing in front of the remains of her house, well within the camp, when a bullet pierced her thigh. The spouting bright red fountain was unmistakable: femoral artery. Normally, one thinks several times and runs a whole gamut of tests before performing vascular surgery on a woman of this age and physical condition. The problem is not so much the surgery itself as the anaesthesia. Fortunately, the young anaesthesia technician and I were half anaesthetized ourselves by this point, our senses numbed by hunger and exhaustion. We went ahead with the operation like automatons, not giving it too much thought.

We were down to an hour and a half of electricity per day, insufficient to recharge the car batteries that provided power for the OR lamp. The fiercely burning propane camping lamps we now used gave off an eerie glow and excessive heat. Sweat rolled down my aching, hunched back, and my face was awash, even though the operation on the hardened atherosclerotic vessel was not difficult. The play of shadows produced by the camping lanterns caused me to stoop even more just to see the fine thread. Still, the operation succeeded, and the old woman took the anaesthesia extremely well, recovering without a hitch. Had we been more conscious of exactly what we were doing, we would probably not have had as good a result. It was the last operation of the Six-Month Battle – number 197; and she was the last of the wounded – number 765. That same day six trucks of food and medical supplies entered Burj el-Barajneh without being fired upon.

The shaming of Syria was succeeding – to a point. By making concessions in the Lebanese refugee camps, Syria was trying to pressure the "democratic" but hard-line factions not to attend the session of the Palestine National Council that was to be held in Algeria. But Syrian President Hafez el-Assad had blundered. He had made it impossible for the "democratic" anti-Arafat groups to maintain their identification with Syria. The PNC session would reunify the PLO, around Arafat, in defiance of Syria. And the Saudi and Algerian ministers in Damascus were eloquent. One held a cheque book (the Syrian economy was in a mess); the other held a blank cheque from the Soviets (Syria's main purveyor of arms).

On April 6, 1987, the day after I operated on the old woman, we served our last half-frozen chicken to the twelve wounded lying in the hospital. Five UN trucks arrived along the main road, carrying food donations from Kuwait and Saudi Arabia. No shooting occurred, and men scrambled over the trucks, unloading the cartons of food. Then a single shot rang out from the Amal positions in the sports stadium, and the bullet split open the head of one of the men. He was the last to die during the battle – number 110. He was from the PFLP-General Command, a fanatically pro-Syrian group. Abdallah, the head of the General Command, made angry radio contact with the Syrian observers who were supposedly also located in the stadium. That was the last sniper fire. The rest of the food was discharged without incident.

April 7, 1987: embarrassed and pressured, Syria intervened, not by sending its troops into Shatila to take control, but by deploying its soldiers around the camp as a buffer force to separate the refugee district from the Amal militia and Lebanese army units, and by reopening the roads. The cease-fire held. The battle, which had begun around Rashidieh and then Burj el-Barajneh six months earlier, was over. The siege would be lifted, even though the men would still be under security constraints. Shatila had resisted and survived.

Oum Mohammed Faramawi came to me to announce the arrival of the Syrian troops. "We are alive, because we are not dead." It was the fatalism of the end of the battle, the struggle to survive for survival's sake, beyond political meaning or symbolism.

Everyone slowly came out from the shelters, the homes, the rubble, the hospital. We gravitated towards the mosque, the walls of which had been blown away long ago by the shelling. We stood there in silence looking into its bowels, into the mass grave that contained the dead of Shatila. The camp had paid a terrible price – more than twenty percent casualties among the population of 3,500. People quietly greeted each other, offering the traditional form of congratulations and thanks for having survived. I looked up and saw Omar. "*Hamdulillah al-salaama.* May God be thanked for your deliverance." We looked at each other and then at the mosque, where Ali Abu Toq and so many others were buried. In joy and sorrow, we fell into each other's arms and wept.

13

Between the Unreal and the Surreal

SILENCE. FOR THE FIRST TIME IN 134 DAYS THE NIGHT passed without a single shot fired or a single shell exploding. Nevertheless, it was difficult to sleep, excited as we were that the battle had finally come to an end and that the blockade of the camp would be lifted. We were still wary of walking about the moon-lit alleyways too freely lest a disgruntled militiaman or soldier, still grieving over the death of a friend, be tempted to seek revenge by firing into the camp despite the cease-fire. Long lines of people snaked around the alleyways, through buildings, behind ramparts, avoiding areas known to be exposed to sniper fire.

People visited each other, ate, smoked, drank coffee, reminisced, wept. Thanks to the food supplies brought in on April 6, we ate our fill that night. Many people passed by the hospital, between rounds of visiting, to ask what and how they should eat. Our stomachs had all shrunk; very heavy meals taken all at once were certain to cause all sorts of discomfort. We recommended that people eat small portions at frequent intervals. Everyone was obsessed with the idea of eating, yet not aggravating the dull, gnawing pangs of hunger with the sharp colic of gluttony.

Cigarettes had also arrived. I had been about two weeks without smoking, overcoming the withdrawal by telling myself that no cigarettes were available. One of the nurses now brought me a pack, not of my beloved Gitanes, but tobacco, nonetheless. After the first couple of puffs, I became light-headed and a wave of vertigo swept over me. Dizzy and reeling, I sat down and waited for the nicotine level to return to "normal" and stabilize my senses.

While Shatila's inhabitants visited each other, we in the hospital prepared for the evacuation of the wounded. Yet another twenty-hour day. I wrote up dossiers for each patient including operative notes, X-rays, and relevant laboratory analyses. It was not so much that the wounded needed evacuation for specialized treatment in other centres – only a half dozen were in such a situation – but I wanted to reduce the workload on the nursing staff, and I did not know when the relief staff would arrive. All too often in the past, after the minor battles, people were afraid to come to work in Shatila; it always took several days to convince them of the stability of the cease-fire. There were also all the non-battle medical patients who needed special care, fresh air, and uncramped living quarters.

On April 8, a horde of women, children, relief workers and journalists invaded Shatila. The narrow alleyways filled with people as friends and relatives came to visit, bring food and gifts, make a pilgrimage to the mass grave. There were tearful, joyous reunions and even more tearful scenes as families gathered in and around the mosque to look at the mass grave where their mothers and fathers, wives and husbands, sisters and brothers, daughters and sons lay. In the traditional gestures of grief, women shrieked, pulled at their hair, rent their clothing, leapt and shuffled in a *danse macabre* while holding photos of their dead loved ones. Several were carried to the hospital emergency room sobbing and shouting hysterically, or limp and flaccid in a faint, and a long parade of visitors overwhelmed the hospital. Then news arrived that the International Red Cross ambulances were on their way to evacuate our wounded.

For the first time in five months I walked out to S-S Street. The men had told me about the destruction over the preceding months of siege and shelling, but no description of the scene could do it justice – desolation and devastation everywhere. Building after building lay in ruin. In the western sector, not a single wall seemed upright or intact. Rubble, mud, gutted trucks – some still smouldering – the general carnage of battle filled the main thoroughfare. Everything was a dirty brown-grey or a charred black. The crystal-clear blue of the sky came as a shock.

Bulldozers were clearing the sand ramparts and debris to open the main street and entrance of the camp. Hordes of women clambered over broken chunks of concrete and twisted iron bars, carrying great sacks of fresh fruit, vegetables, sundry food stuffs, sweets and pastry, coffee and cigarettes. They had hidden not a few bottles of beer, whisky and *arak* among the bundles. The visitors were met by the dazed, haggard, and forlorn residents of Shatila who ambled or staggered out of their holes like moles in shock. A seventy-five-year-old grandmother, clutching the hand of a yellow-faced child, half-crazed, mumbling to herself, stumbled out from the filthy warren of concrete slabs, collapsed roofs, and half-destroyed buildings. She walked past the blown-open sewers, through the clouds of hovering flies, the nauseating smell – the visitors held their noses, but we were inured to it – and on, beyond the checkpoint, out of the camp. "Thank God for your deliverance. Thank God you're safe," resounded everywhere.

Syrian troops and officers were deployed around the periphery of the camp, and as soon as they took up their positions, like any classical army, they began to erect sandbag fortifications. I looked closely at their faces. They stared at the destruction that surrounded them, disbelief in their eyes at the sight of these great crowds of emaciated human beings, dressed in ragged and threadbare garments that hung on their bodies, who seemed to crawl out of the rubble. Syrian officers went up and down the lines, making certain that there would be no breach in the cease-fire. The International Red Cross ambulances arrived, accompanied by Syrian troops to ensure their security and safe passage. No one wanted any "accidents." We eyed the Amal militiamen who had come out of hiding and could be seen standing on the roofs of the still-intact buildings across the street from the camp entrance.

I greeted the Red Cross delegates, some of whom I knew well, and gave them the dossiers of the wounded to be evacuated. We quickly organized the stretchers necessary to carry out those who could not walk, while the ambulant cases hobbled into line on their crutches, many of which were made of half-inch water pipes taken from the Awaini warehouse and fashioned by the camp's plumbers. We had run out of our supply of ordinary wooden crutches half-way through the battle.

We placed a placard bearing an identification number on the chest of each of the twenty-three wounded and ill. No names appeared or were given out for fear of future reprisals. The evacuation went smoothly, and the Red Cross people gave us new blood bags and a few essential medicines. Other trucks and vans carrying medical supplies and food arrived, all safely – no shooting or sniping as they unloaded their precious cargoes beside the gutted carcasses of the trucks that had tried to run the gauntlet less than a week before. The sight seemed unreal. I marvelled at the incongruity of these trucks arriving safely, carrying food and medicines. Food now meant life, whereas only a short time earlier it had meant death.

I thought back to other battles, other evacuations. Things had not always gone so smoothly. I had plentiful stories from the Israeli invasion of 1982, Tripoli in 1983, Shatila. The most striking thing about war, I realized, even when it involves a well-trained and disciplined army, was the confusion: evacuations, botched-up communications, bombings, swarms of civilians fleeing across the countryside.

Visitors kept arriving at the hospital, and they included a "delegation" from the leadership of the National Salvation Front, considered the representative of the camps in Syrian-occupied West Beirut. This time there were members from all the groups, and they were headed by the chief officer of the Popular Front. We talked briefly, and there were understanding smiles, meaningful winks of the eye, and knowing nods of the head. We communicated without words; Syrian agents were all around us. Contacts would continue in Algiers and elsewhere, and within two weeks a reunified Palestine Liberation Organization would hold a new session of the Palestine National Council.

Journalists, local and foreign, including friends from past battles and the wireless hook-up, joined the ranks of visitors. It had become almost routine for some of them to seek me out and bring me gifts (a bottle of scotch, chocolate bars) after every cease-fire.

"Nora, how are you?"

"How are *YOU*? is the question, Chris," she said, handing me a small package. Nora Boustani was Lebanon correspondent for the *Washington Post* and later won the George Polk Prize for her coverage of the War of the Camps. She had managed, with a British television crew, to cross the "passage of death" into Burj el-Barajneh during the final weeks of the siege, and their reports had been instrumental in mobilizing public opinion to apply the necessary pressures to relieve our plight. "Chris, Burj el-Barajneh is in bad shape. But this" — she waved her hands around her — "this is ridiculous! As I came down the street and looked at the sight, I found it impossible to imagine that anyone could still be alive inside. How did you manage to survive?"

Many interviews later, an old friend from Swedish Radio, Agneta Ramberg, arrived. "Giannou, this is wonderful," she said, the light flashing in her eyes. I stared at her.

"What's so wonderful about it? It's a scene of devastation. We have hundreds of dead and wounded, and we've only just begun to eat again." I was a good forty-five pounds lighter than when we had last met.

"No, no," she replied, "but the people here in Shatila walk around with their heads held high. And when they talk, they speak out in a loud voice."

In West Beirut, Amal militiamen had entered and looted Palestinian homes and expelled the families in reprisal for their losses around the camps. Palestinian civilians had had to take refuge in public buildings and unfinished construction sites in parts of the city controlled by the Socialist Party. They were cowed, walking about the streets of West Beirut with their heads down. When they spoke, it was in quiet hushed tones so that no one would recognize their distinctive Palestinian accent. They lived in fear; many had been taken prisoner, beaten, tortured. Women, like Yasmine previously, had been raped. Some had simply disappeared, never to appear again. Everyone lived in sorrow, fear and repression.

In Shatila, the people lived in sorrow, surrounded by mind-boggling destruction, with their dead and wounded in their midst. Bones stuck out under their skin, lice infested their hair, threadbare garments hung on them like scarecrows', and shoes worn through the water and mud of the alleyways and tunnels fell apart as they walked; but they still had their pride and dignity. Most of the 3,500 inhabitants of Shatila could have left the camp before the onset of hostilities. We had all known that a major battle was in store for us and many families did, in fact, move out. But the vast majority chose to stay in Shatila. What had become a meaningless platitude for many others was for them a living reality of their daily existence: they would rather die on their feet than live on their knees. They had refused to surrender, to succumb, and they had maintained their right to resist, to live, to love, to hope, and to aspire to a just existence. And they had paid a terrible price. They had every right to keep their heads held high.

The cease-fire was not broken, and the militiamen and Syrians allowed women and children to freely enter and leave the camp. They carried literally tons of food and household goods into Shatila. Cars, which were not allowed passage onto the main street, discharged their cargoes at the checkpoint, and the men and women carried the goods in. The inhabitants bought and brought in everything imaginable. The young men abandoned their worn, ragtag clothing and could now be seen ambling down the narrow alleyways, through the rubble, dressed in the latest fashions – large, flowing cotton shirts in pastel colours and deep-pleated trousers.

The news from Rashidieh and Burj el-Barajneh was encouraging. The day following the evacuation of the wounded from Shatila, ICRC delegates and ambulances performed a similar task at Burj el-Barajneh. Thousands of people passed the checkpoints every day to enter and leave the Beirut camps. The medical and food blockade had been lifted. "All humanitarian measures" were allowed, according to the official propaganda. The irony was too gross: after all the inhumanity of six months of fighting and siege "all humanitarian measures" were now okay.

The siege continued, only the terms changed. What was now described as a "military blockade" would persist until a "final political solution" could be found. Ominous. Anything of military value could not pass the checkpoint at the entrance to the refugee district. This meant not only weapons or munitions: cement, gravel, sand, and iron bars to repair what was left of the camp's dwellings were prohibited, since they could also be used, theoretically, to build military fortifications, as were radio batteries, which could be used in walkie-talkies. Only women and children had freedom of passage. All males over the age of fourteen were potentially of "military value" and therefore confined within the limits of the camp. We, the 1,500 men and boys, now lived in the 100 by 100 yards remaining of Shatila.

The Syrians gave the hospital a special dispensation, allowing us to bring in spare parts, special material for maintenance work, and fuel for the hospital generator, in limited quantities. It would have made for "bad press" if the hospital were unable to function due to a lack of electrical wiring or spare parts for some of the equipment. The general intent, however, was obviously to prevent any renewed stocking of goods in the camp.

We were eating again. Fresh fruit and vegetables, meat, eggs, chocolate bars were available in abundance. The hospital kitchen staff went back to preparing great feasts. Another special dispensation allowed a number of the male doctors, nurses, technicians, and workers to leave the camp in batches, under the protection of the Syrian *Moukhabarat*. New personnel arrived to relieve the staff who had been sequestered in Shatila for six months. The replacements were all women so that moving in and out of Shatila would not create any problems.

The Syrian soldiers manning the checkpoint, however, weren't very different from the militiamen and Lebanese troops they had replaced, and soon there was a flourishing black market. Bribes were paid, and all sorts of banned goods came in, including ammunition. The soldiers were always asking for various medicines, and prescriptions written by Damascene doctors for medications unavailable in Syria were constantly being sent to me. I provided the necessary medicines, and, in the mutual back-scratching logic that is Lebanon and the Middle East, we brought into the camp all sorts of goods in the name of the hospital. This situation continued for months. With our Ampicillin, aspirin, and cough syrup *baksheesh*, we eventually acquired just about anything we desired, including many prohibited goods – radio and car batteries, extra fuel, burlap bags.

The women resumed their smuggling, hiding items in the mountains of green leafy vegetables and fruit they balanced on their heads or strapped to their bodies under their flowing robes. Not just car batteries, but truck batteries – double the size – and journalists' video cameras. After the first round of filming and interviewing immediately after the cease-fire, the Syrians, who wanted the world to forget Shatila as quickly as possible, prohibited entry by any foreign journalists. Thereafter, newswomen entered the camp as nurses or visiting foreign medical teams, or simply as friends of Régine and Giannou – "the foreigners." Some things in Lebanon never change.

On April 13, Pauline Cutting, Susie Whighton, and the other foreign medical staff left Burj el-Barajneh, escorted by Syrian troops for their protection. Returning to their homes in Great Britain, they told of the death and destruction, horror and hunger of the refugee districts in Beirut. They told also of the predicament facing the population, whose homes had been damaged or destroyed, and the bleak future that awaited them if reconstruction of the districts did not proceed quickly. Pauline also helped set up a special fund for the treatment in Great Britain of children wounded in the fighting.

Listening to the BBC some time later with Abu Mohammed Faramawi, we learned that the Queen had bestowed an O.B.E. (Order of the British Empire) on Pauline. Susie received an M.B.E. (Member of the British Empire), a slightly less prestigious award. I explained to a questioning Faramawi, "Both Pauline and Susie are women. One cannot accuse the British government of traditional aristocratic sexism, but archaic class distinctions obviously still persist. Pauline is a doctor and therefore receives the O.B.E., while Susie, 'merely' a nurse, merits only an M.B.E."

Faramawi had his own explanation: "The British aren't much different than the Arabs."

A new team from Medical Aid for Palestinians (MAP)–U.K. replaced the foreign volunteers in Burj el-Barajneh. They had been brought to Beirut under the guidance of an old friend, Dr. Swee Chai Ang, a diminutive orthopaedic surgeon from Singapore who had organized the evacuation and transfer. A political refugee living in Great Britain, Swee had worked at the Gaza Hospital during the 1982 War and had been there during the Sabra and Shatila Massacre. She had gone to Israel to testify before the Kahan commission of inquiry. The Palestinian "bug" had bitten Swee, as it had Régine. In 1982, Swee knew nothing about the Palestinians and didn't know where Lebanon was, but the massive shelling of Beirut had outraged her sense of justice. Several years later, she was again in the refugee camps of Lebanon and the occupied territories.

Swee is an enthusiastic bundle of energy, and it was a pleasure and a relief to see her again in Shatila. She had worked there previously as a surgeon, just after the first round of fighting and a couple of months before my arrival; now, she became a teamster, driving her ambulance incessantly back and forth between the refugee camps, Mar Elias and the headquarters of Syrian forces in West Beirut. Receiving the necessary permission from the *Moukhabarat*, after horrendous bureaucratic delays, she brought us supplies, new cylinders of oxygen and anaesthesia gas, and generally raised our spirits with her bubbling good nature. Accompanying Swee came two of the newly arrived foreign medical volunteers to work in Shatila. Venke, a Norwegian nurse about twenty-eight years old, had been with us previously along with Kristen, the nurse-anaesthetist, in 1986, and had returned, bridling at the thought that she had not been present during the Six-Month Battle. With her was a tall, lanky Australian in his early thirties – Murray Ludington, our new anaesthetist. There was a bit of work in the operating theatre, but not enough to fully satisfy him. So, adapting quickly and feeling very much at home in the camp, Murray soon joined the workers, lugging cartons of medicines from the main street to the hospital. He also took up plumbing, helping to set up our new drinking water supply, piping it into the camp from the municipal water pipes on S-S Street.

Life was returning to Shatila. Alcohol, hashish, and cocaine accompanied the food, coffee, and cigarettes. Everyone wanted to buy a small portable television and smuggle in a car battery to operate it. There was not much to do at night in Shatila now that the battle had ended and the young men chafed at their lack of freedom of movement. In the new, post-battle, reduced space – 100 yards by 100 yards – if I walked fifty paces from the hospital in one direction or another fifty in the other, I reached the limits of the camp.

For the first few weeks, the men kept busy clearing the rubble and debris from the alleyways, removing the rubbish and refuse from the garbage dump and cleaning Sabra-Shatila Street. But with no building materials, they could not busy themselves with reconstruction, however imperative it was. For the moment, S-S Street was free of sniper fire, and the young men exploited the situation to the utmost, fleeing the narrow, cloistered confines of the camp's alleyways to enjoy the wide-open spaces of this street – fully six to eight yards wide and a couple of hundred yards long – lined by half-rooms and stalls with leaning roofs of mangled concrete and iron bars: the shells of former homes. These they quickly transformed into restaurants and cafés. While the women trundled back and forth between Shatila and West Beirut, the men idled away their hours in the warming spring sunshine, sipping Turkish coffee and playing cards, backgammon and chess. With the unquenchable entrepreneurial spirit of refugees who have to make do, some opened shops that sold grilled meat, sandwiches, and ice cream, or clothing. The young men were quickly regaining weight as they paced up and down, with increasing frustration, along Sabra-Shatila Street in full view of the Amal militiamen and Syrian soldiers who surrounded the camp.

An epidemic of white T-shirts with photos imprinted on them broke out. As after each round of fighting, Shatila's inhabitants had the workshops of West Beirut make shirts with the likeness of the camp's dead martyrs printed on the front. This time was no exception; soon it seemed that the entire camp, including many men from factions other than Fatah, was wearing the photo of Ali Abu Toq. Ali belonged to them all. He had led them all in the struggle for survival; in death he was cherished by all. This was tainted only by the hypocrisy of the dissident officer – as yet not exposed – who had ordered the assassination.

The hospital was busy, as usual, while everyone else in the camp was more or less on vacation – eating, sleeping, and recuperating. During the Six-Month Battle, I had extracted many a tooth to alleviate excruciating pain for many young men. There was nothing much else I could do. Our two female dentists were now submerged with work, dealing with those patients whom I had been able to convince to withstand the pain, rather than remove a salvageable tooth.

Many inhabitants from West Beirut invaded our out-patient clinic daily. Our services and medicines were still free of charge, and the economic situation in Lebanon had deteriorated tremendously over the previous six months. The value of the Lebanese pound had collapsed, dropping from 60 to the dollar prior to the battle, to 120 per dollar by the time of the cease-fire. Now the economic situation rapidly worsened again; by the end of the summer, a dollar would be exchanged for 500 Lebanese pounds. Inflation raged on in triple digits; many Lebanese and Palestinians, especially those on fixed incomes, simply couldn't afford private hospitals and clinics. Great numbers overcame their fear of Shatila and came to our rubble-surrounded, pock-marked, walls-blown-away field hospital. With the cease-fire well established and Syrian forces entrenched, they regained their confidence in a stable security situation, and our out-patient clinic bore the brunt of this.

We now had a total work force of about eighty people in the hospital, sixty-five of them women. Régine and I stayed on. She did not want to leave the camp just yet, and I was still the only full-time surgeon. No one knew what would happen in the near future, and we did not want Shatila to have to face, once again, a situation where it would have to negotiate the evacuation of an ill or wounded patient. My sense of solidarity with these people – through cold, hunger, discomfort, death, tears, and joy – made it impossible for me to separate myself from them as long as the blockade continued. I would not leave the camp until the other men could do so as well.

I had once before been separated from my colleagues by a *deus ex machina* in the form of the Canadian government, which had intervened to secure my release from the custody of the Israeli Army in 1982. Many of my Palestinian, Lebanese, other Arab, Pakistani, and Bangladeshi companions had remained captive for eighteen months in the infamous Ansar prison camp in southern Lebanon. I had, therefore, been separated from my colleagues once before by circumstances beyond my control. I did not wish to separate myself from them this time by an act that was totally within my control.

Our most important work involved measures of preventive medicine to deal with the camp's horrendous living conditions. The rats were thriving; they had bitten many of the young children who were either in the shelters or in the half-demolished houses where families had now taken up residence. The refuse scattered in the alleyways and mixed with the rubble provided excellent breeding grounds in the warming weather for insects and vermin. The men cleared the alleyways as much as possible, piling up high the debris of broken concrete and bricks, and the hospital workers went about daily, spraying insecticide and distributing rat poison. Not only did this allow for better sanitation and easier passage throughout the camp, but the mounds of rubble formed new ramparts, just in case the security situation deteriorated and sniping and shooting began again.

Now that people were out and moving about, there was always the danger that they would use contaminated water from the damaged sewer and water systems. UNRWA sent in a team of health specialists and sanitation engineers to make a study of conditions in the camp. They discovered that two of the public spigots from which most of the camp inhabitants now received their water were contaminated. The pipes had received several pieces of shrapnel, and although the holes were not large enough nor sufficient in number to affect the water pressure when it was running, they allowed the entry of contaminants that dirtied the pipes. The entire network had to be redone.

From the World Heath Organization (WHO), UNRWA supplied us with typhoid vaccines. We organized a round of vaccinations for the camp inhabitants, not wanting to repeat our experience of typhoid fever during the battle, especially now that we had easy access to the western sector, and the cafés and food stalls were established on the main street near the most contaminated water sources. One development led to another, and never gave us respite.

Curative work at the hospital also continued, the sequelae of war trauma. A half-dozen patients had been living for several months with colostomies. They were quickly regaining weight and strength and were soon ready for the relatively minor surgical procedure of closing their artificial anuses. They could now go back to eating a normal diet and having normal bowel movements.

There were other victims of the fighting who needed constant care. Asqol was a ten-year-old boy whose skull had been opened by a shell and his brain splattered across a wall. His recovery was anything but uneventful. Medically speaking, he recuperated splendidly with no complications, recovering consciousness and normal daily activities very quickly. He was, however, a hyperactive child, tremendously verbose. He simply would not stop talking while recovering in the hospital. A great aficionado of melodramatic Egyptian video films, he acted them out, mimicking well-known Egyptian actors. He kept the nursing staff entertained at first, but we were exhausted and he, in spite of his trauma, seemed never to tire and never to want to sleep. The night shift nurses complained to me that his constant banter prevented them from working or resting.

I asked his father if he had always been this talkative and restless – apparently yes. His behaviour, then, was not due to the trauma. He was an only son among several sisters and had always spent endless hours watching the heart-throb idols of Egyptian cinema.

Now Asqol developed epilepsy. The focus in his brain, in all probability, had been present prior to his injury, which simply served to rupture the delicate balance and precipitate his crises. After the ceasefire, I sent him for consultation to a neurosurgeon in West Beirut, who placed him on standard anti-epileptic medication. If he missed or delayed one day's dose (with all his restlessness and acting abilities, Asqol was not a very co-operative patient), it would provoke convulsions, and his family would rush him to the hospital emergency reception. The medication controlled his disease, but he remained as hyperactive and talkative as ever, and his zest for Egyptian melodrama and romanticism never waned. Another problem, albeit small, that we had to contend with.

More problems: people started using butane and kerosene again for cooking, heating, and light. Apparently, they had forgotten how to use them or had become too negligent about minimal safety measures, and there was a spate of burn patients within the first two weeks after the lifting of the siege. Some were quite severe, and one died of his wounds.

Apart from the sequelae of war, we also had our run-of-the-mill chronic cases to treat, cases that never go away, war or peace. Fawzia and her husband had a small vegetable shop beside the garbage dump square. Ibrahim had been treated for tuberculosis several years before and had even entered a sanitorium, but he had not assiduously followed up on his medication, and the humidity of Shatila and loss of resistance from malnutrition during the siege provoked a relapse. His chest filled up with fluid, and I had to tap the thick pus several times. We put him on a heavy multi-drug regime of anti-TB agents, but to no avail. His chest kept filling with fluid. A few months later I resorted to old-time medicine and provoked a surgical pneumothorax – deliberately filling the chest cavity with air to collapse the lung. Thus put at rest, the lung was able to benefit from the anti-TB drugs and his condition improved rapidly. I was relieved that I did not have to resort to yet earlier medical practice and perform a pneumonectomy – removing the lung. Before the discovery of streptomycin and other anti-TB agents forty-five years ago, this was a rather common occurrence when the infection was limited to just one lung. Surrounded by the rubble of Shatila, isolated from the world, it seemed that we were devolving in time.

Many people had returned to live in what was left of their homes. In the mild weather of the Lebanese spring and summer, they covered over the large holes in ceilings or walls with blankets, cardboard, and zinc sheeting. Several squatter families, sharing cramped quarters, quickly occupied the few remaining classrooms of the two schools. Many more, however, were obliged to leave the camp and seek shelter elsewhere. Thus most families split up, the women and children taking up residence in West Beirut or another of the refugee camps in Lebanon, and the men and male adolescents confined to Shatila by the military blockade. Most of the young men still lived underground or in the shells of half-destroyed buildings along the camp perimeter. This was possible during the spring and summer; without repair or reconstruction work, we looked with foreboding to the arrival of next winter.

My villa was a shambles. Two of the walls of the one-room apartment had been almost entirely blown away. The roof was quite simply gone. The place was no longer habitable, and for a while I slept in the laboratory or on one of the hospital beds. Then Régine and I set up temporary residence in the changing-room annex at the top of the stairs leading to the operating theatre. She would return to the hospital late at night after visiting friends somewhere in the camp, while I had usually held court in the administration plus store-room-pantry adjacent to the kitchen. We would have a final demitasse of coffee and then go off to the changing room and spread mattresses and blankets on the floor. I remarked to her that we had become like an old couple, who meet at bedtime, lying next to each other, recounting the events of the day, and then, turning over on their sides, go to sleep.

Abu Mohammed Faramawi had sent his family out of the camp, hoping that the children could make up their school year, and he invited me to stay with him in the second-storey apartment just above the hospital. He slept in one room, and Omar and I spread out mattresses on the floor of the second room for our sleeping quarters. Régine took up residence with the family with whom she spent most evenings anyway.

I was back to a more or less regular work day, sleeping five or six hours a night and taking an afternoon siesta. I would lie on my mattress in the slowly rising heat of the afternoon, recuperating from the stress of the last few months. One afternoon about a month after the cease-fire, a messenger arrived at Faramawi's house, carrying a letter for me. Half asleep, I slowly walked back down the corridor to my mattress. The address on the envelope made me bolt awake.

Dr. Chris Giannou
Shatila Camp
Near Mediterranean Sea
Lebanon

In this shambles of a country, where the central government had only a fictitious existence and most of the ministries did not function on a daily basis or at least had long since given up the pretence of functioning, the mail service was exemplary. Neither rain nor sleet, nor bombs nor devastation could stop the delivery of this insanely addressed letter postmarked Ohio, U.S.A. As I thought about it, it seemed perfectly reasonable that it should arrive. The U.S. Postal Service had sent the letter to Lebanon, near the Mediterranean Sea. There was only one Shatila camp and once the letter got that far, there was no difficulty in finding me in the remaining few yards.

I opened the letter and read, "Greetings to the people of the camps. This is to invite you people to join us in building a better world by co-operation. War is old-fashioned. It belongs to the dark ages. This organization is to promote good will and brotherhood, work and trade." It went rambling on. At the bottom appeared, "P.S. There is hope." The letterhead announced, "International Brotherhood, Sisterhood, Hobby Craft Produce of the New World Government." There was an image of a doll in the upper left-hand corner with the logo, "International Fairy Godmothers and Elves."

The envelope included half a dozen garishly coloured postcards, all carrying photographs of an elderly woman in various romantic poses of the 1930s or 1940s. One showed her standing beside her "International Fairy Godmother" Mini Morris Minor white convertible holding a little doll like the one pictured in the letterhead. On the verso of the postcards were little blurbs telling about this international brotherhood and sisterhood: its charter, motto ("have a heart"), colours (gold and white), its flower (a single red rose), the password (love), and its emblem (the fairy godmother doll). One card explained that the organization "started about forty years ago with the first branch being a secret police force working to get to the cause of crime and the underworld." It continued, "The local police, the national forces and the international police are our guardians of safety and peace ... dues are $1.00 per month." Another assured us that the unions had been invited to join, as had Jimmy Hoppa (*sic*). I slowly put the cards and the letter back into the envelope, lay back down on my mattress, closed my eyes, and took a deep breath.

And then I burst out in uncontrollable laughter. Was I losing my senses? Had the hunger or shock waves of exploding shells affected my brain? Surrounded by an incredible lunar-like landscape of destruction and desolation, trying to sleep not thirty yards away from a mass grave that contained 500 cadavers, I seriously asked myself whether I was still in the real world. Shatila seemed unreal. An elderly woman living in Ohio with her fairy godmothers and elves seemed surreal. Between the two, there had to be something that was real. It was only a question of finding it. My fit of laughter was so violent that Faramawi came in from his room, looking at me strangely. How the hell could I translate and explain this letter to him? I could not hope to begin and did not even try.

The letter from Ohio was not the only mail I received in Shatila. My old élite and prestigious Canadian high school, the University of Toronto Schools, through its Alumni Association, sent me a bulletin on their activities, asking for a contribution. I replied, not knowing if it would arrive, stating that as soon as a bank set up service in Shatila I would open an account and send them a cheque. It seemed the only respectable thing to do.

I was still in search of reality when a U.S. health volunteer working with the American Friends' Service Committee (Quakers) visited me in Shatila. Barbara Pizicani had been working in southern Lebanon for the last two and a half years and was getting ready to leave shortly. We talked about her work in the southern villages and refugee districts. Two weeks later, I saw her on the TV news in a hospital in Sidon. Some militiamen had stopped her ambulance, commandeered it, and ordered her to get out. A group of rival militiamen came on the scene and, rushing to the rescue of this damsel in distress, asked what was going on. Fighting broke out between the two groups, and Barbara was wounded in the abdomen by a stray bullet. The broadcast showed scenes of her in a hospital bed, receiving a long line of visitors – political and religious dignitaries from the region. I wondered how I could contact the hospital to find out if she needed any assistance. A fairy godmother or elf would have been handy indeed, but Barbara recovered without one and was evacuated to the U.S. several weeks later.

Real, unreal, surreal: I certainly had no desire, in the midst of my recuperation, to return to the sterile philosophical meandering of my adolescence. But this was not sterile. I had to come to grips with whatever it was that amounted to the only reality that I now knew. Perhaps, I thought, it is the same reality for everyone, just the distance and angle of observation that changes, creating a receding or advancing perspective. I had not yet receded enough, but I would, eventually. And I would not necessarily like what I saw.

14

Haemorrhage of Human Wealth

THE MILITARY BLOCKADE OF RASHIDIEH, BURJ EL-BARAJNEH, and Shatila continued on through 1987 while negotiations took place to find a political solution that would put an end to the stalemate. The military advance of Palestinian forces to the villages around Maghdushah, east of Sidon, was the first time since the Israeli invasion that an armed Palestinian presence had taken territory from a Lebanese rival, and various Lebanese factions viewed askance this extension of Palestinian military might outside the refugee camps. The Palestinian advance was meant to alleviate the pressure on the besieged camps, and the forces were now ready to withdraw and return to the refugee district of Ain el-Hilweh, but only once the siege of the camps was totally lifted. Determined to force a Palestinian retreat without concessions, Amal and its Syrian backers used the siege of the camps as a pressure point.

In this political game of chess, the thousands of inhabitants of the refugee districts were the pawns. The key to a settlement, of course, was a Syro-Palestinian reconciliation; the reason for the War of the Camps was actually the rivalry for political influence between Arafat and el-Assad of Syria. The ordinary people of the refugee districts, concerned mainly for their own safety and that of their families and homes, were obsessed with living as normal a life as possible – as are most people in the world – while being refugees in a country in the midst of civil turmoil.

We settled in for the continuing blockade. A new political environment existed, however. The new-found unity of the PLO, forged in the co-operative resistance of the refugee enclaves in Lebanon during the War of the Camps, created a new political reality in Lebanon, and in Shatila. The pro-Syrian National Salvation Front became a rump organization; the factions remaining, the hard-line anti-Arafatists, had little popular support, what strength they had deriving solely from Syrian sponsorship. This relieved a great deal of the pressure on the Fatah people. Baha and Amina were no longer ostracized and met daily and openly with the top leadership of the groups now composing the reunified PLO – Omar of the Popular Front, previously the most important element of the pro-Syrian coalition; Abu Imad, head of the Democratic Front; Mohsen, the Lebanese Shi'ite leader of the Palestine Liberation Front in Shatila; and Mohammed, the chief official of the still three-member Communist Party.

Walking over to the Fatah office on my daily "rounds," I arrived just in time for one of these meetings. It began with Abu Ibrahim, the elderly *cahwagi* (literally coffee-man) of the Fatah administrative office, bringing us the traditional cup. (Since the cease-fire a month before, coffee was in plentiful supply, and Abu Ibrahim no longer "unemployed.") Omar twirled his moustache and asked about the finances. "Various countries and international organizations have donated several million dollars for reconstruction," replied Baha. "The DFLP has been in contact with the Syrians."

"No go," said Abu Imad. "I was in contact with Mar Elias this morning. The Syrians absolutely refuse to allow any building materials to enter." He added derisively, "They have no guarantees that we won't use them to construct ramparts and fortifications."

"With the winter rains there won't be a single dry room in all of Shatila and the last of the families will be forced to leave the camp," interrupted Mohsen. "Using the building materials for anything but repair of the houses would be self-defeating on our part. Surely the Syrians must know that."

"We've even conceded that Syrian officers may supervise the use of the materials to insure that no military fortifications are built," said Baha. "But the Syrians also know that it was the housing built under the guidance of martyr Ali that saved us last time. They know that a reconstructed camp doesn't need military fortifications."

With no electricity, a precarious water supply, and the growing frustrations the young faced day in and day out with nothing to do to occupy themselves, these men knew that the destiny of Shatila itself was in question. The camp might well disappear if the social and political challenges were not adequately met. And in their minds, Shatila had taken on an existence of its own, like a cherished parent or child, had become a symbol of their own existence as self-styled revolutionary freedom-fighters. Shatila was becoming a myth.

All were profoundly aware that a return to normalcy in Shatila, with reconstruction of the camp and gainful employment for the young men, depended on a political reconciliation between Arafat and el-Assad of Syria. The precariousness of the situation caused everyone to feverishly explore every avenue of opportunity – and caused anger to boil over. Omar: "The Syrian soldiers are even looking for our secret tunnels. Are they preparing to attack us themselves? The pitiful slobs! They wouldn't stand a chance. They'd have to bring in the air force to bomb us, and even then," he added, scorn dripping from his mouth, "they'd probably miss." A chorus of laughter. "They aren't the Israelis, after all."

I gave my report on the hospital. The operating theatre and ward could continue to function in winter, but we would have to curtail the out-patient department. Floods of water would cascade through the fissures in the ceiling with the first rains. Providing for the personnel would be difficult: nowhere to sleep at night for those off-duty. Medical supplies were adequate, however, thanks to the tireless work of Dr. Swee Ang. "Giannou, Dr. Swee seems like a wonderful person. You both spend so much time in the camps, why don't you settle down here and marry her?" asked Mohsen, a gleam in his eye.

"She's already married, comrade Mohsen. Besides, we don't have enough fuel stocks for the generators." Another chorus of guffaws. Another round of thick Turkish coffee.

Shatila still housed many families, but they could stay there only in the warm summer months. If the refugee district were not to become an entrenched military encampment of 1,200 men, many living underground, then something had to be done, and quickly, while the weather allowed. Abu Imad proposed to create a committee that would study the situation. It rapidly produced long, detailed reports on the socio-economic and security situations and the need for the central Palestinian leaders to quickly come to a reconciliation with Syria, if we were to save Shatila.

The various factions established a new *modus vivendi*. The campaign of denigration against Arafat was muted; both the Popular and Democratic fronts had rejoined Fatah in the PLO, and a united front faced the hard-line pro-Syrian coalition. A strange system of political etiquette determined social contacts. People from different rival factions dealt with each other socially on the basis of personal, shared experiences, not necessarily ideology. Pro-Arafat and dissident fighters who had been on the fronts together during the battle now spent hours talking, drinking tea, playing soccer together. Political rivalry continued, but the men were basically exhausted and had only just begun to relish the simple pleasures of eating, smoking, drinking coffee, and listening to cassette recordings of poetry. Wedding engagements and marriages followed one another in rapid succession. Mundane comforts were the order of the day as a reaction to the physical hardships of life in Shatila.

Not all the men stayed. Basel of the Popular Struggle Front left the camp: the Syrians wanted him. Apparently, some people did not appreciate Basel's contacts with Ali Abu Toq before and during the Six-Month Battle, and he was to be called to account for having overstepped the boundaries of what was considered politically acceptable. The Popular Struggle Front had flirted with rejoining the PLO, then at the last moment refused, preferring to function as a liaison between the reunited PLO and the pro-Syrian National Salvation Front hardliners, but remaining a formal member of the latter. Although his Front supported Basel, it was dependent on Syrian goodwill and so ordered him out of Shatila for "questioning." Basel had attempted to do his best in the defence of the camp. He had known the insides of Syrian prisons before and was not afraid of returning there. But he was certainly going to defend his actions while in Shatila as military head of the National Salvation Front, whether the Syrians liked it or not.

Abu Moujahed and his staff in the Popular Committee faced even more work, cleaning up the camp to rid us of the mountains of rubbish, repairing and in certain areas totally refashioning the network of water pipes. The sewers also needed maintenance. As always, Abu Moujahed was a frequent visitor to the hospital. We consulted on water, electricity, sewers, pesticide spraying, and anything else that needed doing. He visited me late at night, in the hospital kitchen pantry; there was always the midnight meal and tea. Independent-minded, he was as virulent in his attacks on the Syrians as he had been on Arafat's leadership. After water and sewers, we discussed Palestinian politics, the Middle East, the world. Abu Mohammed Faramawi joined us from time to time, as did Dr. Khatib, Abu Imad, Mohsen ... the nights, and innumerable cups of tea and coffee, went on and on.

Abu Moujahed had been superficially wounded in the last week of the battle while trying to unload the food trucks as they came under fire. Later on, he started running a low-grade fever and complained of headaches and fatigue. Our laboratory was now equipped to handle serological exams for typhoid, and Abu Moujahed tested positive. We evacuated him from Shatila, once more through a special dispensation from the Syrian *Moukhabarat*. His absence was sorely felt and the Popular Committee was never as active again; as usual in the Third World, personalities counted for more than institutions. I missed his keen sense of humour and his selflessness.

As the summer months wore on, life in Shatila took on a new routine. Limited to a living space the same size as one city block, plus Sabra-Shatila Street, families still lived among the filthy warrens of concrete slabs, collapsed roofs, and half-destroyed walls. First-time visitors to the camp were always shocked by the surreal Gruyère-cheese ruins, with their pocked walls and scars of bullets, grenades, and rockets. We had lost all visual and sensual contact with the outside world and had long since become accustomed to the squalor. People had adapted to the new normalcy, the state of abnormalcy which is to live among the dead, under siege, surrounded by rubble and débris. But they wore the tatters of their battered lives proudly.

I was still in my quest for the real. In the early morning, before the din of everyday noises rose in the camp, I often went up to the roof of Faramawi's four-storey building. With the cease-fire, we no longer had to fear the snipers' high-powered rifles. I could distinctly hear the sound of car traffic – the noise of engines, the honking of horns, the cacophony of the twentieth-century city – but not a vehicle was to be seen. The surrounding heights blocked the view from the Shatila gully. I had not seen automobile traffic in more than eighteen months. Yet here were the sounds, proving that such a thing still existed, and proving, from my bitter perspective, that there were those who still went about the activities of ordinary urban life, setting off to work at 7:00 A.M., fighting their way through traffic. We, meanwhile, were stuck in this prison, hallucinating about the outside world.

One day, standing by the mosque, I looked up. Clouds had gathered. I looked over to the left where a bright sun shone on the mountain tops. I looked to the right where the sun dazzled over the sea. But overhead, over Shatila, there were only clouds, no sunshine. The damp crept up from everywhere, cold and invasive even in the summer, penetrating my every bone. I shouted out to the people standing around me, "Sun over the mountains and sun over the sea, but no sun over Shatila. Have they extended the siege to the sunshine? Is the sun no longer allowed to shine into Shatila?" I trudged back to the hospital, still ranting. Word got out of my little observation among the camp's inhabitants, and that evening Amina and a few other friends passed by the hospital to see me, just to make certain, politely, of my state of mind.

The Syrian *Moukhabarat* continued to give special passes on a regular basis to the hospital and to the hard-line anti-Arafat, pro-Syrian factions. They allowed doctors, nurses, and technicians in and out of the camp, though sparingly. Fighters of the National Salvation Front factions rotated regularly. Shatila's inhabitants looked condescendingly upon these newly arrived men who, after only weeks of the confined life in the camp, were straining to leave. They had not lived through the battle, nor had they shared in the suffering, cold, and hunger. And yet, when they first arrived they seemed brainwashed, spouting violent anti-Arafat and extremist rhetoric. Once they realized that many of the men had been there for more than eighteen months, and once they shared life amidst the desolation of Shatila, they quickly overcame the brainwashing. When their leaders realized that the men were fraternizing with the "deviationist-enemy," a new rotation would quickly take place, and another group of brainwashed extremists would arrive. Seeing the men come and go at the Syrian checkpoint increased the rancour of those who had defended Shatila. Omar rhetorically asked, as he lay down on his mattress one evening, "Who exactly is keeping Shatila under siege? Amal? The Syrians? The Salvation Front?"

"All three," replied Abu Mohammed Faramawi.

Families ate their fill but still lacked the other basic amenities of life. Social life in the camp continued, in spite of everything. Visits were held by candle-light. The accepted protocol was to ply your visitors with endless cups of coffee and tea and large mounds of fruit and offer several different brands of cigarettes. With little to do in Shatila, people passed many an hour visiting – any and every occasion was a good excuse for socializing – relating past experiences of war and survival, discussing new political developments and what was to become of the camp and us. Those lucky enough to have smuggled a car battery into the camp watched television. Large crowds huddled together on reed mats and mattresses on the floor to watch the nightly news, U.S. or Egyptian films, "Dallas," and the congressional hearings on the Iran-Contra scandal and Oliver North. (This Rambo-like figure provoked the scorn of Shatila's inhabitants, even though the joke had it that there was only one Rambo in the U.S.A. but hundreds in Lebanon. In effect, many men had taken the *nom de guerre* Rambo.) During the day, groups often spilled out into the streets and alleyways, and a round of traditional Arab *debka* dancing ensued, the men snaking around in a circle, hands or arms firmly clasped. The local "orchestra" brought out the instruments from the Fatah store-room in the bomb shelter to provide the music. A large crowd soon gathered, urging on the dancers with frenetic clapping. Anyone passing by could join in.

Summer can be very hot and humid in Beirut, making difficult living conditions still worse. The camp was still without electricity, and without fans or air-conditioners it was difficult to find a cool corner in which to relax. Families could not store much fresh food without working refrigerators. The only available refrigeration and the only air-conditioned room in Shatila were in the hospital. Our generators allowed us to continue our routine, recharge our car batteries, and keep our freezers well stocked. We now had to deal with neighbours bringing little packets of meat and asking us to keep them in the hospital refrigerators overnight. It was impossible to refuse them; we lived in the camp, shared the misery of the camp, were the social-centre of the camp, and could not set ourselves apart from it. We still operated the generators only a few hours each day to save on fuel and because we had constant maintenance problems. We had to ask special permission through the Syrians to obtain spare parts or send out pieces for repair. This wreaked havoc on our water supply, and once we spent several days with water rationing even more severe than we had experienced during the Six-Month Battle. Without water and electricity, the camp's inhabitants felt degraded and humiliated. A deep feeling of bitterness and frustration came over us all.

Visiting hours always found a great crowd in the hospital seeking relief in the air-conditioned eight-bed ward room or simply visiting the female nursing or laboratory staff. Since many families had moved out of the camp, there was greater dearth of single women. Marriages seemed to take place at an ever accelerating pace; the instability of the situation and the numerous battles had lent a sense of urgency to romantic affairs. The young men were obsessed about sex and marriage, and young women often had difficulty in fending off their suitors. The brides and grooms were usually in their teens, a few in their early twenties. There was not much to do in Shatila except conceive children, and the number of pregnant women coming to our maternal and child health clinic increased rapidly.

Even in the chaotic hell that is Lebanon, there was nothing normal about a "checkpoint marriage." As a woman, the bride could enter and leave the camp; the bridegroom could go only as far as the checkpoint – and not too close. He had to remain at least twenty yards away if he didn't want to be accused of threatening to extend "Palestinian armed presence" beyond the refugee districts – even if he was not armed at the time. The religious judge, the *qadi*, could not enter the camp, so he would stand at the Syrian checkpoint with the bride, as the couple shouted their marriage vows over the twenty yards separating them. The *qadi* signed the necessary papers, which the woman – a shuttle bride – carried to her future husband for his signature, and then returned to the *qadi*, who went on his way while the newly-weds traversed the rubble and ruins to their Shatilan honeymoon.

The psychological pressures resulted in many early, ill-considered marriages. The young men frantically sought out anything to relieve the monotony of the tortuous alleyways. Since the relationships they formed were not based on normal expectations in a normal environment, even more social pressures were thrust upon the couples and marriages quickly broke down. There were now many young divorcées as well as widows and widowers. The social fabric of Shatila was slowly but surely coming apart.

As the social-centre, the hospital was the prime courting ground of the camp, creating more problems for me. Middle Eastern society is socially and sexually repressed, and hypocrisy rules sexual relations. Screw around as much as you like – male or female – but close the door. Cultural attitudes consider it bad taste to publicly flaunt affections between the sexes. Men or women may openly embrace or walk with arms interlaced with members of the same sex, but never with the opposite sex – not even after marriage. Many social encounters, and a lot of extra-marital sex, took place in Shatila, but discreetly, behind closed doors, supposedly without anyone in the know. The gatherings in the hospital brought me many complaints as director: was I running a hospital or a brothel? I had no great urge to serve as morals policeman or surrogate father to the female staff, but if I wanted the hospital to continue functioning with the respect of all, I had no choice. Gathering the young women – nurses, pharmacists, cleaners – I lectured them: "I am not your father, brother, or uncle. I don't really care what you do in private, but you all know how easy it is to ruin a young woman's reputation, even if she hasn't done anything." The women sitting before me listened intently as though I *were* their father, brother, or uncle and nodded their heads in silent agreement and consent. "Don't give the scandal mongers ammunition with which to ruin your reputation and that of the hospital. You have enough problems as it is, and so do I." Universal agreement again. I didn't like the way they soaked up my every word purely because of my position of power – doctor, director, male. How to explain it, so that they would assume their own freedom? I stared at them, and they stared back, expectantly awaiting my next word. I gave up and got it over with. "Do whatever you want. Just, please, be discreet about it; for my sake, if not for yours."

The hospital routine continued as usual. Murray the Australian left, replaced by Dr. Kiran Gargesh, an Indian anaesthetist who had been working in Great Britain. Kiran had been in Lebanon the previous year, teaching anaesthesia technicians in the PRCS hospital in Ain el-Hilweh. In Shatila, he learned. A group of Malaysian health workers had been brought in by the London MAP, and one of them was an acupuncturist. The Shatila hospital now had a daily acupuncture clinic, and Kiran was its most assiduous student.

I was beset by my usual administrative problems. Some hospital personnel were unhappy; they were still at work in Shatila, while other colleagues worked in centres in West Beirut and never had to come into the camps. Only Dr. Khatib was his jovial self. He kept busy playing cards, beating everyone in the chess tournaments that different political groups organized (everyone participated regardless of political affiliation. Politics was politics, but chess, after all, was *chess*), and, of course, writing and reciting his poetry. He and his wife had divorced after much soul searching. Like most men in the Middle East, he wanted children badly (adoption as practised in the West is unknown in the Muslim world) but feared that any future pregnancies with his first cousin would result in congenital deformities. Now he was actively courting a new mate.

Someone else was also actively courting. Sherbil, one of the young fighters and a Syrian to boot, wanted to marry Fatima. She had been injured during the fighting and was now back in the hospital to have her colostomy closed. Her father was dead, and her mother and brothers agreed to the marriage. Her uncle, however, was opposed. One afternoon after her operation, when Fatima was receiving visitors, Sherbil and her uncle came face to face and exchanged heated words. A knife was brandished, then a revolver, and a shot was fired – at her bedside in the hospital ward. Both men rushed out to retrieve their automatic weapons and went hunting for each other. Hearing the shot and the shrieking of Fatima and the nursing staff, I rushed over to find out what had happened. Then I went outside and was telling some men to find the security officers of Sherbil's and the uncle's political factions to take charge of the situation, when around the corner of an alleyway came Sherbil running at full speed and brandishing his revolver. I stepped in front of him and he came to an abrupt halt, shooting a round over my head. I stood my ground. "Sherbil, do you want to shoot anyone? Then shoot me. Go ahead, shoot me if you have to shoot anyone." I thought that reason momentarily appeared in his eyes. He put away his gun, turned, and ran off. A few moments later, he came running back down the alleyway, this time carrying his AK-47. I again stood in his way while a few men managed to disarm him. But he once again ran away towards the mosque, still carrying his revolver tucked in his belt.

Seconds later, automatic gunfire riddled the air. Sherbil and Fatima's uncle had caught a glance of each other at opposite ends of a crowded alleyway. Sherbil shot a single round while the uncle emptied a clip of his AK-47. Amidst an incredible panic of shrieking and running, groups of men brought to the hospital the bodies of those who had been caught in the cross-fire.

A battalion of men, women, and children converged on the scene, invading the hospital. People wailed, shrieked, and shouted insults. In the pandemonium, we pushed our way through the crowd, blood slopping across the floor, trying to get to the wounded. Hours later, coming up from the operating theatre, I learned the result: two dead, ten wounded. I examined the uncle, who had been grazed by Sherbil's bullet. It was the uncle's emptying of his entire AK-47 clip, thirty bullets, that had caused all the carnage. He looked at me with sad eyes and said, "I was defending the honour of the family. *Al-hamdulillah*, thank God. Dr. Giannou, you understand why I had to do it?"

I stared at him, bewildered, unbelieving, then lashed out at him. "Screw the honour that costs two innocent lives. *Kos okht Rabak. Ars!* Your God's sister's cunt. Pimp!" Blasphemy and sexism – I mixed the two most common insults in the Levantine lexicon. "Do you really think your niece's cunt is worth all that blood?" I thought back to how I had stopped Sherbil running in the alleyway, realizing that if the uncle had turned the corner and seen us there together, he would have opened fire on us both.

A commission of inquiry composed of representatives of the various factions and notables of the camp considered the case. Sherbil was expelled from Shatila and handed over to the Syrians. The uncle was condemned to death and executed by several men from his faction. I was called upon to pronounce death. As a matter of principle, I am against capital punishment, but this was no normal society and these were not normal times. A plethora of arms in the hands of frustrated young men confined in a very cramped living space, amid political tensions that might flare into open fighting, was a formula for collective suicide if the spilling of blood in personal vendettas was not dealt with severely. We could not allow a breakdown of military discipline and the minimal norms for dealing with one another that had allowed us to survive for the past two years. Most of the camp inhabitants were keenly aware of this and no one thought very much of Fatima's uncle's sense of "honour."

Social upheaval usually accompanies civil strife. The residents of Shatila were rapidly throwing off traditional attitudes and questioning well-established taboos. New situations and conditions of social stress cause people to look more pragmatically at what are normally accepted modes of behaviour. This was true of how people reacted to the incident involving Fatima's uncle. In ordinary, traditional village life in much of the world, including rural areas of Europe, his actions would have been understood and even expected of him. But in Shatila, they were totally unacceptable.

Another symptom of rapid social change in Shatila was the reversal of gender roles. In traditional urban Middle Eastern society, men are the ones who have contact with the outside world. It is their responsibility to work, earn money, and be the force behind social interaction. The women usually stay at home. In Shatila, because the men were not allowed to cross the boundaries of the refugee district, they stayed at home; the women were our contact with outside society. They were mobile, did the chores of shopping, transporting goods, carrying messages to the political leadership in West Beirut, smuggling in money and weapons. The women were our source of social interaction. Obliged to live in such a situation, it was not surprising that people's sense of traditional family honour was changing.

Women had played an important role throughout the siege and the War of the Camps. Part of it involved traditional chores of cooking, baking bread, and taking care of the wounded and the children in the shelters. They also helped build fortifications, fill sandbags, erect ramparts, and dig tunnels. Simply taking food to the men at the camp's defences called for great courage since sniper fire and sporadic bombardments were a constant threat. Some, like Dheeba, were injured and others, like Leila, killed as a result of performing these tasks. And at times of heightened internal friction between different factions, which posed the threat of fighting in the alleyways, it was the women who marched through the streets and alleys, using their moral authority – mother as traditional symbol of authority in a society where mother-son relationships are very strong – to prevent internecine shooting from breaking out.

Although she was not formally prohibited from leaving the camp, I had refused to allow Régine out for a year now. I was certain that she was well known to Amal and I feared for her physical safety in West Beirut. She had become romantically involved with one of the men in the camp and now wished to leave, with him, for France. We kept her departure secret, which pained her greatly because it meant she could say a proper goodbye to only a few people. On the day she left, she disguised herself in the flowing robes and scarf of the *hijab* – the Arab version of the Iranian *tchador* worn by religious women – and went out with the hospital staff on their regular shopping expedition at five o'clock in the morning.

Many young men had tried to escape through Amal and Syrian lines at night, but this was risky unless one had accomplices. Baha did, and after almost thirty months in Shatila, he was replaced by another officer sneaking into the camp while he sneaked out. Régine's fiancé decided to take the road that a few others had tried, not always successfully. He shaved beard and moustache, forearms and legs, and donned the *hijab* himself. Thus disguised as a religious woman, he left Shatila in the midst of a gaggle of women comprising his mother, aunts, and sisters, catching up with Régine in West Beirut. He obtained a visa, and they were off to Paris for their honeymoon. I would miss Régine, but the half-dozen Palestinian scrub nurses she left behind had learned much from her, and the operating theatre continued to function flawlessly – at least one institution that did not depend on the continued presence of a personality.

The summer months dragged on and there was still no relief of the military blockade of Shatila in sight. The young men of the camp resented ever more deeply the constraints of remaining within the physical boundaries of the camp. They had no desire to defend mere stones and half-destroyed buildings; they wanted to defend their families and people, and if the families were no longer present, this would inevitably create enormous problems of discipline and self-control.

Baha's replacement was not up to the task. Baha, for all his inexperience and lack of strength of character, knew Shatila, its frustrations and the limits on political activity. His replacement, on the other hand, came from Ain el-Hilweh, near Sidon, where Palestinian political and military strength, and especially that of Arafat's Fatah, were overwhelming. He found it difficult to adapt to the political constraints of Shatila, where although Fatah was the strongest organization with the most popular support, it was not always possible to say so openly. He had to rely on the political and moral authority of the other factions within the reunified PLO to do what he wanted – in the name of the PLO, not Fatah. His brand of narrow factionalism was just as alien to the spirit of Shatila as was the brainwashed extremism of the dissident fighters brought in from Damascus, and it did not help alleviate the tensions in the camp. Amina and I spent many hours explaining the political and social realities of the camp to him, but we were never sure just how successful we were.

Outside Shatila, the economic situation of Lebanon was rapidly becoming catastrophic. Lebanon imports most of its food and consumer goods, using hard currency, and the vertiginous fall in value of the national currency meant an inflation rate of more than 500 percent over just four months. People bet on how low the pound would fall, or when the dollar would be worth 1,000 Lebanese pounds. The economic chaos had an effect on life in Shatila. The inhabitants still thought in terms of military logistics, and once the food siege had been lifted, we started buying and storing all sorts of produce. But there were few buildings left in the camp suitable for use as warehouses, and much of our food stores simply rotted and had to be thrown out. This meant we had to keep buying new supplies at ever-higher prices. Luckily, virtually everyone in the camp received an indexed salary from one faction or another. Lebanese and Palestinians on fixed incomes outside the camp didn't have the same advantage.

Some Palestinians and Lebanese in West Beirut braved the long trek down the devastated main street to come into Shatila seeking financial aid at the Fatah offices in the camp – a major part of the well-funded Fatah's social strategy. They left immediately after receiving their pitiful sums, but this only served to feed the rancour of those confined to the camp who protected and were the *raison d'être* of the offices that gave out this financial aid to people unwilling to live in the horrible conditions of Shatila. The men's rancour also rose when they saw various officials of the Salvation Front factions return smiling and relaxed after a two-week vacation in West Beirut, Damascus, or the tourist resorts of the Shouf mountains.

Many of the men in the camp sought relief from the harshness of reality in narcotics and alcohol. The terms of the military siege proscribed not only anything of military value, but also drugs, hashish, and alcohol. Nonetheless, the *hashisheen* never seemed to lack, and forged their own concept of "national unity." One fellow might be from Arafat's Fatah and another from an anti-Arafat dissident faction, but this political enmity did not prevent them from smoking hashish together.

Alcohol was smuggled into Shatila's secularized society with a little ingenuity. An opaque yellow plastic bottle of cooking oil would be emptied, washed out, and then filled with whisky to be carried in along with groceries; or better yet, a hypodermic needle would be used to puncture the plastic factory-sealed top of a bottle of mineral water, aspirate the contents by syringe, then fill it, with clear water-like *araq*. It looked like an ordinary bottle of mineral water, still intact. A couple of the more daring souls simply told the soldiers and *Moukhabara*t at the checkpoint that "this bottle of whisky is for Dr. Giannou." Since Dr. Giannou was a Westerner, they could not really apply the same rules of the siege to him as to the Muslim men, and besides, he was the Syrians' source for all the medicines they could not find in Damascus and which were too expensive in Beirut. Soon, half the camp was bringing in beer, scotch, gin, vodka, and *araq* – all in the name of Dr. Giannou.

In August 1987, tragedy struck yet again. A large chunk of masonry with protruding iron rods fell from the second storey of the half-demolished school, impaling a young boy of eight. His death provoked the elders and notables of Shatila to meet and decide on a course of action to deal with the ongoing social crisis. They gathered the camp's inhabitants and held demonstrations. Residents marched through the alleyways and then out into S-S Street, in full view of the Syrian army checkpoint, chanting slogans in favour of "Shi'ite-Palestinian reconciliation and peaceful co-existence between the two fraternal communities." They called the press, and journalists covered the demonstrations. The elders called upon the political factions to publish communiqués, and the hospital put out a report on the difficult health conditions due to the lack of proper housing, electricity, regular clean water supply, and effective sewage system.

The demonstrations and communiqués put the Syrians and Amal in a difficult position. Their stand had been, "Suffer if you must, but suffer in silence. Above all, don't make a fuss about it and remind everyone that the blockade is still on." Lebanese religious and political personalities expressed surprise when they heard about the demonstration. They had thought that since a cease-fire had intervened and Syrian troops had taken positions around Shatila, the siege had been lifted and all was well.

The Fatah dissidents did not want to embarrass their Syrian tutors and tried to dissuade the people from demonstrating. As long as it went unnoticed, the siege situation served the dissidents' political goal of overthrowing the Arafat leadership – at least in Shatila, if not in Tunis. Abu Fadi Hamad, the Fatah-dissident officer in charge of Beirut, visited Shatila from time to time. The military blockade restrictions apparently did not apply to him, and the wagging tongues of Shatila said that he, more than the Syrians, was behind the siege – a Middle Eastern quisling. I ran across him down by the Awaini warehouse while the elders were planning their demonstrations. He had come to strike fear into them, as "the delegation" had done in the last month of the Six-Month Battle, to dissuade them from going through with the demonstration. I thought to myself, "It didn't work then, Hamad. Why do you think it will work now?"

"Giannou, don't do anything stupid. We don't need demonstrations. The Syrians won't be pleased." Like all the dissidents, he believed that I had extraordinary powers over the PLO leaders.

"Hamad, why tell me? Tell *your* people. Come, live in these alleyways with *your* people." I, too, did not appreciate Hamad's healthy, comfortable looks visiting Shatila, coming in and out rapidly, so as not to dirty himself. "Feel their frustration and anger, and then tell them not to demonstrate."

"Come now, you're being more royalist than the king."

"Understand! The people here are quickly losing their confidence in *all* the Palestinian leadership. ALL! Every one of them." Months of rancour poured forth. "They feel that only if they take their destiny into their own hands can they save themselves. They'll still owe allegiance to Arafat, Habash, or your Abu Musa. You pay the salaries!" His expression showed his dislike of my response. "But push them far enough, and they'll take things into their own hands." I was being prophetic without knowing it: Shatila the *Intifadah* before the *Intifadah*.

As I had been told time and time again, in one refugee camp after another, Palestinians had spent so many years, so much effort, suffering, and blood, to create their institutions and give themselves a national identity, that they would never disown the organizational framework of that identity card – the PLO, the organization of their civil society in exile. But they lived a pre-insurrectionary existence until their political consciousness raised their misery to the boiling point. Then they realized they owed allegiance not to any individual leader, but to the symbol of their cause. The demonstrations would take place, decided by the people over and above, and in spite of, what any leader told them. They would risk an insurrection. The Palestinians in the occupied territories would learn the same lesson and apply it in a few short months in the *Intifadah*, the popular uprising.

The inhabitants began to repeat their demonstrations daily, along with press releases. The media battle raged on the airwaves of local radio stations and in the pages of Lebanese newspapers. Political sympathies were mobilized. This is the stuff of Lebanese politics, a war of press releases once the guns of war have fallen silent. After ten days, appeals went forth to other refugee camps in Lebanon and the occupied territories to demonstrate in solidarity with the besieged population of Shatila. Marches and meetings took place in West Beirut and in other areas of Lebanon; strikes were called in the West Bank and Gaza Strip. The public demonstrations in Shatila continued for twenty-eight days and finally stopped only upon the request of the Lebanese Socialist Party, which undertook to serve as intermediary in negotiations between Amal and the Palestinians. We breathed a collective sigh of relief. This apparent breakthrough in the political stalemate galvanized the people of Shatila and raised their morale.

In a series of meetings, charges, and countercharges, a battle of press communiqués, and a war of nerves, the contending sides finally reached an interim agreement on September 11, allowing for "humanitarian measures" in the besieged camps. Amal would allow a trickle of construction materials to enter Shatila for repair of the mosque, the schools and the hospital. A joint Lebanese-Palestinian-Syrian committee would supervise the actual work to ensure that the materials did not go towards military fortifications. It was little help, but better than nothing.

Other measures were supposed to follow, including freer entry and exit to and from the camp, total reconstruction of the three refugee districts under siege and the withdrawal of Palestinian forces from the villages east of Sidon. Factions within Amal disagreed with the accord and thought that the entry of a paltry quantity of building materials was sufficient humanitarian aid and that Palestinian forces should withdraw immediately before they made any more concessions. They wanted to maintain the pressure on the camp. They, and the Syrians, knew that the difficult living conditions in the cramped quarters of Shatila were creating psychological difficulties for the young men, and they wanted to exploit this situation to the hilt.

When the materials arrived, the young men brought the bricks, iron bars, and bags of cement into the centre of Shatila. Mounds of gravel and sand were dumped at the camp's periphery. A couple of days later, snipers opened fire on the men pushing wheelbarrows of sand and gravel from these sites towards the interior of Shatila, killing one. The camp exploded in a rush of activity, the men racing to their defence positions along the fronts. A short, violent exchange of small arms fire took place before a new cease-fire intervened.

The scene repeated itself a couple more times, more wounded and killed. The camp's defenders had orders not to shoot back; any battle would result in the closure of the roads and a total blockade. It was in our interest to keep the road open, but it was terribly difficult to convince the men not to respond when one of their friends was shot and wounded or killed.

Frustration and anger grew. We were sitting on a time bomb. Accusations and counter-accusations issued from the Amal and Palestinian leaderships, each placing blame for the breakdown of the cease-fire on the opposite side. Exasperated, the fighters of Shatila opened up with RPGs and heavy arms fire after yet another person had been killed by sniper fire. The men had studied their target well, and the barrage of fire from the camp caught the Amal militiamen by surprise. They suffered heavy casualties. The October battle lasted ten days, during which we were once again under a total blockade. An outcry arose in the press, communiqué following communiqué from the inhabitants complaining that the delivery of construction materials had only been a ruse. Finally, another cease-fire was announced.

With the new lull, yet another delegation composed of Syrian observers, Amal leaders, and Salvation Front officers was dispatched and approached the checkpoint entrance to Shatila to open the road. The political leadership of the camp went out onto the main street to greet them, but when the two groups were no more than fifteen yards apart, a single shot rang out. The camp people scattered back into Shatila and the delegation scampered for cover. It would be difficult to immediately re-establish the cease-fire.

Mohsen, the Lebanese Shi'ite leader of the Palestine Liberation Front, lay sprawled in the street. The single bullet had passed through his head from side to side. Beside him lay the military chief of the Popular Struggle Front, Basel's successor. The bullet had continued its path and severed his spine.

When the two men were finally pulled in off the street and carried to the hospital, the camp was in turmoil and fighting had broken out again. Mohsen was still alive, but his condition seemed hopeless. I began by operating on the other fellow. I could do nothing for his spine, but the bullet had also shattered both his kidneys. I removed one and two-thirds of the other. For us in Shatila, renal dialysis was a mirage, and with only one-third of a kidney and paraplegic, the man did not last more than forty-eight hours.

I turned my attention to Mohsen. We had spent many an evening together, drinking and talking late into the night. We had been cold together, hungry together. Mohsen was Lebanese and Shi'ite, but his personal convictions and commitment had led him to a position of responsibility in a Palestinian guerrilla group. He had lived through the siege of Shatila while his countrymen and co-religionists pulverized the refugee district. The sectarian fanatics within Amal wanted his blood more than anyone else's. I worked mechanically on his wounds, sucking out pulped brain matter mingled with fragments of bone and blood. Suddenly I stopped, my hands frozen. This was becoming too much for me. I had to force myself to concentrate to be able to go on with the operation.

Every doctor, every surgeon has a personal defence mechanism. Working in a large central hospital, one has to deal with life and death every day, and be able to move from deathbed directly to operating table. When the surgeon operates, cuts into flesh, the emotions are sealed off; the mind passively accepts images and stimuli, then determines action mechanically, automatically. This is how surgeons maintain the ability to function; human reactions come later. To continue to function, to continue to work depends on distancing; most of the patients, if not all, are strangers. There's a reason why it is illegal to operate on a close family member.

After two years in Shatila, I knew everyone and everyone knew me. We had shared so much and gone through so much together. I was operating on my friends, on people whom I knew intimately, loved and respected. I thought back many months to the deep emotions I had felt when examining Yasmine after her rape, or operating on Somaya while her two children lay dead. I no longer had any defence for myself. I feared being driven to paralysis as a surgeon by my grief and not being able to take care of my patients. Holding Mohsen's head in my hands, his brains spilling out, was I supposed to operate or weep?

With how much more blood would I have to wash my hands? How many more friends would I have to bury? How many more would I save? *Could* I save them? I felt myself rapidly nearing the breaking point.

From the summer of 1987 until December, 60 died and another 100 were wounded in the skirmishes and sniping. It was a slow, steady haemorrhage of Shatila's human wealth. The men could no longer go out on S-S Street; sniper fire would immediately drive them under cover. We were confined to the remaining unexposed alleyways of Shatila. The camp was truly being turned into a sardine tin. Negotiations for a political solution continued, but the siege of Shatila was not yet over.

15

Leaving Home

A CONSTANT FACTOR IN MIDDLE EASTERN POLITICS IS THE hypocrisy that produces the gap between policy as declared and policy as implemented. Although the Syrian army surrounding the camp was supposed to be neutral, it was anything but. The special permissions and dispensations delivered by the Syrian *Moukhbabarat* permitting the movement of some men in and out of the camp unmasked the falseness of this neutrality. Members of the hard-line pro-Syrian factions came and went, apparently without any problems from the Amal militiamen. In effect, the blockade applied only to the men of the reunified PLO, the majority by far in the camp, and the civilians, as a means of "persuasion" to win over their "sympathies."

Whenever skirmishes and sniper fire began, a cease-fire was implemented and strictly respected within a half hour – if the Syrians wanted one. If they did not, then the fighting continued for days on end, with Shatila totally blocked off. The pressure continued, rendering life yet more difficult, making the inhabitants hostages to the political concessions Syria demanded of the Palestinian leadership: serve as obedient proxy – like the Amal militia – for Syrian political aims in Lebanon; renounce an independent role in political and diplomatic manoeuvres; recognize Syrian supremacy in setting policy for any Middle East peace negotiation – concessions that the Palestinians were not about to make.

Our demonstrations and sit-ins had provoked one political crisis and forced a round of negotiations among Palestinians, Syrians, and Lebanese, but the implementation of the interim accord had stopped with the resumption of sniping and skirmishes. The morale that had risen so high with the entry of the first bags of cement and truckloads of sand for repairs had fallen to new depths of despair.

Although all three refugee districts – Rashidieh, Burj el-Barajneh, and Shatila – were still formally under siege, only Shatila bore the burden of this military activity. We were still the smallest, the weakest, the most strategically placed, and there was not much left of the camp for defence purposes. Isolated by the ongoing siege, the gutted ruins of Shatila were far from the public eye.

One day in November, Youssef, a young fighter with Arafat's Fatah who had now missed three years of school, passed by the hospital to complain of fever and fatigue. When I questioned him about his symptoms, he intermingled his answers with insults directed at the Syrians, Amal, the dissidents, the Palestinian leadership, Arafat, God, and their honour, calling into question the chastity of their mothers and sisters, and the sexual activities of their fathers and brothers. He wanted to go back to school. "All you have to do is leave Fatah and join the dissidents," I provoked him.

"Dr. Giannou, I'm seventeen. When I was twelve, during the Massacre, the Phalangists entered our house and shot my mother and father as we stood in our living room. The bastards burst in through the door and just opened fire. I was buried under the bodies of my mother and father; their blood ran over me. When other Phalangists came in the house, I played dead. I stayed that way for hours. That's why I'm alive today. I owe my life to my parents' death." Youssef swallowed hard before going on. "Where were the Syrians then, Dr. Giannou? Where were they during the whole war of 1982? I took up weapons in '85 to defend myself and Shatila and the memory of my parents. You know how much we've suffered since. I was not going to die, defenceless, like my parents. It's a point of honour. I've lost three years of studies, it's my whole future. I don't care about Arafat, or Abu Musa, or Assad, or anyone. But I'm not going to sell myself to Abu Musa's dissidents just so I can leave Shatila and go back to school. That's not why I took up arms in the first place."

"I know, Youssef. Unfortunately, not everyone thinks like you."

In this cynical little game that is the stuff of politics in general and Middle Eastern politics in particular, we in Shatila were at the same time pawns and protagonists. There were daily personal crises that tore at the fabric of every individual, forcing us to ask ourselves why exactly we were doing what we were doing. Everyone reacted differently.

"This is a fratricidal war that we have been forced into, Giannou," said Dr. Khatib one afternoon as we shared tea in between rounds of coffee on Faramawi's balcony. "The poor fighting the poor, neighbours fighting neighbours. We've had so many intermarriages, shared dreams and hopes, pain and suffering. Half the victims of the '82 Massacre were Lebanese Shi'ites." He inhaled deeply on his cigarette, put it out, and lit another. "They've let themselves be used by the Syrians."

"So have a lot of Palestinians, Mohammed," I replied.

"True, we have our own political whores. But that makes the Syrians all the more pimps."

"It's very sad," added Abu Mohammed Faramawi. "The Lebanese Shi'ites have sacrificed more for the Palestinian cause than many Palestinians. The villagers in the south took in our *fidayeen*, fed them, hid them, protected them; the Israelis bombed the hell out of them. They really sacrificed a lot for us. We tried to make it up to them, took up their social and political cause, trained them, protected them here in Beirut during 'the Events'; even died for them. We've shared so much blood. Today, we believe there are Palestinians and Shi'ites who've made mistakes. We must overcome ours, they theirs. And we must convince them of that. We are the survivors, not just of Palestinian dead, but of all those who have died with and for us. We live for them, in place of them; and for our children, for their children. You know" – Faramawi always spoke to me frankly, revealing his deepest thoughts, even if it might shock the sensibilities of some of his more extremist (country-less) countrymen – "that's exactly what I'd like to tell the Israelis. Too many dead: we have to build for all our children, for all the survivors, theirs and ours. But we need a just peace that respects the rights and equality of all. I'll always remember the 400,000 Israelis who demonstrated in the streets, protesting their government's complicity in the Massacre in 1982. They understood. I'll also remember that no Arab government allowed their people to demonstrate – they even suppressed them." Faramawi's Marxism was always humanist, humanitarian. He was not dogmatic, nor a utopian; his experiences had made him a cynic – but a wishful cynic. "That's why, because of their memory – Ali Abu Toq, Mohsen, the Lebanese and Palestinians and Kurds and Egyptians who died in the Massacre, killed indiscriminately, the Jews gassed by the Nazis, all the victims, from all injustice – we can't surrender, we can't give up. No matter how bad it gets."

Our situation mirrored that of Lebanon; no matter how bad things became, they could always get worse. The ordinary greeting "How are you?" asked by visitors to Shatila provoked the standard response, "Oh, we're alive." And that of course was the secret: life and the will to live.

It was becoming more obvious that it was Syrian policy that was continuing the siege, even though the Amal militia, hard-pressed by socio-economic problems in the Shi'ite community, wanted to lift it and put an end to the War of the Camps. Syria would not attack the camp directly, but simply allow the situation to deteriorate – socially, economically, medically, physically – hoping that the psychological rot would eat away at the resistance of the inhabitants, demoralizing them into submission. As Syria the supposed arbitrator became Syria the antagonist, negotiations to end the stalemate involved more and more actors. Algerians, Libyans, Saudis, Iranians, and Soviets all served as intermediaries. The pressure grew, both on the Syrian regime and on Shatila.

Sniper fire further restricted the limits of Shatila. The checkpoint marriages became impossible. No male could safely stand in the street near the checkpoint long enough for the brief ceremony. Not only were S-S Street, the lung of the camp allowing the men to get a breath of air and enjoy a little bit of space, and perimeter of the camp off limits, but the only passage into Shatila, at the Syrian checkpoint, was itself not free of the snipers' lethal fire, periodically targeting women and children carrying groceries in full view of the Syrian troops stationed there.

The rubbish siege returned. Snipers took aim at young men at the camp's periphery trying to carry out garbage, so the rubbish began to pile up again in the central square. The rodent population flourished in spite of our supply of poison, and swarms of flies and mosquitoes hung in the air even after we had sprayed with insecticide. Gastroenteritis and skin diseases were rampant once more. The humidity in the trough that is Shatila was overwhelming, and an epidemic of influenza laid low the entire population of the camp at one time or another. Another small outbreak of typhoid fever added to the general physical and emotional deterioration of the community.

Hysteria began to reach epidemic proportions. Men, women, and children threw temper tantrums and then either fainted or thrashed about wildly. Every such attack turned into a social crisis as friends and relatives, shouting and shrieking, invaded the emergency reception. Sometimes the hospital staff, not immune to the phenomenon, participated in the shouts and shrieks.

People could not go up to the roofs of their dilapidated, half-destroyed homes to patch over a hole because of the danger. The autumnal rains arrived and water cascaded into rooms, slowly dribbling down the fissured and fractured walls. Half the hospital rooms were unusable. We sloshed through the alleyways back and forth between the hospital buildings in rubber boots; moved medicines and food supplies away from the damp and watery walls; placed pots and pans to catch the water dripping from the pharmacy and kitchen pantry ceilings. With every rain storm, we had to check the pharmacy to make certain that the sewers had not backed up and the effluent endangered our medical supplies.

Mildew and fungus reappeared, colouring ceilings and walls a delightful green – the only organic green in Shatila. There was no grass and only two barren trees within the confines of the camp, although clearly visible were the luscious vegetation of the Lebanese mountains and the forest delimiting the "Green Line" dividing Beirut into West and East in the southern suburbs. No birds lived or even perched in Shatila. We could make out the rumble of car engines and the honking of horns in the early morning hours, but we never heard the sweet song of birds. At night, in the deathly silence pervading the alleyways, the only sound was the pattering of scampering rats.

Every aspect of the situation was deteriorating rapidly. The respected leadership was decimated: Ali Abu Toq was dead; Abu Moujahed, then Basel, then Baha had left the camp; only a few of us remained who had the authority to deal with the social and psychological problems and impose the necessary discipline, and we ourselves were in dire need of help.

Even the outside world seemed to ignore us. The League of Arab States held a summit conference in Jordan in early November. Topic number one on the agenda: the Gulf war between Iran and Iraq. Topic number two: the eventual re-integration of Egypt into the Arab fold. The Palestinians, Shatila, and the other besieged camps had become invisible again; at least, that was the wish of the Arab regimes. We felt very alone, isolated and abandoned; even under the bombs, it hadn't been this bad.

Worse still were the strict orders not to return fire should sniping occur. We all understood the sniping to be a provocation, a deliberate attempt to elicit a response that would degenerate into a battle, close off the road, and demoralize us even more. Sometimes, a man seeking revenge for the injury or death of a friend would patiently wait and snipe at the Amal positions, and then the Amal militiamen would spend hours shooting into Shatila, seeking their own revenge. The Syrians did nothing. The skirmishes repeated themselves with sickening frequency.

No peace and no war, only a continuing haemorrhage of our lives and our sanity. In mid-November 1987, a few men, without the knowledge of their political and military superiors, prepared a military adventure to open hostilities and break out of the camp, even fighting Syrian troops if necessary. They planned to disobey orders not to reply to sniper provocations, and not simply to disobey by returning the fire, but to mutiny and charge forward under their own *ad hoc* command. They wanted to take the military initiative – open hostilities – and thereby take the political situation into their own hands. With 10,000 Syrian troops stationed in West Beirut, and the camp still encircled by Amal and the Lebanese Army Sixth Brigade, this would have been suicide.

We discovered both the planned mutiny and its instigator, the now-deranged brother of the man killed beside Mohsen. For days he went without sleep or food, his eyes at times brilliant and sparkling with talkative mania as he explained in hushed tones his preparations for attack, at times glazed and dull with the depression of mourning and exhaustion. He refused treatment, but I managed to trick him, exploiting his trust in me to disarm and then sedate him before arranging his evacuation to a psychiatric hospital.

With hundreds of young men cooped up in an exceedingly small area, their nerves on edge and feeling frustrated, any argument carried the risk of settlement by guns, of which there was no lack. The men became ill-mannered and intolerant; political friction, ever present, provided as good a pretext as any to let off steam. A simple argument over a hashish cigarette could, and did, result in one man shooting another. Each fellow's comrades-in-arms came out in his support – with arms.

Late November 1987: in an attempt to forget, if only for a moment, the men brought out their instruments and started a round of dancing. A crowd of more than 100 people soon gathered. Then someone threw a hand grenade, injuring thirteen. Luckily, no one was killed. The injured belonged to different factions – pro- and anti-Syrian, pro- and anti-Arafat. Nonetheless, everyone rushed to get their weapons – a red alert – thinking themselves to be under attack by another faction. It took us hours, scrambling through the alleyways filled with men armed to the teeth, to convince everyone to put away their guns. No one was under attack, and yet we all were. "Was it a provocation by some Amal or Syrian agent trying to demoralize us?" Abu Mohammed Faramawi asked rhetorically.

"Or was it insanity?" I snapped.

A few days later, in the silence of the night, another successor to Basel in the Popular Struggle Front was found lying in the mud in an alleyway, his body riddled with bullets. The assassin had used a silencer-equipped automatic pistol – the better to respect the quiet of the deserted alleys. Shatila was rapidly descending into social anarchy. We had become cannibals, eating ourselves up, everyone willing to shoot at everyone else simply out of frustration. "People treated like animals," I told anyone within earshot, "also tend to behave like them." It was not a question of the will to live and resist, but rather of the human capacity to withstand unmitigated stress, suffering, deprivation, and death.

Negotiations for a political settlement were deadlocked, and we believed that the world had finally and truly forgotten us. For the first time in two and a half years, desperation set in. All our information showed that Burj el-Barajneh and Rashidieh were large enough geographically and demographically to withstand the pressures on them and maintain a semblance of normal social life. Shatila seemed damned and doomed.

Tragedy rapidly followed tragedy. A woman burned to death trying to heat her home with a leaking butane gas cylinder. Ali Abu Toq's former confidant and bodyguard died, asphyxiated by a leaking gas heater. A fourteen-year-old girl was killed by a sniper after having just passed the Syrian checkpoint. Skirmishes recurred. A group of four friends, one with a sister married to an Amal official, contacted, through the sister, her husband to arrange to sneak out of the camp at night, passing through the Amal lines. Instead of gaining safe passage, the men were captured and tortured to death, their disfigured bodies left in a rubbish heap by the airport road. These four men had been in Shatila for more than two years. In the midst of the bombing, in the throes of the hunger and cold, they had never thought for one moment of escaping. But their frustration and disgust had finally broken them.

Amidst the reeking garbage littering the muddy lanes of Shatila, life had never seemed darker. We had lived a shabby existence, but we had never given up hope. We had surprised ourselves at our capacity to improvise and make do. Now, after the awesome ordeal of multiple battles and sieges, we faced the naked reality of the solitude and squalor of our existence. We had been pushed to the limits and were in danger of cannibalizing ourselves. We *truly* were alive only because we were not dead.

November 25, 1987: a hang-glider incursion of a Palestinian fida'i into northern Israel, attacking an Israeli military outpost and killing six Israeli soldiers and wounding another six before the fida'i was killed in turn. In the ethos of Lebanon, where daily life throughout the country is profoundly militarized, this daring attack against a military objective created a tremendous surge of popular enthusiasm.

Lebanese and Palestinians in Lebanon have for years lived with the daily threat of devastating Israeli air raids. The disparity in technology is a source of constant frustration. Obsolete Arab anti-aircraft batteries fire uselessly at high-technology supersonic Israeli aircraft that stay out of reach. To the people of Lebanon, a low-technology hang glider infiltrating Israel's sophisticated defences was a victory of the primitive over the supermen.

On December 9, 1987, following rapidly on this incident, and at the very moment when Shatila seemed to be on the verge of sinking under the weight of its own misery, frustration, and neglect, the *Intifadah* began, pitting low-technology slingshots against the high-technology weapons of the occupation army. The local Lebanese media – press, radio, television – went wild with praise and expectation. News spread rapidly of the young Palestinians in the occupied territories of

Gaza and the West Bank facing the modern Israeli army with their stones. Weeks passed, and the uprising continued. Like the people of Shatila, the Palestinians of Deheisha in the West Bank and Jabalya in the Gaza Strip preferred to die on their feet rather than live on their knees; they had learned from the resistance of the besieged refugee camps in Lebanon, which had refused to submit to an Arab diktat. People had decided that they were unwilling to continue to live under occupation and under an Israeli diktat, no matter how many died or how many were deported or how many bones were broken or how many houses were dynamited. The young men throwing stones had lost their fear of the enemy. They kept alive the tenacious spirit of the will to survive and live in freedom and justice. The *Intifadah* had begun, and there was no end to it in sight. As the number of martyrs increased, and as the revolt continued and gained in strength, new life and hope returned to Shatila. Hope beyond despair: the hope of the stones of the *Intifadah* vanquished the despair amidst the rubble of Shatila.

The people in Shatila stayed glued to their radios, following the events in the occupied territories. The rumblings from the occupied West Bank and Gaza Strip – periodic demonstrations, stone throwing, strikes – were nothing new, of course. Throughout 1987, however, the incidents seemed to increase in frequency and intensity, often in solidarity with the besieged refugee districts of Shatila, Burj el-Barajneh, and Rashidieh. (The Palestinians under Israeli occupation dared to demonstrate their solidarity with us; those under the control of Arab regimes dared not. Arab repression tends to be more ferocious than Israeli.)

In Shatila, the sniping continued, but although bleak, our outlook improved as people's morale rose. Demonstrations and sit-ins resumed, inside the camp now since we could not even reach S-S Street. Press releases and communiqués announced the solidarity of the three besieged refugee districts in Lebanon with those under siege in the West Bank and Gaza Strip. Demonstrations also occurred in West Beirut and in other Lebanese cities in solidarity with the *Intifadah*. Lebanese political and religious leaders – including the Amal leadership – proclaimed their support of and respect for the stone throwers. Yet, despite their proclaimed solidarity, Amal continued to encircle Rashidieh, Burj el-Barajneh, and Shatila, and to hold Shatila in a tight grip of deadly sniper fire. Communiqués followed each other on the radio and in the press, complaining of the situation in the beleaguered refugee districts, both in Lebanon and in the occupied territories. I published press communiqués describing the horrendous living conditions, the health problems, and my thoughts. But as the weeks passed and the uprising continued, the expectation transformed the political climate.

January 15, 1988: Soheir, twenty-five years old and nine months pregnant with her second child, was entering Shatila around noon, weighed down by her bundles of groceries. She passed the Syrian checkpoint and was about to turn off the road through the first block of flattened buildings to enter the camp when a sniper's bullet struck her. The men in the camp could not be controlled and a firefight broke out. Employing a covering barrage of rocket-propelled grenades, two men jumped out into the open and carried Soheir into the camp to safety.

She had lost a great deal of blood by the time she finally arrived at the hospital. The bullet had severed the major artery in her right thigh, and we worked quickly to staunch the bleeding. I made certain of saving her life and limb and then turned my attention to her baby. The profuse haemorrhaging had affected the fetus, who was now in grave distress. I performed a Caesarian section before returning to clean out the rest of the wound in her thigh. In the end, I managed to save Soheir's life and leg, but lost the boy. Her husband was relieved. "The most important thing is to save my wife. We can always have more children."

The Popular Committee and Shatila's elders published an insulting press release, complaining bitterly of the shooting of pregnant women by Amal. They put it quite bluntly: although Syria and Amal called Israel the enemy, their actions against the Palestinian refugee districts in Lebanon were worse than those of the Israelis.

On January 17, 1988, Nabih Berri, the leader of Amal, called a press conference. Under the pressure of public opinion, the press campaign, and the final humiliation of wounding a pregnant woman, he announced a unilateral and unconditional lifting of the siege on all three refugee districts. He ordered his militiamen and the soldiers of the Lebanese Army Sixth Brigade to withdraw from around the camps and allow free access to them. This, he stated, was in solidarity with the popular uprising of the Palestinian people in the occupied territories. He would leave to the conscience of the Palestinian leadership the question of Palestinian troops occupying villages east of Sidon. He was not asking for a *quid pro quo*, but was unilaterally putting an end to the War of the Camps.

It was an astute political move. By making this concession in the name of "solidarity with the Palestinians," Berri and the Syrians had removed a political pressure point in their battle with the Palestinian political leadership, gained respect, and given up nothing of any real value. Berri had outmanoeuvred Arafat.

But the political astuteness wasn't Berri's only motive. He had problems within his own movement and needed a respite. Amal was disintegrating. It had always been a heterogeneous group with many factions, some of which had never agreed to participate in the War of the Camps. Others had actively aided the Palestinians, helping to smuggle weapons and ammunition into the camps. Factional feuding threw into question Berri's leadership of Amal, and he needed some strong political accomplishment to help re-establish his authority. Amal had suffered very heavy casualties and thousands of its members who did not want to get caught up in the hell of the War of the Camps had defected, joining the ranks of the Hizbollah. The fundamentalist pro-Iranian Shi'ite "Party of God" had opposed the War as a matter of principle and had condemned the Shi'ite-Palestinian fighting. Putting an end to the War of the Camps was a popular move and was met with a great sense of relief by all in West Beirut.

The Shi'ite community, the power base of Amal, was in turmoil. Comprising about one-third of the Lebanese population and the largest single religious group, the Shi'ites had borne the brunt of the Israeli invasion and three years of occupation in South Lebanon. They had organized a popular resistance and waged a guerrilla war against Israeli troops, who had finally withdrawn from most of South Lebanon in 1985. Now this Shi'ite population felt a deep empathy with the active resistance of the Palestinian *Intifadah* stone throwers who had also overcome their fear of the Israelis. This created tremendous grass-roots pressure on the political and religious leaders of the Lebanese Shi'ite community to put an end to the War of the Camps.

The announcement that the siege was to be lifted left us in shock. We had become so sceptical and cynical that we could not believe it until it actually happened and we saw the militiamen withdraw. But the logistics were rapidly put into effect, and on the night of January 19 the last of the militiamen and soldiers withdrew from their positions. Abu Mohammed Faramawi commented, over yet another demitasse of Turkish coffee, "Wait until the morning. We'll see if there are any militiamen left."

There were none left. The last of them danced as they withdrew, relieved that their nightmare, as well as ours, was over. Syrian troops were deployed to include the area around the refugee camps of Shatila and Burj el-Barajneh within the territory covered by their security plan for West Beirut. They did not actually enter the camps. Amal also withdrew from around Rashidieh, where militiamen of Hizbollah took over their positions.

We could go out to Sabra-Shatila Street again. Men were free to come and go, went out to the cinema, to shop, to discothèques. Families moved back into the camp and quickly started to repair the remnants of their homes and lives. Another wave of journalists – U.S., French, and British, TV and newspaper correspondents – flooded into the camp. The images of the remains of Shatila flashed across the globe. Once again, if only momentarily, the world remembered Shatila.

From April 7, 1987, until January 20, 1988, we had lived under a military blockade. The outpouring of joy and relief after the Six-Month Battle had been overwhelming, but now that the war and siege were finally over, the joy and relief were tainted with the bitterness of the last months. So much blood had been spilled uselessly, and we had come perilously close to collective suicide. The very essence of the social fabric that had made possible the resistance and survival of Shatila had begun to unravel. Now we were saved – from the siege, from the snipers' bullets and from ourselves. The popular uprising in the occupied territories had saved Shatila just as surely as the earlier example of Shatila had helped spark the *Intifadah*.

Like everyone else cooped up for months and years in Shatila, I had dreamed of leaving, dreamed of the freedom to come and go. I wanted to get out of Shatila, I needed to get out. I had come close to paralysis as a surgeon, useless to serve those in need. Now I could not imagine leaving, because each day that I had lived there, I had experienced things that once would have been unimaginable to me. Leaving Shatila also meant leaving Beirut, a city where too many Western hostages had been taken by too many different groups and where there were too many people who might not appreciate what I had done in the last twenty-seven months. And leaving Beirut meant that I might not see my beloved friends in Shatila for years, if ever again. I could rationalize and say that I had to leave to recuperate, but that didn't prevent my feeling a certain guilt. I held a Canadian passport and could leave; my friends couldn't. I had to go. I couldn't go.

January 27, 1988: exactly one year after the death of Ali Abu Toq, I left Shatila. I couldn't bring myself to go before the first anniversary commemoration of Ali's death, and afterward there would be too much pressure from friends, and myself, to stay. The right yet painful choice was to leave on that day. The siege was over. The road had been open for a week. Other doctors could come and go freely. The ill could be taken elsewhere if need be, and we could hope there would be no more wounded. And I needed a respite.

My suitcase had rotted away from the dampness and mildew. A friend bought me a replacement in West Beirut about half the size of the first, and I quickly packed my sparse wardrobe and a few books. Abu Mohammed Faramawi, in whose house I had operated and cared for my patients and slept for so long, looked at me in disbelief. He finally realized that it was time for me to leave, and with Dr. Khatib, we went down the stairs to the hospital where I greeted the three patients who still lay in their beds. Word had got out that I was leaving, and by the time I retraced the path through the hospital complex and took one last look at our accomplishments and sacrifices, people filled the alleyways.

Colleagues and hospital staff, families and children, elders and students, political officers and ordinary fighting men – just about every single one had been at one time or another a patient of mine, either in the operating theatre or in the out-patient clinic – came to say goodbye. Kissing everyone on both cheeks, it took quite some time for me to reach the mosque. A final glance at the graves covered with garlands of flowers, the photos of the martyrs hanging along the walls, and I went on through the labyrinth of the ruins, towards the main street.

Sabra-Shatila Street throbbed with a massed crowd. Political leaders and officials from Mar Elias had arrived for Ali Abu Toq's first anniversary commemoration ceremonies. I had made the appropriate choice. It seemed right that I should be leaving Shatila one year to the day after Ali had left us. It took still more time to say farewell to the crowd. Every time I finished embracing one group, another appeared. People wept, embraced; Omar, Abu Imad, and Baha's replacement made speeches. Abu Moujahed was there.

As the surrounding crush of people pushed and shoved, Amina tightly clutching my arm, I made my way to the waiting convoy of diplomatic, Red Cross, and journalists' cars that was to accompany me, for reasons of security (this was Lebanon, and on the day of my departure a West German was taken hostage in West Beirut), to the airport where I would catch a plane to Cyprus, the first stop on my way home. The Greek embassy had sent a car complete with bodyguard (there was no longer a Canadian embassy in Beirut); friends from the press and the ICRC had come as well. The caravan of vehicles slowly started off. Sitting in a car for the first time in twenty-seven months, looking but not taking it all in, I caught only glimpses of the area beyond the Sabra camp as we drove towards the airport road.

Epilogue: The Moral Boundaries of Shatila

LIFE GOES ON IN LEBANON AND THE MIDDLE EAST. AFTER the War of the Camps and the lifting of the siege in January 1988, Syrian-instigated fighting between Arafat loyalists and Fatah dissidents began in May and carried on through the summer, resulting in the fall of Shatila and Burj el-Barajneh to Syrian control. Fighting also broke out in the Shi'ite-populated southern suburbs of West Beirut in the summer of 1988, and the Hizbollah militia wrested control of the area from Amal. At its 19th session in Algiers the Palestine National Council declared the constitution of the State of Palestine on November 15, 1988. Horrendous shelling between East and West Beirut during the first six months of 1989 set the scene for another constitutional agreement to put an end to the civil war, and yet another assassination of a newly elected president. Several weeks of fighting in East Beirut between rival Maronite forces killed and wounded as many as the six months of shelling, and the constitutional agreement could just as easily be the victim as the victor of the renewed hostilities. And the *Intifadah* in the occupied territories continues into its third year with no end in sight.

I still hear news of many of the people I lived with in Shatila. Amina, Basel, and Omar are safe, in a manner of speaking, in Ain el-Hilweh, southern Lebanon. Dr. Mohammed Khatib remarried, left the PRCS, and is now working in an UNRWA clinic in West Beirut. Abu Moujahed, Faramawi, and Abu Imad are in Mar Elias, trying to organize the reconstruction of Shatila and Burj el-Barajneh. Baha is in a Syrian prison, captured while trying to return to the Beirut camps during the internecine Palestinian fighting; his replacement was wounded and, with Amina and the other loyalists, evacuated to Sidon under Arab League auspices. Assassins killed the Shatila Hospital chief of nursing in a Beirut street. Samir, the child of Oum and Abu Abed, recovered from his head wound and went to France, along with Rana, for further treatment. He returned to Lebanon and, while visiting relatives in Sidon during the summer of 1989, was playing in a garbage dump where he found a grenade. It exploded and killed him on the spot. Life in Lebanon does go on.

I have thought long and hard about Shatila, Beirut, and the Middle East. As Professor Richard Day, a psychologist at the American University in Beirut, puts it, "For anyone who has lived in Beirut, their view of the world around them will never be the same again." To an outsider, it probably seems like a hopeless mess. But there exists an order that underlies the apparent chaos. The explanation of that order has not been well served by the Western media. Larry Pintak, former CBS television correspondent, relates in *Beirut Outtakes:* "It was an axiom of Beirut coverage that New York television producers weren't much interested unless you had pictures of people with guns shooting at each other. Diplomatic intrigue and erudite analysis usually bit the dust if there was no 'bang, bang' involved. Given a choice between a crucial political development and mindless violence, mindless violence won out every time."

The problem goes beyond Shatila and Beirut. I would add that Western media coverage has helped to reinforce prejudices and perceived stereotypes and continues to do a great disservice to the public's understanding of the Middle East. Even, and especially, when it comes to the U.S. government's role in the area. All the more reason to explain why the U.S.A. at first tried to bring down the regime of Ayatollah Khomeini and then acquiesced in selling it arms; at first refused a preponderant Syrian role in Lebanon, and then acquiesced to the Syrian-supported candidate for the Lebanese presidency; continuously refuses the Palestinian demand for self-determination, and then acquiesces to an Israeli government that refuses American peace plans. Confusing? The First World War began in the Balkan powder-keg. If there is a Third World War, a nuclear holocaust, it will begin in the Middle East atomic powder-keg. And just as with the Balkans in 1914, everyone will find the Middle East confusing.

More "media-ted" perceptions: the press coverage of the *Intifadah* portrayed it as something new; it was not, but only perceived to be so. Hundreds of stone-throwing Palestinian youths have captured the imagination and anguish of millions around the globe; young boys raise a banned flag or throw Molotov cocktails or burn tires; Israeli soldiers charge with tear gas or respond with rubber- or plastic-coated steel bullets or live ammunition or break the bones of the youths. The images are familiar to all, but this is only ten percent of the *Intifadah*. The media coverage is superficial. Superficial also is the characterization of the repression of the *Intifadah* as a matter of re-establishing "law and order."

In reality, the occupied territories were always in turmoil, rebellion always just under the surface. In the spring of 1982, just prior to the Israeli invasion of Lebanon, open revolt had broken out. I visited the hospital's Lebanese neighbours in Nabatieh every evening to watch the televised news; to watch young Palestinians in the occupied territories throw stones, burn tires, raise the banned Palestinian flag; and to watch Israeli soldiers fire tear gas, break bones, and shoot live ammunition. In two months, twenty-seven young Palestinians were shot dead. This was in 1982, almost six years before the uprising.

A number of Israeli pundits contended that the real aim of the invasion of Lebanon in 1982 was not to destroy the menace of the PLO in Lebanon, but rather to shut up the rambunctious population in the occupied territories and crush their morale with a Palestinian defeat. They argued that the 1982 war was misunderstood history, that a military solution to a political problem would not succeed. Israel had to come to grips with Palestinian nationalism and the occupation of a large hostile civilian population. Thinking back on Algeria, Vietnam, Zimbabwe, and South Africa, it seems to me not so much that history repeats itself, but rather that politicians repeat, with astounding stupidity and myopia, the errors of history.

Israel has not come to grips with the occupation of another people, but that other people has now come to grips with Israel. Reflecting the pundits' opinion of the 1982 invasion, Israeli military and intelligence agencies today describe the uprising as "an expression of Palestinian nationalism, that as a political problem has no military solutions, only political ones." According to Israeli Chief-of-Staff Dan Shomron, "The *Intifadah* cannot be ended through military means short of transfer [mass expulsion], mass starvation or physical liquidation, that is – genocide...."

Fully ninety percent of the activities of the *Intifadah*, that part not well described in the Western media, is the reorganization of Palestinian society along lines of a consensus grass-roots democracy through local popular committees. Palestinians in the villages, refugee districts, and cities of the occupied West Bank and Gaza Strip have created committees to deal with education, health, agriculture, food distribution, self-defence, and political policy. This has been achieved in spite of, and in the face of, curfews, closure of schools and universities, mass administrative detention, deportation, and the lack of a free press and freedom of assembly.

An Israeli journalist has written that what the Palestinians are now doing is exactly what happened in the *Yishuv* – the Jewish community in Palestine prior to the establishment of Israel – during the struggle against the British in the 1940s. "We [the Israelis] can no more end the *Intifadah* through emergency laws and regulations, force and repression, than the British could end our nationalist struggle through similar means." Meeting such political and civil action with brute force only reinforces the will to continue such action. Older Israelis realize this; it is how they reacted to British force. And they realize that this is how Palestinians are reacting to Israeli force.

Just as Shatila has become the symbol of an entire people denied its very existence as a people, so the *Intifadah* has become the symbol of a people's desire for dignity and self-determination. Shatila's inhabitants had to organize all services themselves, a self-sufficient, isolated community of 3,500 people living in 200 vards by 200 yards, under attack, under siege: the *Intifadah* before the *Intifadah*! In the same way, the 1.7 million Palestinians of the 2,200 square miles of the West Bank and the Gaza Strip have had to organize their society, under attack, under siege. "Resistance is the mechanism for building a state, a national identity, and dignity; the *Intifadah*, the daily struggle, becomes a model for the future state." The importance of the *Intifadah* lies in what Edward Said has written: "Liberation is not something to be won all at once at the end of the struggle, but little by little during the struggle and expressed in daily relationships between people."

The Israeli-Palestinian conflict has been going on for decades. What is new today, I believe, is that both Palestinians and Israelis face existential questions – questions that are tearing apart both societies and that have already provoked attacks by extremists of both sides on members of their own communities. I have found chauvinists to exist among both Palestinians and Israelis.

The Palestinians of 1947, who owned ninety-four percent of the land of Mandate Palestine and made up the majority of the population, did not understand how the UN could apportion the land without the agreement of the population. Since then, Palestinians have had to come to grips with the reality of Israel and the impossibility of recuperating all of their historical homeland. They have learned, after living cheek by jowl for more than twenty years with Israelis, about Israeli society, a functioning liberal democracy with all its positive aspects and its faults and shortcomings. They know that they could never face an Arab, Third World, or South African army with mere stones. They have also learned about and become sensitive to the tribulations of Jewish history in Europe: persecution before and during the Inquisition, the expulsion (along with the Muslims) from Andalusia/Spain, the pogroms, and that unique event, the Holocaust.

Palestinians have argued that they were not responsible for any of this, and that whenever persecuted Jews had to flee Europe, they found refuge in the Muslim countries of North Africa and the Middle East, with the exception of the one time that the flight was coupled with nationalistic intentions of its own – political Zionism.

Their homelessness of more than forty years, and a paradoxical historical parallelism that has replaced the myth and image of the "wandering Jew" with that of the "wandering Palestinian," have convinced many Palestinians that, rightly or wrongly, they must come to terms with a people who, in spite of the mutual antagonism, have much in common with them. (Having attended a number of meetings between PLO and Israeli officials in Europe and North America over the last year, I know that the Palestinians and Israelis get along much better together in both the formal conferences and the informal drinking sessions afterwards than either do with Americans or Europeans.)

Palestinians have made their choice, difficult as it is for many to accept. The Palestine National Council and the clandestine Unified Leadership of the Intifadah have opted for a partition of historical Mandate Palestine – two states, Israel and Palestine, living in peace side by side, in reciprocal recognition, with the possibility of an economic common market between them, which might also include Jordan and other states in a Middle Eastern "Benelux." The decision to relinquish one's claim over all one's homeland was not an easy one. Indeed, it is not accepted by all, but today, it is the official policy of the Palestine Liberation Organization. For the PLO, the policy of exacting justice for one's people has become one of securing peace for one's people.*

Just as the Arab Palestinians of 1947 did, the Jews of Palestine faced a political dilemma. A slight majority of the *Yishuv* accepted partition.

*The controversial Palestinian charter that calls for the "destruction of the Zionist state" is not only "*caduc*," as Yassir Arafat said to French President Mitterand, but also a "*canard*," in the words of Yehoshafat Harkabi, former head of Israeli military intelligence. "It constitutes a dream but no longer a policy," according to him. On the other hand, Israeli Prime Minister Shamir's Herut Party in April 1988 passed a resolution calling the East Bank [Jordan] a part of "the Land of Israel."

The extreme right wing refused; they wanted all of Eretz Yisrael. The left wing refused partition; they didn't want a Jewish state but rather a democratic binational state. Today Israelis, and Jews in general, face existential questions that relate to the kind of Israel they want and the type of society Israel is becoming. Do they want all the land, Eretz Yisrael? Or do they want a "Jewish state"? Do they want a liberal, tolerant democracy, or an exclusivist messianic society? There is a crisis in national identity and therefore a conflict of loyalties. If Israelis decide to keep all the land, then they must decide what to do with 1.7 million Palestinians in addition to the 750,000 who now hold Israeli passports. Give them full political and civil rights, and they will become forty percent of the population in what would be a de facto binational democratic secular state – the exact policy, until recently, of the PLO for twenty years – and no longer a "Jewish state." Do not give them rights, and you have the Middle Eastern equivalent of apartheid. Expel them, en masse ("transfer" is the euphemism of Israeli political jargon and the concept is so jarring that the English word, not the Hebrew, is used), and there is no longer a tolerant liberal democracy. Maintain the status quo, as Messrs Shamir et al. would like, and the *Intifadah* will continue because Palestinian nationalism will continue, and television audiences around the world will continue to receive nasty, truthful, albeit superficial, images. The moral rot will continue, and both Israel society and the Jewish diaspora will continue an ever-divisive debate on what to do.

The more and better I know Palestinians and Israelis, the more it seems to me that they have come to resemble one another, as though each were looking into an historical, cultural, and political mirror. They look so hard at times that they do not recognize the other in their own reflection. The propagandists see only the terror of the "other," without seeing their own. The history of terrorism in the contemporary Middle East is a long one. The litany of achievements of Jewish terrorist groups differs from that of the Palestinian only to the extent that it has been more politically successful, and thanks to the relatively short memory span of western public opinion, has tended to escape censure.

I understand, if I do not accept, the violence and terror that extreme frustration brings forth; on the part of Jews after the Holocaust, and of the Palestinians after their dispossession. Individual frustration victimizes, ultimately, individuals.

Another reflection in the mirror: I described a family in Shatila that was the epitome of the Palestinian political "stew": the father the leader of the pro-Syrian Saiqa, the wife an officer of the neutral, critical but unionist DFLP, and the son a fighter with the Arafat loyalists. The Israelis do not allow the Palestinians to outdo them. The brother of the right-wing Israeli Foreign Minister, Moshe Arens, is an American Peace Now activist, and the minister's son is a member of an extreme left-wing anti-Zionist party in Israel. After all, this is the Middle East.

The protagonists may well resemble one another, but the situation of occupier and occupied is asymmetrical, of course – the Jews victims of Europeans and the Nazis, and the Palestinians "victims of the victims"; a sophisticated, First World, state-of-the-art army, and a ragtag, Third World, militarily ineffective guerrilla force; one society based on modern management techniques, the other trying to throw off the legacy of centuries of the backwardness of Ottoman obscurantism and bureaucracy. A practical solution to the Middle East conflict, however, must be based on symmetry and reciprocity.

The struggle for human and civil rights is a part of the history of Western civilization. But this history also contains a long litany of victims – Jews, indigenous peoples, blacks. In contemplating the importance of the Middle East, I ask myself, "How will Western civilization meet the challenge presented by its current victims, the Palestinians? Can we gain any lessons from this to prevent other victimization in the future?"

A propaganda debate is a facile one; the propagandists do not help. They speak with what Hemingway once called "that beautiful detachment and devotion to stern justice of men dealing in death without being in any danger of it." The conflict of the *Intifadah* and its repression is a lethal debate. Israelis and Palestinians need an end to this violent debate if they are ever going to exploit fully their tremendous human potential. A lasting peace can only be a just peace, and justice must be based on reciprocity and equality of rights. There can never be a secure Israel if there is not a secure Palestine. How to achieve both is the true debate. Everything else is propaganda.

As I write this, it is now two years since I left Shatila.

This book is "the duty of the living to the dead," but also the duty of the privileged, the free, with Canadian passports to those without privilege but who maintain, in the face of untold danger and suffering, their humanity. "As long as the price of freedom is equality, and vice versa, there will always be situations where to survive is to betray the dead, and others where, to approve one's own death is a political necessity," wrote Heiner Müller, East German dissident playwright. During the last ten months of the imprisonment of the military blockade, a friend of Régine's from the French embassy had come regularly to visit us. The embassy's liaison for humanitarian social and health work in Palestinian refugee camps in Lebanon, she regularly brought me reading matter. One book in particular caught my interest: Jean Genet's *Un Captif Amoureux*, a posthumously published memoir of his experiences among the Palestinians, and especially his visit to Sabra and Shatila immediately after the 1982 Massacre. The title means the enamoured captive, the prisoner in love. Régine's friend wrote an inscription: "*D'une passante, à un autre captif*" – from a passerby, to another captive. The book drew me, but I could not bring myself to read it while I was still in Shatila.

Reading Genet's book months later in North America, and writing my own, I came to understand how truly his title resounded. I needed to leave the physical limits of Shatila, but I knew that I could never leave its moral boundaries. I had to go, I couldn't go. I left, and yet no. In some sense, Shatila and I are now inseparable, and I, far away, still a captive.

Glossary of Political Groups

Please note that although this glossary is more extensive than the names of factions given in the text, it is not complete for the Lebanese or Middle Eastern political scene. Despite that, I hope it will give the reader an idea of the different currents and ideologies at play.

Palestine Liberation Organization, Arafat "loyalists" during War of the Camps:

Fatah (Palestine National Liberation Movement): largest, most popular support and best financed; headed by Yassir Arafat; actually a broad coalition including all shades of opinion from Muslim fundamentalists to Marxists, with a common denominator of independent Palestinian nationalism.

Palestine Liberation Front (PLF) – Abu Abbas faction: minor group, supposedly Marxist in ideology.

Arab Liberation Front: pro-Iraqi, minor group; led by Ahmed Abderrahim.

The Palestine National Salvation Front (PNSF) (from 1984 to 1987):

Popular Front for the Liberation of Palestine (PFLP): most important left-wing faction, two major currents – pan-Arabist and Marxist; led by Dr. George Habash; rejoined PLO ranks in April 1987.

PFLP-General Command: minor extremist group; led by Ahmed Jibril; financed by Syria, Libya, and recently Iran.

Popular Struggle Front for the Liberation of Palestine (PSFLP): minor Marxist-nationalist group; led by Dr. Samir Goshe.

Palestine Liberation Front – Yacoub faction: minor group, supposedly Marxist; rejoined PLO ranks in April 1987 and attempted to reunify PLF.

Saiqa (Palestinian branch of the Syrian Ba'ath Party): minor group; little popular implantation; cover for Syria within Palestinian ranks.

Fatah dissidents of Abu Musa: chauvinist scission from Arafat's Fatah, 1983; existence dependent on Syrian rivalry with Arafat.

Democratic Front for the Liberation of Palestine (DFLP): major orthodox Marxist faction; left PLO at time of creation of PNSF but refused to join, instead allied with Communist Party in Democratic Alliance; led by Nayef Hawatmeh; rejoined PLO in April 1987.

Palestine Communist Party (PCP): existence negligible in Palestinian diaspora, very important in occupied territories; joined PLO for the first time in April 1987.

Revolutionary Palestine Communist Party: chauvinist scission of PCP; negligible existence anywhere; Syrian-supported.

Fatah-Revolutionary Council – Abu Nidal group: minor but extremist and violent faction; major perpetrator of terrorism against Jewish and European targets as well as PLO moderates for more than fifteen years; recently has undergone major scission and internal purges; originally financed by Iraq, then Syria, Libya, and perhaps Iran.

Islamic Fundamentalists – in occupied territories: Islamic Jihad has joined with PLO leadership; Khamas group has remained outside PLO; minority groups but increasing in importance, especially in Gaza Strip.

Unified National Leadership of the Intifadah: clandestine leadership of major PLO groups in occupied territories (Fatah, PFLP, DFLP, PCP) and nationalist Islamic fundamentalists.

Lebanese National Movement (LNM): broad coalition of largely secular Lebanese political parties, each with an armed militia, led originally by Kemal Jumblat, assassinated in 1977; group includes:

Lebanese Communist Party – traditional leadership was Christian, large number of Shi'ite members.

Progressive Socialist Party – mostly Druze Muslims, led by Walid Jumblat, son of Kemal.

Nasserists – collection of groups espousing pan-Arabist ideology; secular; well-implanted in Sunni Muslim community.

Syrian National Social Party – pan-Arabist; believe in Greater Syria; particularly powerful in Greek Orthodox community.

Amal Movement of the Disinherited: founded in 1978, originally supported by Fatah and Arafat; became overtly sectarian Shi'ite Muslim and pro-Iranian after the Islamic revolution in Iran, 1979; after 1982 Israeli invasion became pro-Syrian, and Syria's prime ally in Lebanon.

Hizbollah-Party of God: pro-Iranian Shi'ite fundamentalist group; includes large number of disgruntled Amal militiamen and former Communists; core of diffuse grouping of minuscule radical factions responsible for taking of Western hostages.

Phalangists: major right-wing Maronite Christian party; founded in 1936 and based on Franco's fascist Falangistas; Israel's Lebanese ally.

Lebanese Forces: amalgam of right-wing Christian militias unified through force of arms by Bashir Gemayel, assassinated president-elect; Lebanese ally of Israel.

Marada: pro-Syrian right-wing Maronite militia, headed by former President Suleiman Fanjieh, who in 1976 invited Syrian troops into Lebanon to help put an end to civil war.

Chronology of Main Historical Events

1922-23	Establishment of British and French mandates over Lebanon, Syria, Transjordan, and Palestine
1943	Independence of Lebanon
1947	United Nations partition plan for Mandate Palestine; establishment of Israel; first Israel-Arab War resulting in hundreds of thousands of Palestinian refugees
1949-52	UNWRA sets up refugee camps in Lebanon, Syria, Jordan, West Bank, Gaza Strip
1956	Egypt nationalizes Suez Canal; second Israel-Arab War – British-French-Israeli attack on Egypt
1964	League of Arab States establishes Palestine Liberation Organization
1967	Six-Day (third Israel-Arab) War; Israel occupies Sinai Peninsula (Egypt), Golan Heights (Syria), West Bank (Jordanian control), and Gaza Strip (Egyptian military authority)
1968	Battle of Karameh – Palestinian guerrilla groups resist Israeli Army, enter, and take control of PLO
1970	Black September: fighting between Jordanian army and Palestinian *fidayeen* after hijacking of four airplanes to Jordan; PLO expelled from Jordan, sets up bases in Lebanon to continue guerrilla attacks against Israel; Israeli retaliatory air raids against South Lebanon
1973	Egypt and Syria attack Israeli-occupied Sinai and Golan heights (fourth Israel-Arab War); Suez Canal defences overrun by Egyptians; Arab oil embargo
1975	Outbreak of Lebanese civil war
1976	Syrian army enters Lebanon at invitation of Lebanese president to help put an end to civil war; at first attacks LNM/PLO coalition, two years later fights right-wing Maronite coalition
1978	First Israeli invasion of Lebanon (fifth Israel-Arab War)
1979	Camp David peace treaty between Egypt and Israel; Egypt expelled from Arab League

1980	Iraq invades Iran, beginning of Gulf War
1981	July – after fierce fighting between Israeli and PLO forces in Lebanon, including Israeli air raid on civilian area of Beirut, American diplomat negotiates a cease-fire on Lebanon-Israel border
1982	June – after assassination attempt on Israeli ambassador to London by radical anti-PLO Palestinian group, Israel invades Lebanon (sixth Israel-Arab War); three-month siege of Beirut; evacuation of PLO and Syrian forces from Beirut; Sabra and Shatila Massacre
1983	Phalangist-controlled army in control of West Beirut; Syrian-inspired dissidence breaks out in Fatah and PLO; fighting in Beqa'a Valley and Tripoli, North Lebanon; results in expulsion of troops loyal to PLO chairman Arafat
1984	February – popular uprising in West Beirut ends Phalangist control
1985	Armed popular resistance against Israeli troops obliges them to withdraw from most of South Lebanon, taken over by Amal, Hizbollah, and Communist Party; PLO enclave in Sidon and Rashidieh refugee camp near Tyre May – Amal militia attacks Sabra, Shatila, Burj el-Barajneh, beginning War of the Camps
1986	January – Four-Day Battle at Shatila April – Twenty-Day Battle at Shatila July – Thirty-five-Day Battle at Shatila September – Six-Month Battle begins at Rashidieh, then Burj el-Barajneh in October, finally Shatila in November
1987	April – cease-fire at Burj el-Barajneh and Shatila, lifting of food and medical blockade; re-unification of PLO during Palestine National Council meeting in Algiers December – outbreak of *Intifadah*, popular uprising in Israeli-occupied West Bank and Gaza Strip
1988	January – Amal lifts siege of Shatila and Burj el-Barajneh May – Syrian-instigated fighting in Beirut camps; Shatila

and Burj el-Barajneh fall to Syrian control; Arafat loyalists expelled
December – Palestine National Council meeting in Algiers declares constitution of a Palestinian state

Selected Bibliography

This bibliography is very personal and is by no means intended to be exhaustive.

Lebanon

Evron, Yair. *War and Intervention in Lebanon: The Israeli-Syrian Deterrence Dialogue.* Baltimore, Maryland: Johns Hopkins University Press, 1987.

Khalaf, Samir. *Lebanon's Predicament.* New York: Columbia University Press, 1987.

Khalidi, Walid. *Conflict and Violence in Lebanon: Confrontation in the Middle East.* Cambridge, Massachusetts: Harvard University Press, 1983.

Mackey, Sandra. *Lebanon: The Death of a Nation.* New York: Congdon & Weed, 1989.

Petran, Tabitha. *The Struggle over Lebanon.* New York: Monthly Review Press, 1987.

Pintak, Larry. *Beirut Outtakes: A TV Correspondent's Portrait of America's Encounter with Terror.* Lexington, Massachusetts: Lexington Books, 1988.

Salibi, Kamal. *A House of Many Mansions: The History of Lebanon Reconsidered.* Berkeley, California: University of California Press, 1988.

Yermiya, Dov. *My War Diary: Lebanon June 5-July 1, 1982.* Boston: South End Press, 1984.

Palestinians and Israelis

Abu-Lughod, Ibrahim (ed.). *The Transformation of Palestine: Essays on the Origin and Development of the Palestine Conflict.*

Evanston, Illinois: Northwestern University Press, 1987.

Aruri, Naseer (ed.). *Occupation: Israel over Palestine*. Belmont, Massachusetts: Association of Arab American University Graduates, 1983/89.

Beinin, Joel, and Zachary Lockman (eds.). *Intifadah: The Palestinian Uprising Against Israeli Occupation*. Boston, Massachusetts: MERIP and South End Press, 1989.

Beit-Hallahmi, Benjamin. *The Israeli Connection: Who Israel Arms and Why*. New York: Pantheon, 1987.

Benvenisti, Meron. *West Bank Data Project: A Survey of Israel's Policies*. Washington, D.C.: American Enterprise Institute for Public Policy Research, 1987.

Binur, Yoram. *My Enemy, My Self*. New York: Doubleday, 1989.

Brenner, Lenni. *The Iron Wall: Zionist Revisionism From Jabotinsky to Shamir*. London: Zed Press, 1984.

Chomsky, Noam. *Peace in the Middle East: Reflections on Justice and Nationhood*. New York: Vintage, 1974.

Chomsky, Noam. *The Fateful Triangle: the United States, Israel and the Palestinians*. Boston, Massachusetts: South End Press, 1983.

Cobban, Helena. *The Palestinian Liberation Organisation: People, Power and Politics*. Cambridge: Cambridge University Press, 1984.

Flapan, Simha. *The Birth of Israel: Myths and Realities*. New York: Pantheon, 1987.

Gresh, Alain. *The PLO – The Struggle Within: Towards an Independent Palestinian State*. London: Zed Press, 1987.

Halevi, Ilan. *A History of the Jews: Ancient and Modern.* London: Zed Press, 1987.

Harkabi, Yehoshafat. *Israel's Fateful Hour.* New York: Harper & Row, 1988.

Heller, Mark. *A Palestinian State? The Implications for Israel.* Cambridge, Massachusetts: Harvard University Press, 1983.

Hirst, David. *The Gun and the Olive Branch.* London: Faber and Faber, 1977/84.

Jiryis, Sabri. *The Arabs in Israel.* New York: Monthly Review Press, 1976.

Khalidi, Rashid. *Under Siege: P.L.O. Decisionmaking During the 1982 War.* New York: Columbia University Press, 1986.

Khalidi, Walid (ed.). *From Haven to Conquest: Readings in Zionism and the Palestinian Problem until 1948.* Washington: The Institute for Palestine Studies, 1987.

Lesch, Ann M., and Mark Tessler. *Israel, Egypt and the Palestinians: From Camp David to Intifada.* Bloomington: Indiana University Press, 1989.

Morris, Benny. *Birth of the Palestinian Refugee Problem: 1947-49.* Cambridge: Cambridge University Press, 1988.

Palumbo, Michael. *The Palestinian Catastrophe: the 1948 Expulsion of a People From Their Homeland.* London: Faber and Faber, 1987.

Quandt, W.B., F. Jabber, and A.M. Lesch. *The Politics of Palestinian Nationalism.* (Rand Corp.) Berkeley: University of California Press, 1973.

Rodinson, Maxime. *Israel and the Arabs.* Harmondsworth: Penguin, 1968.

Rodinson, Maxime. *Israel: A Colonial-Settler State*. New York: Pathfinder Books, 1973.

Rokach, Livia. *Israel's Sacred Terrorism: A Study Based on Moshe Sharett's "Personal Diary" and Other Documents*. Belmont, Massachusetts: AAUG Press, 1980.

Said, Edward W. *The Question of Palestine*. New York: Vintage Books, 1980.

Said, Edward W., and Christopher Hitchins (eds.). *Blaming the Victims: Spurious Scholarship and the Palestinian Question*. London: Verso Editions, 1988.

Sayigh, Rosemary. *The Palestinians: From Peasants to Revolutionaries*. London: Zed Press, 1979.

Shlaim, Avi. *Collusion Across the Jordan: King Abdullah, the Zionist Movement and the Partition of Palestine*. New York: Columbia University Press, 1988.

Stone, I.F. *Underground to Palestine and Reflections Thirty Years Later*. New York: Pantheon, 1978.

War of the Camps

Ang, Swee Chai. *From Beirut to Jerusalem: A Woman Doctor with the Palestinians*. London: Collins, 1989.

Cutting, Pauline. *Children of the Siege*. London: William Heinemann Ltd., 1988.

Periodicals

From the Hebrew Press: The Shahak Papers (monthly): pub. in Jerusalem; available from American Educational Trust, P0B 5306, Washington D.C. 20009.

Israel & Palestine Political Report (bi-monthly): Magellan Publishing, 5 rue Cardinal Mercier, Paris 75009.

Journal of Palestine Studies (Institute For Palestine Studies) (quarterly): 3501 M St, NW, Washington DC, 20007.

MERIP Reports (Middle East Research and Information Project) (monthly): 1500 Massachusetts Ave, NW, Washington DC 20005.

Middle East International (semi-monthly): 21 Collingham Rd, London SW5; 1700 17th St, NW, Washington DC 20009.

Documents

United Nations Resolutions on Palestine and the Arab-Israeli Conflict. Washington D.C.: Institute for Palestine Studies, 1987, 2 vols.